Judicial Dispute Resolution (JDR)

Judicial Dispute Resolution (JDR)

New Roles for Judges in Ensuring Justice

Lawrence Susskind, William Tilleman, and Nicolás Parra-Herrera

A

ANTHEM PRESS

Anthem Press
An imprint of Wimbledon Publishing Company
www.anthempress.com

This edition first published in UK and USA 2023
by ANTHEM PRESS
75–76 Blackfriars Road, London SE1 8HA, UK
or PO Box 9779, London SW19 7ZG, UK
and
244 Madison Ave #116, New York, NY 10016, USA

British Library Cataloguing-in-Publication Data
A catalogue record for this book is available from the British Library.

Library of Congress Control Number: 2023901194
A catalog record for this book has been requested.

ISBN-13: 978-1-83998-866-0 (Hbk)
ISBN-10: 1-83998-866-5 (Hbk)
ISBN-13: 978-1-83998-898-1 (Pbk)
ISBN-10: 1-83998-898-3 (Pbk)

Cover Credit: George Farmer and Christinia Tilleman Greep

This title is also available as an e-book.

CONTENTS

FOREWORD

Justice Russell Brown

Justice of the Supreme Court of Canada and Honorary Professor of
Law at the University of Alberta

I am pleased and honored to have been asked to offer a brief foreword to this important new book on the experience, practice and possibility of JDR.

Irrespective of country of origin, lawyers in the Western tradition have long understood the civil action as critical to civilized co-existence. For us, a claim brought before an independent arbiter, expert in the law, is civilization's substitute for vengeance and therefore essential to social order. Our fellow citizens look to the decisions of courts to learn how the law applies to the citizen, so that they may order their conduct and affairs so as to comply with the law. Through the independent operation of the courts, *society* also orders *it*self in the certain knowledge and belief that all can have a remedy for a wrong, and that no one, no matter how powerful, is above the law.

For decades, however, and for various reasons, the law's capacity to discharge this function in a timely and accessible way has been constrained. Resourcing is limited. As a result, courthouse construction and judicial appointments have not kept pace with population increase. The law governing many areas of private activity has become more complex, and trials have lengthened as a consequence. Family litigation has proliferated in a system that was not designed with families in mind. The cost of legal services is prohibitive for most people. And criminal justice, with its constitutional imperative of a speedy trial, (quite rightly) tends to receive the highest priority.

Those of us who still militantly believe in justice and in the system that administers it should hope and press for brighter days. Unless all have reasonable access to justice and, where necessary, to the civil action, we risk finding ourselves living in a society where the strong and well-resourced will always prevail over the weak. Hence Chief Justice Dickson's caution, over 30 years ago:

> [T]here cannot be a rule of law without access, otherwise the rule of law is replaced by a
> rule of men and women who shall decide who shall and who shall not have access to justice.
> (Supreme Court of Canada 1988)

The stakes, therefore, are high. A system key to preserving and advancing civilized society is at risk of failing those whose support sustains its public legitimacy. Preserving it to date has taken resources, effort and imagination (Farrow 2014). More of each is required, perhaps especially of imagination.

Enter Professor Lawrence Susskind, Justice William Tilleman (my former colleague at the Court of Queen's Bench of Alberta) and Nicolás Parra-Herrera. In *Judicial Dispute Resolution: New Roles for Judges in Ensuring Justice*, they present Judicial Dispute Resolution (JDR) as an emerging practice (particularly in four Canadian provinces) that provides litigants with an alternative means of resolving the civil action. It preserves (albeit often in a changed form) relationships. As my Court once said, "[t]rue reconciliation is rarely, if ever, achieved in courtrooms" (Supreme Court of Canada 2017). It helps families come to terms with past grievances and new relationships. It allows claimants to relate, and defendants to comprehend, the losses that the law doesn't recognize or sufficiently value.

At the same time, the authors—a co-founder of the Program on Negotiation at Harvard Law School, a pioneer and leader in the practice of JDR at his court, and a doctoral candidate at Harvard, and a professor of negotiation, mediation and dispute system design in Colombia—acknowledge that JDR, if it is to be understood as an aspect of the judicial role, remains controversial. That normative objection is met with practical accommodation: JDR cannot descend into a mandate to clear the docket, but must lead to a result that is fair and just; JDR is not for every judge, and certainly not for judges who are inadequately trained.

The authors then marshal their considerable experience, insight and skill to offer something of a "use, care, and maintenance" manual for JDR: the qualities of the JDR judge (and for that matter of the lawyer), the vexing question of confidentiality, suitable and unsuitable cases, juggling complexity, the role of precedent, intake systems, triage, specialized JDRs, preparation and online JDRs. It represents a valuable resource for all concerned—from court administrators, judges, mediators, arbitrators and lawyers, to students and instructors in law schools and other university departments or faculties such as business or criminology.

The overall result is a comprehensive and indispensable resource. I warmly congratulate the authors on this achievement.

ACKNOWLEDGMENTS

This book could not have been written without the support and contributions of many parties in JDR, their counsel, justices and chief justices, law students and research colleagues. We are grateful to each of them, especially counsel Amy K. Murphy, Jamie K. Warne, Keith Marlowe, Paul Kazakoff, Dennis Groh, Phyllis Smith, Christine Silverberg, Quinn Kuefler, Peter Gibson, Alison Gray, Barry Alloway, Robert Maxwell, Matthew Laurich, Damon Bailey, Trent Johnson, Paul Stein, Valerie Prather, Tara Pipella, Patricia E. Olyslager, Derek Allchurch, Doreen Saunderson, Domenic Venturo, James Rose, Carol Drescher and Susan Borsic for making themselves available for interviews, when necessary, and for providing insights about their JDR experience. We also appreciate the support of Associate Chief Justice Nielsen, Associate Chief Justice Rooke, U.S. District Court Chief Judge Brian Morris and Chief Justice Mary Moreau for relocating Justice Tilleman's banked time to teach the JDR class at Harvard Law School (HLS) and for rearranging his time to do SPEC JDRs during the COVID pandemic.

Many thanks to the HLS students who authored the cases listed in the Appendix and whose interest in alternative forms of dispute resolution give us faith that future lawyers will be even more imaginative, collaborative and dialogical. Thanks to Rachel Viscomi, who made sure we had a place to meet.

Special thanks to Paula Raymond and George Farmer, who not only clerked and assisted with the SPEC JDRs but helped coordinate the HLS research seminar.

Finally, for the photos, we want to thank Nicole Farmer and George Farmer, who did such an excellent job of capturing in real-time the collaborative mood that characterizes most JDRs.

Chapter 1

INTRODUCTION

There is a growing concern worldwide about ensuring fairness and justice in society, especially on behalf of those at the margins who have the least resources. In this book, we examine the responsibility that courts, particularly judges, have in guaranteeing justice. Judges could do more to meet the rising demand for justice by helping parties resolve their differences, not just by picking a winner and a loser—which is what litigation usually does—but by stepping in to assist the parties in resolving their differences themselves.

Since the early 1970s, judicial scholars in the U.S. and Canada have documented the costly failures of litigation—in terms of time, finances and shortfalls in achieving justice—and encouraged lawyers to find better ways to resolve their clients' legal claims. Typically, judges and attorneys are opposed to the notion of judges stepping down from the dais to help parties settle disagreements. Canada, however, has embraced this practice. We look closely at a series of Canadian civil cases in which judges use Judicial Dispute Resolution (JDR) in just this way. Since JDR is almost always confidential, direct access to participant interactions and detailed descriptions of how the process works have not been available. Our case studies, though, through the intervention of Justice Tilleman and with the permission of the parties involved, are included here and lay bare the actual JDR courtroom experience.

JDR is a dispute resolution process in which a judge adopts the role of mediator to facilitate problem-solving conversations between disputing parties. In many instances, the judge is called upon to provide a personal assessment for the parties of what the likely outcome will be at trial if they can't resolve their differences themselves. At the outset of the process, the parties can decide whether or not they want their JDR judge's decision to be binding, dubbed Binding Judicial Dispute Resolution, or BJDR. If not, the process is Non-Binding Judicial Dispute Resolution, or just JDR.

A JDR judge's efforts to mediate go beyond what a private mediator typically can offer. The involvement of a sitting judge tends to enhance the credibility of the mediation process in the eyes of the disputants, and guarantees them a reasonably accurate prediction of what Oliver Wendell Holmes Jr. called "the oracles of the law." Knowing the likely outcome of their case if it goes to trial often pushes parties to reach a voluntary settlement. If they do not settle in JDR with their chosen judge, they are free to revert to litigation. In that case, a different judge would hear their case, and any discussions that took place during the JDR would remain confidential.

Thus, there are clear differences between JDR and traditional mediation. First, in JDR, litigants are more likely to take seriously what a judge says the results of their litigation are likely to be, than what a private mediator—regardless of their past experience—predicts. In other words, in JDR, parties get what they think is a credible appraisal of what they are likely to end up with if they don't settle voluntarily. In negotiation theory, this is called their Best Alternative To A Negotiated Agreement, or BATNA. In JDR, parties with realistic assessments of their BATNA are likely to move toward a shared sense of what an agreement needs to accomplish. Second, JDR assists in working out the terms of a mutually acceptable agreement, but it does so in the setting of a courthouse, which brings a sense of gravity to the process and an increased motivation to succeed. Importantly, there is no cost for the judge's involvement. Third, mediators are trained to search for mutual gain or "win-win" outcomes while most judges are not. JDR judges, however, are an exception. JDR is certainly less costly than private mediation or one of its hybrids like mediation-arbitration (med-arb). In med-arb, at the request of the parties and their lawyers, the mediator switches into the role of arbitrator, and makes a binding decision. Often, the parties are advised not to reveal everything about their real interests during the mediation portion of the process because the mediator might use that information to their disadvantage in formulating a subsequent arbitration decision. In JDR, either the mediation ends and a new non-ADR (alternative dispute resolution) judge takes over (with no discussion of what happened earlier) or the parties decide they want the mediated decision to be binding.

For scholars and professionals who study and practice ADR, JDR sounds, at first blush, similar to another ADR method called "mini-trials" practiced in the U.S. A mini-trial typically starts with the parties presenting their strongest arguments in summary form to a non-binding arbitrator or a panel of neutrals to see whether they can convince them (or each other) to drop their claims or work out a settlement privately, especially in complex cases. The neutrals managing the proceedings—often a panel of three former judges—provide commentary with some authority after a mini–look at the case. They sometimes forecast what they think the likely court outcome will be and suggest why the parties might want to settle, but mostly they comment on the strengths and weaknesses of each side's arguments. This is similar to what a sitting JDR judge might do if asked by the parties to do so, but the ADR judge will not necessarily have specialized background in the substance of the dispute. A mini-trial is abbreviated and does not take place before a sitting judge. The neutrals provide an authoritative analysis of the strengths and weaknesses of the legal claims offered, but there is no cross-examination. Parties are usually represented by counsel and the process assumes that counsel will be in a better position to advise their client on the desirability of settlement or litigation in light of what they have all heard, especially the forecasts offered by the neutrals. A major difference is that JDR judges interact mostly with the parties, assisted by their attorneys. JDR is client-focused, as opposed to lawyer-focused. One last distinction: in a traditional mini–trial, the outcome is an opinion, not a decision; parties can move on as they like, and the neutrals do not seek to mediate among the claimants or suggest the terms of a settlement.

Difficulty in gaining access to the courts and paying for representation is a global problem. Long delays are common, and trials and appeals increase the uncertainty of the outcome and frustration of the parties. In the Province of Alberta (as well as several other Canadian provinces), however, litigants who choose JDR are guaranteed that a judge will be available to help them settle their dispute. The JDR success rate is remarkable: 90 percent of parties reach a relatively quick settlement, saving weeks of the court's time and giving the litigants control over the outcome. The therapeutic benefit of each party telling a judge their version of what happened is not insignificant.

The Canadian practice of JDR illustrates a new way for judges to ensure that justice is done. We examine the practice of JDR in Canada—particularly Alberta—but we also want to help our readers think globally and comparatively about JDR. Although we are drawing from cases in Canada, our goal is to extrapolate from these lessons to other jurisdictions. JDR might have a different name in other countries, but there is no reason to assume that the process can't enhance the administration of justice worldwide. China, Australia, Singapore, New Zealand and a number Latin American countries report that they are already using some version of JDR. In this book, we explain how JDR emerged in Alberta using the personal story of the current Associate Chief Justice of the Court of Queen's Bench who was already a sitting judge in the early 1990s.

We hope this book will be used to teach law students internationally, though our primary audience is practicing lawyers and their clients. Building on nine detailed JDR case studies, we explore JDR as a means of enhancing the quality of justice by opening a new channel for experimenting with a dispute resolution or management procedure that might leave the parties more satisfied, less emotionally drained and sparing their resources. We compare JDR to pretrial or settlement conferencing, especially in the U.S., and to private mediation outside of court (ADR), internationally. In the Appendix we offer a Teaching Guide for instructors who may use our JDR case studies in a variety of law school classes (e.g., family law, contract, medical malpractice, wills and estates, environmental disputes and others).

The purpose of this book is to look closely at JDR mostly through the Canadian experience. We hope it is helpful for litigants (or potential litigants) who are considering their ADR/JDR options. Law students and practicing attorneys need to understand the somewhat different role and responsibilities they have in an ADR/JDR context. Hybrid dispute resolution processes, like JDR, call for hybrid skills or, as Julie MacFarlane puts it, the cultivation of conflict resolution advocacy, which is particularly needed in judicial settlement processes, sometimes labeled as judicial mediations, judicial settlement conferences, or JDR. This is the hybrid model we want to explore here, and we want to reflect on how this experiment has unfolded —its benefits and downsides— in specific context (Macfarlane 2012).

We explore JDR's Canadian origins and its early promoters. A fuller understanding of the intellectual beginnings of dispute resolution and JDR makes it clear why these processes were inaugurated and what agendas they served. The practice of JDR has flourished beyond Alberta, particularly in Québec and Ontario, which was a steady and early proponent. The innovative judicial mediation process now used in Nova Scotia, for example, began in an online form, without oral evidence. In that context, the judge and parties interact via a chat function to resolve disputes.

JDR is easily adaptable to any of the United States' judicial districts because the Federal Rules of Civil Procedure, particularly Rule 16, allow the court to facilitate settlement. So, any U.S. judge can choose JDR when they realize they are encouraged to be the master of their own courtroom, with the authority to promote settlement on a case-by-case basis. In other countries, JDR-like efforts have led to a variety of independent dispute-settlement practices that we explore in the book.

Our coauthor, Canada's Justice Tilleman met with a U.S. judicial colleague to discuss the idea of her mediating cases, and the option of resolving even her most difficult cases through ADR (therefore, JDR). When she asked how she could possibly make a final decision when attorneys continue to bring certain cases back repeatedly for "reconsideration" or a "motion for a new hearing," Justice Tilleman looked at the huge case file on her floor and recommended she call the counsel and parties involved into open court and offer them binding or non-binding mediation, explaining that judicial mediation (or JDR) would conclude each case. "Listen, Your Honour," he said, "this can easily be done with just the consent of the parties." She couldn't hide a beaming smile and her excitement at the prospect.

Throughout the book, we point out JDR's general distinctions from ADR: JDR offers the imprimatur and jurisdiction of the court along with a judge who has authority to grant settlement orders at the end of the mediation. The sitting judge knows the law and is able—through their combined mediation-judicial expertise—to help parties set relevant and realistic expectations and to resolve their substantive disagreements.

Practical tips are included for those preparing for a JDR: how to interact with a judge; when to bring clients to scheduled sessions; what materials the court requires; what elements are confidential; under what circumstances witnesses can attend, and much more.

We also explore JDR's constraints, one of those being confidentiality. Limited documentation has led to misunderstandings and uncertainties about how JDR works. The lack of formal scholarship on the subject motivated us to write this book and include the case studies. Our limited sample of cases means that our findings and prescriptions are provisional, but provide a good starting point for future theoretical and empirical studies.

That a failed JDR will require a new judge may strike some as a waste of resources. Nevertheless, it ensures that parties can freely share information during their JDR and know that it will not be used against them in court. Other relevant concerns about JDR involve potential problems associated with judges privately caucusing with clients and their lawyers, or if pro se, how a record should be kept.

We want to respond up front to the skeptics likely to argue that JDR offers no guarantee that disputes will be resolved quickly and harmoniously. That's true; JDR is not the solution to every problem in the dispute resolution field. It is—to cite Frank Sander again— just one more room in (or door to) the courthouse, where parties can address and resolve their conflicts with a judge's help. JDR does not ensure that justice is served; it is unlikely, though, that JDR will lead to unjust outcomes in the eyes of either party, or from the standpoint of the public-at-large. Thus far, the results are promising.

Another possible criticism is that JDR cases are settled behind closed doors. The parties are often feel safe pursuing their dispute in private, but one of the hallmarks of the judicial system—creating and applying precedent—is lost. There is no written decision that stands as the basis for future mediations, and there is no record to show what past precedents played a role in each mediated outcome. Our research indicates that the tradeoff is worth it, but we address the role of certain kinds of precedent in JDR, and explain why the results in one JDR should not be used to settle another.

The book concludes with a discussion of online judicial dispute resolution (OJDR) and what it takes to initiate such a program from scratch. Two events have caused this technological turn in the development of JDR: the internet and e-commerce. As Ethan Katsh and Orna Rabinovich-Einy suggest, e-commerce, globalization and online inter-connection call for a new wave of experimentation in handling disputes (Katsh and Orna-Rabinovich 2017). Online dispute resolution (ODR) systems have been a response to this, and JDR is ideally suited for this uniquely twenty-first century means of settling disputes. The 2020 COVID-19 pandemic was an important push in this direction, forcing courts to rethink how to allocate their time and resources and how to improve access to justice during lockdowns. OJDR emerged as a clear solution. OJDR is ODR conducted remotely by a judge, allowing each party the benefits of a courtroom experience from the comfort of their home. This book draws on the experience of Justice Tilleman, who has been a prime mover in the development of OJDR.

Taking A Dispute Systems Design Perspective to JDR

The Canadian JDR experience is not limited to opening a new "door," so to speak, in the courthouse so that parties can mediate their disputes before a sitting judge. It is also about designing a new more comprehensive court system. This requires thinking simultaneously from two perspectives: JDR as a process and JDR as a system. It is one thing to assess the outcome of a particular dispute resolution effort, like a single instance of JDR. It is something else entirely to assess a system that handles a continuous stream of relatively similar cases or legal disputes. In the first instance, legal analysts can talk to the participants and sometimes even watch the proceedings. They ask the parties and their lawyers for their opinions on the outcome, compared to what they or others expected or predicted if traditional litigation had proceeded. They can tally actual costs, and less obvious impacts, and make judgments about the overall benefits each of the parties achieved. In the end, they can determine whether a single dispute resolution effort produced results the parties felt were fair, and an independent analyst finds efficient. This is the main lens we use in this book.

Looking at JDR as a system, it is much more difficult to evaluate the efficacy and the impacts of a whole dispute-handling system—such as a specialized court that hears dozens of relatively similar cases every month—than it is to assess an individual dispute resolution effort. It is not obvious how to make an overall judgment of a system that incorporates many different judgements from the standpoints of many different parties. The average result may well hide more than it reveals: parties might be satisfied with the direct outcome of their JDR, but there might be unintended consequences they are unaware of. The public cost of confidentiality, for example, might represent a serious loss. Or, it could be the other way around: there might be unforeseen benefits of a system that seeks to expand the use of JDR. A commitment to JDR might lead to a shift in mindset among lawyers and court system users. This, in turn, could enhance the quality of justice produced overall. One key question remains: from whose perspective should the results of a dispute-handling system be evaluated?

We studied the nine JDR cases in great detail, but also tried to assess JDR more generally, as a new approach to handling a wide range of civil cases that come before the court. In their book, *Dispute Systems Design: Preventing, Managing and Resolving Conflicts,* Lisa Amsler, Janet Martinez and Stephanie Smith—reviewing the relatively new field of dispute system design (DSD)—make a distinction between DSD as the thing that is built and DSD as a process of managing institutionalized arrangements for dispute resolution (Amsler, Martinez, and Smith 2020). You can design a dispute handling system, you can run one, or you can do both. In this book, we have focused on both: the way individual judges piece together their own approach to mediating disputes that come before them, as well as the way the court system with large manages the JDR option provided in Canada.

Amsler, Martinez and Smith describe the common elements of all dispute handling systems: goals; stakeholders; context and culture; processes and structure; resources; and success, accountability and learning. While they don't evaluate JDR, they do report on DSD in quite a few sectors (e.g., labor relations, family law, environmental regulation, transitional justice, etc.), proving the relevance of their analytic framework. Applying it to the JDR systems we have observed reveals Canada's JDR goals as: (1) ensure more quality and more affordable access to judicial services to all citizens; (2) allow parties greater control over their disputes and, thus, more satisfying outcomes than traditional litigation; (3) reduce the court's burden by settling cases in much less time than it normally takes to hear them to their conclusion; and (4) increase the likelihood of compliance without enforcement because settlements are voluntary.

The stakeholders in the JDR system are, of course, the two or more parties to the litigation. However, we also see the judiciary as a stakeholder representing the public-at-large. Presumably, there are still other stakeholders: the experts who testify at trial; private mediators and arbitrators outside the court system who would like to handle the cases; court administrators; law professors; and the media.

The context and culture of the JDR system are confusing. The judge comes down from the dais to help the parties settle their dispute by switching into a mediation role. The search for settlement alters the lawyers role to one where they must still advise their clients on the law, but the parties engage each other and the judge directly. Legal arguments and reference to precedent do not apply. The parties are encouraged to search for mutually satisfactory agreements. And, no winner or loser is declared at the end. We will discuss another important aspect of JDR: it allows parties to approach conflict resolution that is more consistent with aboriginal and restorative justice, emphasizing conversation and participation among parties more as allies who care about their well-being and less as adversaries.

Although JDR takes place in the courthouse, there are no spectators, and it involves a lot of private caucuses. Court costs—including the judge and intake assessment by court staff—are covered by the government, and the parties pay for the services of their own counsel. JDR judges may ask for input from experts, but they are not cross-examined by the parties' lawyers. JDRs tend to take days rather than the months—even years—that would have normally been set aside to litigate the same cases. Accountability is achieved through private settlement agreements prepared by the parties that are sometimes signed by the JDR judge. Prior to the writing of this book, there wasn't much shared JDR knowledge within "the JDR system" because judges may not discuss their experiences with each other. JDR's high settlement rate shown by the data gathered by the Canadian courts thus far and almost no re-visits to the court to enforce voluntary JDR agreements, indicates that the parties and judges involved feel justice was achieved.

We did not study cases that went to JDR, failed to reach agreement, and then proceeded to litigation. Nor did we examine JDR outcomes in all the provinces in which it is currently being used. Our work stands as an initial review of JDR and its potential, rather than a complete evaluation as a dispute handling system. By comparison with Professor Susskind's oft-cited, in-depth analysis of negotiated rulemaking (Susskind et al. 1993), which includes many more detailed case studies, we have a pretty clear record, from a range of perspectives, of an ongoing dispute resolution experiment in which a long-standing system for handling civil cases was modified several times, and produced results that suggest the experimental approach "worked" pretty well.

In the U.S., Congress passes laws while the administrative apparatus of the federal government must enact regulations spelling out the details of how new laws will be implemented. The rule-making process is itself regulated by law (i.e., The Administrative Procedure Act). The U.S. Environmental Protection Agency, in an effort to avoid the extended legal delays that surrounded almost all of its efforts to pass new environmental laws, began experimenting with a process of inviting representatives of all the relevant stake-holding groups to participate, with the help of a neutral facilitator, in early efforts to draft new, consensus-based rules (Susskind and McMahon 1985). This collaborative process worked fairly well (in more than two dozen experiments) and Congress passed The Negotiated Rulemaking Act of 1990, adding a consensus building option to the larger system of administrative law in the U.S. Organizing and evaluating the negotiated rule-making experiments (concerning actual not hypothetical laws) took many years. Integrating the findings of multiple independent evaluations was contentious. But, in the end, a purposeful dispute system design effort led to a change in the way administrative law in the U.S. is practiced. The experiments were undertaken carefully, and the results were evaluated using standard applied social science methods.

JDR is not just a method; it can be considered a whole system—a process and a result—that integrates two domains that typically have been considered separately: the administration of the courts (including the role of judges) and the quality of justice produced by ADR methods.

Chapter 2

JUDICIAL DISPUTE RESOLUTION (JDR) AROUND THE WORLD

JDR, in one form or another, has been around for hundreds of years. The earliest examples involve Anglo-Saxon adjudication and arbitration that took place between the seventh and eleventh centuries A.D. (Sanchez 1996). In more recent centuries, judges have been called upon to settle, not adjudicate, all kinds of disputes, especially within families. In Canada, for the last thirty years, mini-trials (without juries) were promoted by the late Alberta Chief Justice William Ken Moore (Moore 1995). Throughout the 1980s, in both Canada and the U.S., the legal system placed increasing emphasis on what based on Frank Sander's ideas was coined as "the multi-door courthouse" and Judith Resnik called with some critical bite "the managerial judge," encouraging the use of ADR to move cases off the court's docket (Sander 1979; Resnik 1982, 1995).

Sander's idea had an impact in the U.S. In 1980, Congress passed the Dispute Resolution Act "to provide financial assistance for the development and maintenance of effective, fair, inexpensive, and expeditious mechanisms for the resolution for minor disputes." Then, in 1983, the Federal Rules of Civil Procedure were amended; Rule 16 endorsed the discussion of settlement at pre-trial conferences encouraging the parties to think hard about whether their dispute would be better resolved through voluntary resolution mechanisms than formal litigation.

The history of JDR in Canada is still an unfolding story aimed at imagining ways of empowering judges and parties to resolve their disputes and achieve a greater sense of justice.

The goal in a JDR remains to resolve a legal matter without consuming the usual level of court resources, while giving control back to the parties, control they relinquish when they choose to litigate. Giving the parties more authority and ensuring that they are treated fairly and respectfully is often the key to a greater sense of closure and satisfaction.

Anglo-Saxon Beginnings

In Valerie Sanchez's history of early ADR, she notes that Anglo-Saxon courts used a wide array of dispute resolution mechanisms akin to modern-day negotiation, mediation, arbitration and JDR. The emergence of Christian teachings paved the way for less vindictive conflict resolution that focused more on achieving peace. Sometimes, before an arbitrator decided a case—or even after they had done so—they tried to promote settlement. That is, before "judgements were finalized by oath-swearing, the 'third-party decisionmaker' often persuaded the losing party to come to terms with the winning party, fostering their reconciliation" (Sanchez 1996). This is an early historical account of a judicial decisionmaker (i.e., arbitrator or adjudicator) acting as a facilitator of settlement negotiations in the same way a JDR judge would today. The arbitrator provided the parties a provisional reality-test by telling them how the dispute would probably be resolved, but allowed them an opportunity to bargain in the "clear light of legal certainty" (Sanchez 1996). This left the parties with a clear choice: accept the most likely result of litigation or reach a better outcome themselves. Thus, JDR-like methods were used in the seventh century. Since then, judges, adjudicators and arbitrators, particularly in Canada, have often fostered settlement agreements before final decisions were imposed (Landerkin 2003).

Child Custody Disputes and Family Courts

In the nineteenth century, courts began addressing family disputes—synonymous with family life—in new ways. Social organizations like churches, schools and community groups provided mediation to struggling families. In the 1930, for instance, U.S. divorce courts recommended mediation and in some states like California, parties had the option of a conciliation process (American Arbitration Association 2003).

This new direction in child custody disputes also anticipated the emergence of JDR when it sought to help the parties maintain a working relationship for as long as possible. Thus, a more conciliatory approach to dispute resolution emerged—one less likely to tear relationships apart (Mintz 1992). During the Progressive Era in the U.S. (1896 – 1916), family courts provided even more informal, collaborative and conciliatory space to work out family conflicts. Societal problems, particularly in Canada and the U.S., were often attributed to dysfunctional homes. This led to the creation of "Socialized Tribunals" that redefined the role of judges (and courts) in family disputes:

> Socialized tribunals, where magistrates had the power to relax the usual rules of evidence and make judgments "in accordance with the social needs of the family" and where trained workers could mediate out-of-court settlements, would be far more conducive to domestic reconciliation than litigious hearings." Domestic relation courts, so the reformers said, would save money. Litigants could come to court without counsel; there would be no costs, and no occasion for pleadings. Like the justices-of-the-peace system, this court created its own procedure to carry out its purposes (Landerkin 1997).

In 1997, Hugh Landerkin, a judge of Calgary's Provincial Court of Alberta and a JDR scholar, completed his graduate thesis on JDR. It was subsequently published under the title "Custody Disputes in the Provincial Court of Alberta: A New Judicial Dispute Resolution Model" (Landerkin 1997). He proposed a judicial decision-making procedure in family disputes, drawing on W. K. Moore's Queen's Bench pre-trial model, that would proceed through three-stages: First, the Court adopts a standardized affidavit so that it can obtain relevant factual information about the dispute and the child. Second, the judge assumes the role of a mediator. This provides an important balance between the right of guardians to private ordering and the inherent checks afforded by public ordering of a court system. If no settlement is reached, the judge can offer a mini-trial hearing and render a non-binding judicial decision, which may nudge the parties toward a settlement on their own. In this third phase, the judge seeks to employ "all his or her knowledge and experience to help the parties reach a wise solution without the necessity of trial adjudication. The judge [uses] mediation skills to work with the parents, in open court, on the record, without hearing evidence, in an attempt to resolve the difficulties" (Landerkin 1997). If no settlement is reached, the parties proceed to trial before a new judge.

The child custody cases and socialized tribunals initiated a transformation of the judge's role. The judge was not only allowed to mediate, but was encouraged to bring his or her knowledge, experience and wisdom to help the parties formulate their own settlement. In Landerkin's view, JDR should always precede the assignment of a trial date, and in Canada since the early 1990s, that continues to be the case. Litigants who file for divorce find themselves in a dispute resolution process. The supportive role of the Court is emphasized, unlike traditional litigation.

Landerkin's JDR model builds on other pre-trial prototypes (Moore 1995): (1) the judge acts as a mediator; (2) the judge uses his or her knowledge to facilitate and encourage parties to settle; (3) the judge offers a non-binding decision, giving the parties a "reality check," or what negotiation theorists call a clearer BATNA; and (4) the judge allows the parties the option of going before a new judge if they are unable to settle. "The Alberta Court, with little or no statutory history, felt that it was in a good position to resolve family disputes. Some call this case management; some call this pre-trial conferencing; some call this settlement conferencing; some call it case conferencing" (Landerkin 1997). In Alberta, the federal judges of the Court of Queen's Bench (now King's Bench) call it JDR.

Mini-trials as Prototype JDRs

Associate Chief Justice Rooke suggests that another possible origin of JDR in Alberta was the advent of the mini-trial:

Alternatives to adjudication in the [Alberta Court of Queen's Bench] have been judicially led since 1992. Indeed, this is the start of a number of symbiotic processes that … led to JDR becoming institutionally normative. First, the judiciary initiated the JDR program. Second, a judicially led early alternative to adjudication (the minitrial) led, in turn, to a judicial expansion of the alternatives to include judicial mediation, binding JDR and hybrids of each. Third, as the first alternative service led to the expansion to other alternative services, the demand for JDR increased. Fourth, as the demand increased, it was followed by individual and systematic quantitative and qualitative successes. Fifth, this success was achieved in large part by the level and depth of judicial participation. Sixth, success has led to more demand. Seventh, through the evaluation of the JDR program, based on the empirical survey research reported in the evaluation report, the judiciary are now in the process of looking at recommendations to ensure that the important positive elements of the JDR program make it a growing, integral part of the resolution of disputes in [Alberta

Court of Queen's Bench]. Thus, it is asserted that the judicial role in the JDR program has been instrumental in contributing to JDR becoming institutionally normative within the court. (Rooke 2010).

A directory published by the Alberta Law Reform Institute in 1990 pointed to a number of ways in which trials could be made more settlement-prone and thus efficient: (1) mechanisms to reduce long trials; (2) mandatory pre-trial conferences; (3) case management and (4) mini-trial processes (Alberta Law Reform Institute 1990). The evolution of JDR in Canada is mixed with the emergence of mini-trials in the U.S. Around 1991, the Court of Queen's Bench of Alberta in Calgary and Edmonton announced that it was offering mini-trials to facilitate the settlement of disputes. A similar path has been taken by several other provinces (Alberta Law Reform Institute 1990; British Columbia Supreme Court Rules; Saskatchewan Rules of the Court of Queen's Bench; Manitoba Queen's Bench Rules; Ontario Rules of Civil Procedure).

In fact, the term mini-trial is something of a misnomer, as discussed in the introduction. Mini-trials are primarily voluntary interactions that sometimes lead to non-binding arbitration. Generally, they encourage parties and their lawyers to hear the arguments the other side intends to make and to work out their differences accordingly. The idea was borrowed from the American courts, specifically from California (Moore 1995) and imported into Canada with a few differences. Justice Moore notes: "[u]nlike the classic form of arbitration, there is no final and binding result in the Alberta mini-trial process. As with other ADR procedures, the object of the mini-trial is to permit both parties to see how their cases will play before a [judge], without the formality, inconvenience, publicity, or irrevocability of an actual courtroom trial" (Moore 1995). In a way, mini-trials are like rehearsals. Parties can hone their arguments and hear an independent commentary on what will likely happen in court, without suffering the consequences of an actual ruling. Mediation is rarely involved.

Canadian mini-trials (1) bring the parties together in the presence of a judge; (2) enable the parties, through their counsel, to put forward their arguments; (3) obtain a non-binding opinion as to what the judge believes will happen at trial and (4) promote or facilitate settlement discussions. Thus, from the beginning it was assumed that the presentation of evidence and arguments would take place before a sitting judge (not a private arbitrator or arbitration panel) and that the judge (in a JDR fashion) would offer to mediate once the parties had a clearer sense of the likely outcome of their litigation (Moore 1995).

Mini-trials in the Canadian context offer numerous advantages. First, they can narrow the issues in dispute—even if they don't lead to settlement—and they can facilitate the quick exchange of information. Second, since the judge conducting the mini-trial will not hear the case if the parties don't settle, the parties and their lawyers don't have to worry about revealing their arguments' strengths and weaknesses to the court that will issue a final ruling. Third, judges are not allowed to discuss any of their non-binding opinions with anyone on the bench. Fourth, for many counsel and parties, hearing the non-binding opinion of a judge is tantamount to having their day in court, without the risks of losing the case. Fifth, the non-binding opinion of a judge can make it easier for lawyers to explain to their clients that they may have unrealistic expectations about the likely outcome.

Mini-trials and JDRs have their similarities; perhaps the key difference is that a mini-trial judge is more or less limited to listening to an expedited presentation of the legal claims on both sides and offering a non-binding opinion about what will probably happen if the case goes to court. The mini-trial, even in Canada, rarely leads to mediation by the sitting judge; that only happens when the parties choose JDR. The JDR judge functions as a mediator: telling the parties what factual materials to prepare and share ahead of time; caucusing with and without both the parties and their lawyers at various stages in the agreement-seeking discussions; calling for and reviewing materials provided by expert witnesses; evaluating possible settlement options with one or both sides; and ultimately offering either a binding or a non-binding opinion. Everything that happens during the JDR remains sealed, though the judge may keep his or her own notes in case they are needed during subsequent enforcement conversations (Moore 1995).

The Idea of the Multi-door Courthouse and the Evolution of JDR

Harvard Law Professor Frank Sander believed that each dispute has its singularities and that not all disputes should be resolved through trial. He argued that the court system should "fit the forum to the fuss," following Maurice Rosenberg's phrase, and he imagined the so-called "multi-door courthouse" where disputes are screened and then directed through a negotiation, mediation, arbitration, fact-finding, or trial "door" (Sander 1979; Sander and Goldberg 1994). In other words, going to court should not mean that the parties are heading to trial. The most important question, then and now, is how can the court system know which kind of resolution method is most appropriate for each dispute?

Alberta was at the forefront of the "multi-door courthouse movement" in Canada. As Associate Chief Justice Rooke pointed out, initially, some judges were hostile about ADR, but now many are openly promoting and practicing it. In Rooke's words, "The result is that it is now beyond question that active judicial participation in settlement procedures, broadly or narrowly defined, is a part of the dispute resolution program in the court. Simply put, with all trained and/or experienced JDR judges participating, JDR has become and is part of the judicial function in the court." He went on to say, "By the end of 1999, JDR had 'been largely institutionalized in the superior courts of the Prairie Provinces' with the [Alberta Court of Queen's Bench] becoming the First court in Canada to incorporate 'JDR weeks' into their regular sitting schedules" (Rooke 2010).

The emergence of ADR in North America, which has focused mostly on Court-Annexed Mediation (CAM) by trained mediators rather than by sitting judges, is often incorrectly assumed to be the source of JDR in Canada. In fact, it was the idea of the multi-door courthouse—emphasizing the "helping role" the court system can play in addressing societal problems—that was the primary inspiration for JDR. ADR contin-ues to represent an effort to reduce the cost of litigation and enhance the efficiency of the court system. JDR, while also a contributor to greater court efficiency has, from the beginning, stood for securing justice with a more appropriate process when the opportunities present themselves.

The court system needed to be redesigned; not only to reduce the increasingly heavy judicial workload and rising court costs, but to improve the quality of justice from the standpoint of the litigants. This transformation would allow dispute resolution services to fit the unique needs of each case. Sander opened the way for experimentation with the design of the whole court system, not just for the use of new dispute handling procedures in particular cases. After Sander, the courts could be seen as "justice brokers" referring disputes to most appropriate resolution processes (Zariski 2018). The multi-door courthouse underscored the idea of the court as a site for innovation and experimentation. In Canada, that's what JDR represents.

Chief Judge Brian Morris of the United States District Court, District of Montana, suggested to one of us, that federal court judges might operate more like JDR judges in Canada. They probably have more discretionary authority than they think: In his words:

> The ability of federal district court judges to refer cases to settlement conferences as part of the Rule 16 process or its case management authority represents one of the most powerful tools available to promote fairness, reduce case processing time, and address the prohibitive cost of civil litigation. Federal courts should make available the experience and skill of magistrate judges and Article III judges to conduct settlement conferences to allow the parties to resolve disputes on their terms.

Based on our conversation with Judge Morris, we believe that judges in the United States, after learning more about JDR in Canada, might be inspired to move beyond settlement conferences to something more like the flexible JDR system in Canada (including Binding and hybrid JDRs). Obviously, JDR practices can not be transferred directly to the US, but there's a lot that could be learned from the Canadian JDR experience and applied in the US. What distinguishes JDR in Canada from ADR in the US at present are firstly, in Canada, judges step down from the dais in cases where they have been asked to mediate (following the beginning of the trial or any court application) and work as facilitative mediators as long as the lawyers and the parties agree. Facilitative mediation and judicial conferencing are not the same thing. Secondly, the JDR judge seeks to help parties construct a settlement on their own terms (independent of the points of law or past precedent that would normally dominate the discussion if settlement of the litigation were the only goal); thirdly, in Canada, there is a joint problem-solving setting created inside the courthouse (including a judge-run JDR intake system). Judges with just settlement conferencing experience would need more mediation training.

The Managerial Judge

In 1982, Yale Law Professor Judith Resnik pointed to, and was critical about, an important shift that was occurring in the role of judges: moving from a classically disinterested role to a more hands-on managerial role. The classical view assumes judges are disengaged with no particular interest in specific disputes or disputants. Resnik's diagnosis showed that judges not only adjudicate disputes on their merits, but are also actively concerned about reducing or managing the court's burden, its workflow, and the demands on its staff." Judges are managers of the litigation process, which might invite sacrificing justice for efficiency. Thus, they must constantly "negotiat(e) with the parties about the course, timing, and scope of both pretrial and posttrial litigation" (Resnik 1982). Judges are managers of the litigation process.

This new managerial orientation made judges more aware of the deficiencies of the trial system, which were increasingly costly, lengthy and adversarial. The system was not concerned with how parties felt about the outcome; it took no responsibility for the relationships between the parties after an outcome was reached, regardless of the difficulties the parties might face in ensuring compliance in situations where those who "lost" decided to fight back. To alleviate docket caseloads, "judges ... turned to efficiency experts who promise(d) 'calendar control.' Under these experts' guidance, judges began to experiment with schemes for speeding the resolution of cases and for persuading litigants to settle rather than try cases whenever possible" (Resnik 1982). This certainly involved experimentation with JDR and a shift away from adjudication, but the motivation was to make it easier for the courts to operate efficiently, not to improve the quality of justice by having the court system take more responsibility for meeting the needs of the disputants.

It is difficult to trace the genealogy of the managerial perspective in the U.S. and Canada. One view highlights the role of the U.S. Congress which authorized the supreme court to write new rules of civil procedure: the court should "prescribe the rules for the conduct of their business" (U.S.C. 1976). The Court granted permission to district courts, which in turn empowered local courts to focus more on reducing court workloads, increasing the speed with which cases were heard, and encouraging the use of ADR to keep cases out of the court all together. The Rules of Civil Procedure call for "the just, speedy and inexpensive determination of every action" (Federal Rules of Civil Procedure). Additionally, in 1967, Congress established the Federal Judicial Center, which offered training to judges in the techniques of docket management (U.S.C. 1976).

Unfortunately, this mindset-shift did not come with clear standards or guidelines for determining which form of dispute handling should apply in each case. Nor did it come with a clear mandate that the quality of justice (in the eyes of the parties) should be given the same concern as the increased efficiency of the court system. Judges were offered training in docket management, but they were not offered (or required to obtain) training in JDR, or when and how to use ADR. The fact is judges and court system managers were told that settlement is a better outcome because it is quicker, cheaper and less burdensome on the court system (Resnik 1982). Unfortunately, there was no evidence to back up this assertion.

Judicial Dispute Resolution in Other Parts of the World

Other countries beyond the U.S. and Canada have their own versions of JDR, or at least a rudimentary form of it. Brazil, Colombia and Chile vest in judges the power to promote and enact measures to resolve disputes efficiently, allowing judges to conciliate. In India and Israel, courts are allowed to send cases to court-recognized mediators who are not sitting judges, more in the U.S. style of ADR but called JDR in those countries.

The People's Republic of China has a system closer to the Canadian model of JDR. According to Kwai Hang Ng and Xin He, the civil trial in China is a good example of combining mediation and adjudication in an integrated trial process leading to the settlement of more than 60 percent of all cases (Hang Ng and He 2014). At the beginning of civil hearings, the judge announces the planned phases of the trial (i.e., court investigation, discussion, mediation and decision). Thus, the same judge—not a different one as in Canada—serves as an adjudicator and as a mediator during the trial. Hong Kong's system allows the parties who have filed an action to mediate during the early stages of the process, where the judge might encourage mediation but would probably not facilitate it (Lee 2014). In Singapore, the State Courts Centre for Dispute Resolution, established in 2015, employs mediation, among other methods, to manage cases without resorting to trial. If the claim exceeds $60,000, parties are referred to the appropriate mode of court dispute resolution (CDR) unless they opt out, very much like Sander's multi-door courthouse (Singapore State Courts).

In Australia there have been initiatives of court-conducted mediations, more commonly led by court officers, registrars, or deputy registrars than judges. The exception is Victoria where a former Victorian Attorney General studied the Canadian model, endorsed judicial mediation, and said: "Well over 80% of matters that go before judge mediators are resolved and resolved very quickly. Why? Because you have the imprimatur of a judge resolving these matters" (Spencer 2006).

Philippines' judicial system is committed to promoting party autonomy in the resolution of disputes and encourages a three-stage process using ADR methods. In the first stage, the judge leading the CAM refers the parties to a mediation center. If this fails, the judge initiates a JDR process and becomes the mediator. If the case is not settled, the mediator judge refers the case to another judge who will try the case (Philippine Justice Administration).

In China, judicial mediation has been used consistently. According to recent studies, Chinese justices are motivated by alleviating their heavy caseloads, resolving cases quickly, and preserving social stability. In China, there are no such institutional firewalls, judges are both the mediator and adjudicator (He 2022, 1194). But rarely express their opinion on the merits of the case, which does not mean judges do not present settlement proposals to the parties. Judicial mediation has been prioritized since the 1940s as a basic policy because it facilitates information and improves communication among parties. This prioritization was later reinstated in the Civil Procedure Law of the People's Republic of China (1982) and has become part of the distinctive characteristics of China's judicial system (Chen 2015). Chinese judicial mediation, therefore, was seen as part of a larger project of maintaining social stability and shaping a harmonious society, but for others, it is seen as an exercise of state power rationalized as part of tradition and custom. In his detailed empirical analysis of how judicial mediation works in China, however, Fan observes that mediation has been on a decline since President Xi Jinping rose to power (Fan 2023).

There are few countries that have added ADR and case management to their court systems and included a Canadian-style JDR option. Sourdin and Zariski write about "multi-tasking judges" in many parts of the world, but they are referring mostly to judges encouraging—not providing—ADR, as in the U.S., in an effort to reduce the cost and time it takes to litigate (Sourdin and Zariski 2013). If JDR in Canada is motivated primarily by a desire to improve the quality, not just the efficiency of justice, our findings may inspire judges, lawyers and court administrators around the world who are still operating exclusively as adjudicators to reconsider their options. Judges are transforming, as Macfarlane argues, their approach to disputes and the skills they use to manage them. They are also shaping themselves as facilitators and mediators of settlements and crafting new roles for judges (Macfarlane 2012; Macfarlane 2008). JDR as practiced in Canada is an example of this trend.

Chapter 3

THE HISTORY OF JDR IN CANADA

Canada's efforts to resolve and manage legal disputes have included mini-trials, pre-trial conferences, settlement conferences, as well as binding and non-binding JDR. The Court of Appeal in Quebec and the Court of Queen's Bench of Alberta initiated ADR efforts in the mid-1990s. Although there are differences among some local and provincial court practices, there is a clear commitment to move away from purely adversarial to more collaborative means of resolving legal disputants. But how did this collaborative drive emerge?

"JDR has a common legal root in both the U.S. and Canada. In the U.S., it is Rule 16 of the U.S. Federal Rules of Civil Procedure (FRCP) on pre-trial conferences, scheduling and management established in 1938. One of the purposes of a pre-trial conference in any jurisdiction is to facilitate settlement, and the statutory authorization to open up extrajudicial dispute resolution techniques comes under the umbrella of pre-trial management—or settlement conferences. Particularly, Rule 16 (a)(5) provides that the judge may in its discretion direct the attorneys for the parties and any unrepresented parties to appear before it for a conference with a purpose "facilitating settlement." One of the most pressing questions since the emergence of settlement conferences is how much judges should be actively engaged in facilitation and what was the appropriate role judges should embrace (Menkel-Meadow 1985). As stated by Maurice Rosenberg, the pre-trial conferences derived from Rule 16 were, for some states mainly to clarify issues and improve the conditions for an eventual trial (trial orientation), whereas, for other states, the primary objective was to get rid of the trial and settle (settlement orientation). The pretrial conference "confronts the judge with so many choices as to the intensity of his participation, and does so in an atmosphere less inhibited than at the trial (Rosenberg 10-11, 1964). These choices aimed at lowering delays in case resolution, handling cases more effectively, and inviting more settlements. Encouraging judges to be actively involved in settlement discussions is not restricted to the US. In England and Wales, Rule 1(4)(2)(f) of the Civil Procedure (1993) establishes the duty to manage the cases by "helping the parties to settle the whole or part of the case" (UK Civil Procedure Rules 1998). The introduction of the Civil Procedure Rules 1998 has encouraged experimentation in negotiation settlements and court mediation projects (e.g., National Mediation Helpline and court-referred mediations). But these reforms gravitated around judicial encouragement of mediation instead of judicial-oriented mediation (Prince 2009). Settlement conferences and procedural reforms have been part of a trend to inspire JDR efforts and are one of the bedrocks of JDR in Canada and the annexed JDR-like dispute processing methods in the U.S. The other foundation is Frank Sander's idea of a a variety of dispute processing captured in the idea of a "multi-door courthouse."

In Canada, the implementation of the multi-door courthouse idea, a focus on the judge's managerial role, and the emergence of ADR in general, were spurred by a report in 1989 by the Canadian Bar Association Task Force on ADR. The report was intended to not only promote reform of the judiciary, but also as a means of changing lawyers' minds about the merits of ADR and JDR. The Bar Association argued: "If lawyers appreciate that their primary function is problem-solving, 'alternative dispute resolution will not be viewed as superior or inferior to, or indeed even separate from, court adjudication'" (Canadian Bar Association 1996). The intent of the Bar was to make a case for ADR as a fundamental part of the judicial system, not as an alternative to it. Although ADR is usually understood as a non-court option, there might be other ways of engaging the judiciary, not necessarily as alternatives to court—like JDR. This expansion of alternative methods is shifting some lawyers' thinking about the dispute resolution skills they need, and led the Bar to include pre-trial conferences, settlement conferences or JDR, mini-trials and mandatory mediation on the list of ADR options. Canada moved quickly, as Justice Alan Linden explains:

> We in Canada are lucky with our legal system. It's been a very fine system. It served us extremely well, but it, too, is beginning to show wear and tear. Not so much of time, but of numbers. As the cities are growing, as the numbers of lawyers grow, as the types of disputes that come up in our society increase in number and in complexity, greater and greater pressure is being placed upon the legal system to respond to it and a lot of methods are really not working as well nowadays. It's just taking us too long and costing too much…
>
> Conflict is becoming more and more a part of our life. So often it seems there are battles that don't seem to go anywhere … There are, of course, benefits to … [the adversary system] but there are also costs, and in particular these days, the costs of lawyers who, if they wish, can battle the way for months and even years before trial and during trial. There are so many issues now that can be raised that people can drown one another with costs and we as judges, I think, and as people who are in charge of the legal system, have got to start getting hold of it (Rooke 2010).

Justice Linden concluded by pointing out not only a new way of thinking about dispute resolution, but also a new way of thinking about the judges' role in relation to ADR: "I believe that it's important for judges to be involved if we can devise within the system techniques to bring the parties together" (Rooke 2010).

This ADR moment led to more dispute resolution initiatives across Canada. The Divorce Act of 1985, for example, required lawyers to certify that they had talked with their clients about dispute resolution alternatives. In 1986, the Zuber Report for Ontario recommended that the Court offer a range of dispute resolution mechanisms, including mediation and arbitration.

By the 1990s, a wave of judicial experimentation had hit most Canadian courts. The influence of the ADR debates in the U.S. must be acknowledged, but it was judicial flexibility that made it possible to introduce what some provinces called "settlement conferences" and others named "JDR" (Otis 2006).

It is worth noting that settlement conferences as they are practiced in the U.S. are not quite the same as JDR. Unlike BJDR, in settlement conferences the judge cannot provide a binding opinion on the substance of a case and the ultimate decision is still left to the parties. Sometimes settlement conferences are conducted by retired judges as in the Judicial Settlement Conference Program in Virginia's Judicial System. But, even if a settlement conference is conducted by a sitting judge in the U.S., they don't lose their jurisdiction over the case if the settlement fails.

Some Canadian legal scholars suggest that JDR was originally offered in the 1980s, although it is not clear exactly what form of ADR they are referring to (Agrios 2004). The term "JDR" had not yet been coined at the time, but mini-trials were, indeed, offered (Rooke 2010). Whether provinces called them JDR, settlement conferences, or pre-trial conferences, in the Canadian context, there might be significant differences among these forms of ADR, as explained before.

Alberta

Alberta was the first province to coin the term JDR (Landerkin 1997; McEwan 1999). In 1993, JDR was offered in the provincial and federal (Queen's Bench) court system. This decades-long history, plus its more recent emphasis on settlement, make Alberta a JDR pioneer. In 2004, about 80 percent of the cases referred to JDR in Alberta settled (Agrios 2004). JDR gained traction in part because of the efforts of Queen's Bench ACJ Rooke. He believed in resolving disputes and wrote his LL.M. thesis on the subject of JDR. As the Associate Chief, he also promoted the JDR SPEC program discussed in Chapter 16.

The Alberta courts have published guidelines that explain what parties can expect if they use JDR, although individual courts operate slightly differently. This can be some-what confusing because the guidelines also serve as a roadmap for new judges who do not have experience conducting JDRs. In the Edmonton court, the guidelines state, "the purpose of judicial dispute resolution is to reach a settlement on all issues or to resolve as many issues as possible with the assistance of a judge of the Court. JDR is voluntary and all parties must agree to the process. The JDR meeting is strictly confidential, and all parties must be present" (Agrios 2004). On the Queen's Bench Court website, there is a different definition: "Judicial Dispute Resolution (JDR) is a confidential pre-trial settlement conference led by a Justice of the Court of Queen's Bench. The objective of a JDR is to resolve the dispute so a trial will be either unnecessary or at most limited to those issues on which the parties do not agree" (Court of Queen's Bench of Alberta).

For the most part, the mechanics of JDR are equivalent to the way settlement conferences and pre-trial settlements are administered. Perhaps the most striking difference is Alberta's two types of JDR: non-binding and binding (BJDR). According to ACJ Rooke, [BJDR] seems like an oxymoron in concept, but it works with great success ... and [is in] great demand by the parties" (Rooke 2010).

> ... parties meet with Justice to confidentially discuss the background of the case and what the parties feel is important in the case. The participants will then discuss possible solu-tions. If no agreement is reached, the Justice may give a non-binding opinion of what deci-sion they would make if this case and these facts were presented at trial. The Justice's non-binding opinion may help the parties and their lawyers reach a resolution without

having to go to trial. A settlement is only reached if everyone agrees. Binding JDRs are also available at the Court of Queen's Bench. In these cases, the parties agree that the Justice's opinion will be binding (Court of Queen's Bench of Alberta).

Thus, the characteristics of JDR include filing pre-JDR briefs, and focus on (1) self-determination; (2) confidentiality; (3) judicial mediation; (4) binding vs non-binding judge's opinions and (5) the facilitative vs. evaluative style of the mediating judge. The binding and non-binding alternatives give more [choice] to the parties … and the judge can still have the last word on how to resolve the dispute (by shifting to a more adjudica-tive mode at the request of the parties) (Otis 2006; Agrios 2004).

Below is the most detailed regulations of JDR in Canada. We include them *in toto* because there is nothing else quite like them and other jurists will want to study them. These are Alberta's Rules of Court.

Subdivision 2
Judicial Dispute Resolution
Purpose of the JDR

4.17   "The purpose of this Subdivision is to provide a party-initiated framework for a judge to actively facilitate a process in which the parties resolve all or part of a claim by agreement.

Judicial dispute resolution process

4.18(1)   An arrangement for a judicial dispute resolution process may be made only with the agreement of the participating parties and, before engaging in a judi-cial dispute resolution process, and subject to the directions of the presiding judge, the participating parties must agree to the extent possible on at least the following:

    (a) that every party necessary to participate in the process has agreed to do so, unless there is sufficient reason not to have complete agreement;

    (b) rules to be followed in the process, including rules respecting

        (i)   the nature of the process,

        (ii)   the matters to be the subject of the process,

        (iii) the manner in which the process will be conducted,

        (iv)   the date on which and the location and time at which the process will occur,

        (v)   the role of the judge and any outcome expected of that role,

        (vi)   any practice or procedure related to the process, including exchange of materials, before, at or after the process,

        (vii) who will participate in the process, which must include persons who have authority to agree on a resolution of the dispute, unless otherwise agreed and

        (viii) any other matter appropriate to the process, the parties or the dispute.

(2)   The parties who agree on the proposed judicial dispute resolution process are entitled to participate in the process.

(3)   The parties to a proposed judicial dispute resolution process may request that a judge named by the parties participate in the process.

Documents resulting from judicial dispute resolution

4.19   The only documents, if any, that may result from a judicial dispute resolution process are
    (a) an agreement prepared by the parties, and any other document necessary to implement the agreement,
    (b) a consent order or consent judgment resulting from the process, and
    (c) a transcript of proceedings made in open court at the time of the judicial dispute resolution process which records the outcome of the judicial dispute resolution process.

Confidentiality and use of information

4.20(1) A judicial dispute resolution process is a confidential process intended to facilitate the resolution of a dispute.
(2)   Unless the parties otherwise agree in writing, statements made or documents generated for or in the judicial dispute resolution process with a view to resolving the dispute
    (a) are privileged and are made or generated without prejudice,
    (b) must be treated by the parties and participants in the process as confidential and may only be used for the purpose of that dispute resolution process, and
    (c) may not be referred to, presented as evidence or relied on, and are not admissible in a subsequent application or proceeding in the same action or in any other action, or in proceedings of a judicial or quasi-judicial nature.
(3)   Subrule (2) does not apply to the documents referred to in rule 4.19 [Documents resulting from judicial dispute resolution].
(4)   Subrule (2) does not prevent the use of statements made or documents generated for or in the judicial dispute resolution process to prove the fact that a settlement was reached or the terms of a settlement.

Involvement of judge after process concludes

4.21(1) The judge facilitating a judicial dispute resolution process in an action must not hear or decide any subsequent application, proceeding or trial in the action without the written agreement of every party and the agreement of the judge.
(2)   The judge facilitating a judicial dispute resolution process must treat the judicial dispute resolution process as confidential, and all the records relating to the process in the possession of the judge or in the possession of the court clerk must be returned to the parties or destroyed except

    (a)   the agreement of the parties and any document necessary to implement the agreement, and

    (b)   a consent order or consent judgment resulting from the process.

(3)   The judge facilitating a judicial dispute resolution process is not competent to give evidence nor compellable to give evidence in any application or proceeding relating to the process in the same action, in any other action, or in any proceeding of a judicial or quasi-judicial nature.

In fact, Alberta takes JDR so seriously that the court may order J/ADR on its own motion in certain circumstances (see 4.16(4) below):

4.16(1)   The responsibility of the parties to manage their dispute includes good faith participation in one or more of the following dispute resolution processes with respect to all or any part of the action:

    (a)   a dispute resolution process in the private or government sectors involving an impartial third person;

    (b)   a Court annexed dispute resolution process;

    (c)   a judicial dispute resolution process described in rules 4.17 to 4.21;

    (d)   any program or process designated by the Court for the purpose of this rule.

(2)   On application, the Court may waive the responsibility of the parties under this rule, but only if

    (a)   before the action started the parties engaged in a dispute resolution process and the parties and the Court believe that a further dispute resolution process would not be beneficial,

    (b)   the nature of the claim is not one, in all the circumstances, that will or is likely to result in an agreement between the parties,

    (c)   there is a compelling reason why a dispute resolution process should not be attempted by the parties,

    (d)   the Court is satisfied that engaging in a dispute resolution process would be futile, or

    (e)   the claim is of such a nature that a decision by the Court is necessary or desirable.

(3)   The parties must attend the hearing of an application under subrule (2) unless the Court otherwise orders.

(4)   A case management judge or a case conference judge may, on application or on the Court's own motion, by order direct that the parties participate in a dispute resolution process.

(5)   In determining whether an order under subrule (4) should be made, the case management judge or case conference judge may consider all relevant circumstances, including

    (a)   the issues in the litigation,

    (b)   the nature of the cause of action and the relief claimed,

    (c)   the identity, relationship and means of the parties,

    (d)   whether the action has proceeded to a stage at which alternative dispute resolution is likely to be successful, including whether record production and questioning are sufficiently advanced to support the dispute resolution process, and

    (e)   whether any of the factors in subrule (2) justify delaying, modifying or dispensing with the need to participate in a dispute resolution process.

(6)   As part of an order made under subrule (4), the case management judge or case conference judge may give directions respecting any aspect of the dispute resolution process, including

    (a)   the identity of a neutral third party to be involved in the process,

    (b)   where an equal sharing of the expenses is not appropriate, directions apportioning the responsibility of each party for the expenses of the neutral third party and other disbursements relating to the process,

    (c)   the time, location, structure or conduct of the process, and

    (d)   the consequences of the failure of any party to comply with any directions, or to pay its share of the expenses (emphasis added)."

Quebec

In 1997, the Quebec Court of Appeal initiated an ADR program (created by Justice Louise Otis and endorsed by Justice Yves Michaud) that allowed judges to act as conciliators in family matters. It was subsequently expanded to cover civil and commercial disputes and later adopted with some minor changes by the Quebec Superior Court trial judges (Otis 2000).

The procedural mechanics of the Quebec program were straightforward and, more importantly, embodied the essence of contemporary JDR:

> If both parties agreed to undergo judicial conciliation, a session would be scheduled for them with Justice Otis, who at the time was the only judge conducting such sessions. "With the growing popularity of the programme and the positive reputation it has acquired since its beginning, the court no longer has to take an active part in finding cases because more and more parties voluntarily file requests for judicial conciliation (…) If both parties agreed to undergo judicial conciliation, a session [is scheduled] (…) A judge conciliator, chosen by the court clerk administering the programme, will conduct the session and, with the help of the parties, establish the rules to govern the session. The process can include caucusing, joint sessions, meetings with lawyers, video or phone conferences. If an agreement is reached, the parties will put down in writing the terms of the agreement which will then be sent to a panel of the court so that it may be (…) rendered enforceable. This offers a great advantage for parties who then have in hand an agreement that has the force of a judgment and which can be executed as such. Should no agreement be reached, the judge (…) who conducted the conciliation session cannot take part in any hearing relating to the matter. The session is confidential and any notes taken during the process will be destroyed at the end of it (…) Justice Otis, the architect of the system, and Lysanne Legault, the coordinator of the programme, insist that the role of the judge conciliator is facilitative, they do acknowledge that in some cases evaluative mediation takes place, because of particular circumstances, or the style of some judge conciliators. In any event, if an evaluation is given, it is done so only to help parties gain perspective. (…) Throughout the mediation process, the judge conciliator enjoys judicial immunity, which protects him from civil liability, but this does not protect him from disciplinary actions." (Otis 2006).

Based on this description, it is clear that the Quebec Court of Appeal judicial conciliation program follows the main characteristics of JDR as it is practiced elsewhere in Canada:

- *Self-determination of the parties* (the parties must consent to undergo judicial conciliation)
- *Judicial mediation* (the judge conducts the conciliation or settlement conference)
- *Facilitative style* (the role of the judge is mainly facilitative)
- *Evaluative style exceptionally* (the judge can offer evaluative judgments to give parties perspective and reality-test their assessments)
- *Procedural flexibility* (the judge and the parties establish the rules that will govern the session)
- *Plurality in the modalities of conferencing* (the judge can use caucusing, joint sessions, or meeting with lawyers)
- *Virtual or physical interaction* (the judge can use video, phone, or other non-physical modes of communication as it is the case in online judicial dispute resolution)
- *Enforceable agreement* (if an agreement is reached, parties must write it down so that it can be enforceable by the court)
- *Impartiality and neutrality in an eventual trial* (if no agreement is reached, the case cannot be heard by the same judge who acted as the mediator)
- *Confidentiality* (any notes, testimonies and conversations shall be confidential).
- *Immunity* (the judge acting as a conciliator has judicial immunity, but is liable for disciplinary action)

In 2006, six judges acted as conciliators in the Court of Appeal. Although some of these judges have formal training in mediation, it is not a requirement.

In 2001, the Superior Court followed the Court of Appeal's example and began offering settlement conferences. A year later, language about settlement conferences was added to the Canadian Code of Civil Procedure. According to the code, the purpose of settlement conferences is "to facilitate dialogue between the parties to help them better understand and assess their respective needs, interests and positions, and explore solutions that may lead to a mutually satisfactory agreement to resolve the dispute" (Canadian Code of Civil Procedure). In 2002, the Court of Quebec followed the lead of the Superior and Appeal Court and organized its own judicial mediation program. The most important feature of the Court of Quebec program is that the parties can request mediation at any point during the trial, and conciliation assistance is provided by a second judge (Otis 2006).

Ontario

In Ontario's trial courts the story is different. Pre-trial conferences are quite common and their purpose and mechanics are spelled out by the Ontario Rules of Civil Procedure (rule 50). These conferences might be led by a judge or a case management master who can explore a range of methods for resolving contested issues and consider settling only some elements of a case. The pre-trial conference—where lawyers are not necessarily required to attend—is "an opportunity for any or all of the issues in a proceeding to be settled without a hearing and, concerning any issues that are not settled, to obtain from the court, orders or directions to assist in the just, most expeditious and least expensive disposition of the proceeding" (Ontario Rules of Civil Procedure). The procedures, though, are flexible with only four requirements: (1) a joint request for assistance must be made by the parties (self-determination); (2) confidentiality must be ensured; (3) a judge must be the mediator; and (4) independence and impartiality are required if a trial follows.

The Quebec system indicates why the differences between JDR and pre-trial conferences are salient. A pre-trial conference may be conducted without the parties being present, unlike JDR. Pre-trial conference rules do not specify whether parties must cover any of the costs or whether or not previous proceedings must be suspended before dispute resolution efforts can begin; in JDR, parties do not pay court costs and previous proceedings must be suspended. Pre-trial conferences (and settlement conferences in Quebec) are aimed at producing less expensive alternatives to a trial. These are tools judges can use to manage their case load. The point of JDR, in contrast, is to clearly facilitate communication between the parties and generate a solution that satisfies both sides.

In 1995, the Court of Appeal of Ontario published a statement indicating it was ready to incorporate judicial mediation into its operations—an action taken by Justice Jean-Marc Labrosse and Justice Karen M. Weiler. Yet, from 1995 to 2000, there were very few judicial mediations. In 2000, a pilot-program for family law matters was initiated and by 2003 had become permanent.

In 2011, the Ontario Bar Association Board of Directors charged its Judicial Mediation Task Force with the mission of (1) developing a comprehensive understanding of the JDR landscape; (2) determining whether and, if so, how, JDR could improve access to justice; and (3) offering recommendations to relevant policymakers to further the goals of access to justice and enhancing the reputation of the administration of justice. The Task Force played a large part in promoting the popularity of judicial mediation in Ontario (Ontario Bar Association 2013).

British Columbia (B.C.)

In 2004, the B.C. Court of Appeal introduced a two-year pilot project offering pre-hearing judicial settlement conferences for the first time, based in large part on the experience of the Quebec Court of Appeals (Leacock 2004). As of 2021, settlement conferences still exist in B.C., governed by the Court Rules Act Rule 9-2, and can be ordered by a judge or requested by the parties.

The purpose of the pilot was primarily to save time and money. To participate in the process both parties must consent, but the court has the power to reject the petition if it considers the case unsuitable for settlement. The conference is presided over by a judge who facilitates based on the Practice Directive from the court. The process is confidential, and if an agreement is reached, a formal judicial order is entered. If an agreement is not reached, the judge is excluded from the panel presiding over the appeal that follows.

Besides settlement conferences, B.C. adopted an experimental approach to dispute resolution that has had an impact on subsequent online tools used for communication and convenience. In 2021, B.C. adopted Canada's first online tribunal, an important innovation in online dispute resolution (ODR). According to the Stanford Legal Design

Lab, "Canada—in particular B.C.—has been the leading light in using online tools for providing dispute resolution to citizens" (Stanford Legal Design Lab). For instance, the Civil Resolution Tribunal (CRT) is "Canada's first online tribunal and, currently, the only ODR system in the world that is fully integrated into the justice system. The CRT allows the public to resolve their condominium property and small claims disputes fairly, quickly, and affordably" (Salter 2017).

B.C.'s first ODR initiative was not the CRT. In 2011, Modria Technologies—a company led by Colin Rule, who designed eBay's Dispute Resolution Settlement system—developed the Consumer Protection dispute resolution system. The same year, the British Columbia Property Assessment Appeal Board (PAAB) began using online systems to handle disputes over residential property tax assessments. These two prototypes encouraged B.C.'s Ministry of Justice to develop a more expansive system of ODR, leading to passage of the Civil Resolution Tribunal Act in 2012 (Salter 2017). Three years later, the Act was amended making CRT a mandatory forum for condominium property disputes and small claims disputes in B.C. (up to $5,000). In, 2018, B.C. further amended its CRT Act to cover motor vehicle injury disputes up to $50,000.

B.C.'s incursion into ODR now has a lot to do with JDR. When the COVID-19 pandemic hit, court processes across Canada, including JDR, had to be reimagined for virtual use. B.C.'s CRT helped other provincial courts envision JDR in the virtual realm.

Brief Note on Other Provinces

The provinces of Saskatchewan, Manitoba and Prince Edward Island have offered JDR since 1984, but under the labels of Civil Pretrial Conferences or settlement conferences (Richler 2011). In Manitoba, the court recently initiated a Judicially-Assisted Dispute Resolution option. Nova Scotia, New-Brunswick and others have developed similar pretrial or settlement conferences. As all of these descriptions suggest, the locus of judicial experimentation and the push for ADR in Canada have come at the local level in the trial courts. In Alberta and Nova Scotia, the courts adopted hybrid procedures ranging from judicial settlement conferences to binding JDR.

Recapitulation: Judicial Mediation in Canada

It appears that all of the court-sponsored ADR programs in Canada share the following characteristics: (1) self-determination (party-initiated processes); (2) judicial mediation (judge-led facilitation to bring parties together); (3) facilitative approach (facilitation is the default rule in terms of style, while the directive approach or providing binding evaluation is the exception) ; (4) procedural flexibility (judges and parties can shape the design of their dispute resolution efforts); (5) plural modes of structuring the encounters between the disputants; (6) physical interaction between the parties was the default norm, but virtual encounters surfaced recently; (7) court enforcement of the terms of settlement; (8) confidentiality; (9) no fee imposed by the court; (10) neutrality and impartiality if dispute resolution fails and trials follow; and (11) accountability (the judge has immunity but also must be accountable for the proceedings) (Zariski 2018).

Associate Chief Justice Rooke found most of the cases sent to JDR had been in the legal system for years and ended with a settlement rate of around 80 percent. This should not, however, lead to the conclusion that JDR is operating at its best. In fact, judges need additional training not only to raise the success rate, but to satisfy parties that a judge presiding over the JDR proceeding is a good thing.

Judges influence how disputants talk with and relate to one another. Their presence gives parties assurance that they are in good hands and carry some authority from the bench to the JDR table. This has persuasive appeal to parties as well as their attorneys (Sela and Gabay-Egoz 2020). JDR allows judges to insert their legitimacy and credibility into what occurs during settlement. Of course, some parties prefer JDR primarily because it eliminates costs, delays, risks of trial, stress and the formality of lawsuits (Rooke 2010).

There are some interesting variations in the administration of Canada's ADR programs: the option of binding vs. non-binding judgments; the use of facilitative, evaluative, or hybrid techniques by the mediating judge; judicial immunity, disciplinary immunity, or hybrid protection for mediating judges; mediating judges appointed by the court versus selected by the parties; expansive versus limited flexibility on the part of the judge and the parties; and pre-session or no pre-session communications between the mediating judge and the lawyers in a case.

In Canada, there are no national JDR standards or overarching ethical rules governing its practice; the training of judges in JDR is practically inexistent. The individuals who determine whether and how judges conduct JDRs are the leaders of the court system. Provincial and local regulations also play a role, as do the motivations of the individual judges who are inclined to provide JDR services.

Beyond Canada's judicial mediation—through JDRs, settlement conferences and mini-trials—is its pioneering of ODR, as seen in the Civil Resolution Tribunal and in online judicial dispute resolution (OJDR). (This is described in more detail in Chapter 19, especially as it unfolded under the COVID-19 pandemic). The question remains though, how well do JDR and other efforts by mediating judges respond to the weaknesses of litigation and the shortcoming of the judicial system?

Chapter 4

JDR'S RESPONSE TO THE
WEAKNESSES OF LITIGATION

Apart from fighting just for the sake of it, or the questionable morality of giving priority to the rules rather than the needs of the litigants, relying on adjudication simply takes too long and costs too much. In the words of former Supreme Court of Canada Justice Estey: "Disputes, unlike wine, do not improve by aging. Many things happen to a cause and to parties in a dispute by the simple passage of time, and almost none of them are good. Delay in settlement or disposal of conflicting claims is a primary enemy of Justice and peace in the community."

The Queen's Bench judges in Alberta agreed. They wanted to achieve better results, not just reduce court costs and delays. According to Associate Chief Justice Rooke:

> To define "success" in a broader way, with reference to a pre-trial resolution of litigation, recognizes the myriad of benefits to litigants and the judicial system, in avoiding the costs and risks of an all-or-nothing outcome at trial. The benefits and purposes of—the success sought from—ADR, and JDR in particular, are many. The benefits include: "lower court caseloads;" "more accessible forums;" "reduced expenditures of time and money;" "speedy and informal settlement;" "enhanced public satisfaction with the justice system;" "tailored resolutions;" "increased satisfaction and compliance with resolutions;" "restoration of... values;" responding to "complaints about the current judicial system," including the cost (time and money spent) to resolve the dispute; the incomprehensibility of the process (issues relating to the lack of participation of the affected parties); and the results (issues related to the imposition of a "remedy" by a "stranger" from a predetermined and limited range of win/loss or "zero-sum" options) (Rooke 2010).

ADR began as a response to purported weaknesses of litigation and the lack of institutional alternatives for settling disputes. One of its harshest critics, Yale Professor Owen Fiss, stated that the ADR movement mistakenly assumed that settlement and reconciliation would always produce better results than litigation and adjudication (Fiss 1984). Fiss was concerned that securing peace would displace securing justice and he did not think settlement would do a better job of preserving relationships between disputing parties, especially in the following scenarios: when there are power or distributional inequalities among the parties; when there is a need to supervise the implementation of the judgment; when the stakeholders and parties of a dispute are difficult to identify because the parties are social groups or multi-agent organizations; and when the law is not entirely fixed, demanding, therefore, an authoritative interpretation of the law by courts (Fiss 1984). He argued that by promoting ADR (especially by independent mediators) the court would be deprived of its opportunity to interpret the law and orient society, if necessary, to social change. More, he argued that ADR can be a form of avoidance, preserving the status quo and not engaging with (and making effective) the public values embedded in the texts that order society. In short, Fiss thought that settlements based on less than the ideals enshrined in our legal texts was to renounce the essence of civil litigation as a means of bringing society closer to its chosen ideals through authoritative interpretation of public values. For Fiss, law's promises are not aimed at necessarily achieving peace, but rather justice—an ideal best captured in litigations like *Brown v. Board of Education* that fought against discriminatory social ordering.

Fiss's clash with ADR's promoters was informed by the divide between ADR as a private conception of dispute resolution governed by an efficiency logic and litigation as a means of dealing with societies' differences governed by a logic of public values. He was not, however, talking about JDR as we now understand it. In JDR, the dualism between private and public is blurred: JDR resolves private disputes in a private setting before a judge who still represents public values and helps the parties articulate their interests in a court context.

First, JDR is not an alternative to the courts. It doesn't drive cases away from the legal system; it embraces them, particularly by helping parties find resolution and get on with their lives. It still gives them their day in court, emphasizing the judge's role and how their dispute would likely play out in court.

Second, JDR offers the judge and the parties a wider array of dispute-handling strategies. It is not skeptical of the judge's role or the court's ability to handle its workload, as might be the case with some ADR efforts in which the dispute is taken out of the judges hands entirely.

Third, JDR is not an alternative to adjudication. Parties do not have to choose between JDR or a binding adjudicative process; they can opt for binding-JDR (BJDR) but then choose a voluntary and mutually acceptable agreement before the judge issues a binding decision. JDR looks somewhat like ADR in that the parties control the outcome, and the goal is not to pick a winner and a loser. The difference is actual judges leading the settlement conferences or the mediation. From our research thus far, we find JDR ADR—leaves parties feeling more like they had their day in court. And they're reassured that if the dispute is not resolved through JDR, they may take their case before a new judge at a trial.

In short, JDR is a very special kind of ADR, one that is not, strictly speaking, an alternative to courts and adjudication. The focus is as much on justice as on peace. The judge has an opportunity to interpret the law, and can take steps to correct any institutionalized discrimination—as Fiss would prefer—in the design of the settlement process. The judge can also raise relevant precedents in caucuses with the parties and their lawyers (Agrios 2004).

The Chief Justice of the Court of Queen's Bench in New Brunswick states that JDR "avoids the considerable uncertainty of trials. To paraphrase Ms. Gump in the movie Forrest Gump, 'trials are like a box of chocolates, you never know what you are going to get inside.'" JDR overcomes the uncertainty of a trial by giving the parties control over the outcome, while also offering disputants the box of chocolates they might prefer if they don't get their desired results.

ADR or Litigation?

In 1988, Marc Galanter asked how scholars, judges and parties should assess the quality of ADR mechanisms and outcomes, and how to compare them to the results of litigation (Galanter 1988). He suggested there should be two parts to any such comparison. The first, related to "production," is whether a dispute processing mechanism can generate more with less—the measure of success in production. Does it allow the court to handle more cases at a higher speed and a lower cost? Can it save institutional resources? Merely achieving more with less, however, doesn't speak to the "quality" of justice—the second part of his comparison—especially in the eyes of the parties. The quality of justice measures the superiority of the outcomes achieved through ADR, or JDR in our case, as compared to litigation in comparable situations (Galanter 1985).

Production and quality can be used to compare JDR and litigation, even though they are difficult to measure in practice. We have only rough and partial estimates, since we can't compare time and money saved through a JDR unless the case subsequently goes to court. According to Rooke, mediation—be it judicial or non-judicial—is effective in 80 percent of the cases in which it is used as an alternative to litigation (Rooke 2010). Rooke's numbers were subsequently verified by similarly high rates of success in John Agrios' report: "[t]he JDR statistics are kept by the trial coordinators on a fairly informal basis and they show settlement rates ranging anywhere from 73 to 83 percent" (Agrios 2004). Agrios admitted these numbers might be a bit unreliable, but he was fairly confident that at least two-thirds of the disputes that go to JDR are settled. The JDR findings parallel even more optimistic mini-trial reports, indicating a success rate of about 90 percent (Moore 1995). Nevertheless, the production argument favoring JDR versus litigation is insufficient. Qualitative (or justice) benefits are even more important.

Robert Baruch Bush has identified fifty statements he believes can be used to measure ADR quality (Bush 1988), which we believe can be adapted to JDR. His statements fall into six clusters:

- *Individual satisfaction:* satisfying the desires and needs of the parties, namely, a just and expedient resolution to their disputes in a fair, efficient and inexpensive process.
- *Individual autonomy:* strengthening the ability of the parties to solve their own disputes and allowing them to prescribe their own norms of conduct to manage and resolve conflicts.
- *Social control:* enhancing the control of private and public institutions over sources of social change.
- *Social justice:* mitigating inequalities in the distribution of resources, power and rights.
- *Social solidarity:* increasing social solidarity and connections among individuals and groups by creating a space for dialogue (. . .)
- *Personal transformation:* opening up possibilities for individuals to experience growth, self-improvement and moral betterment.

All fifty of these statements (in all six clusters) can be unpacked as shown in the chart below (Bush 1988). Or, they can be analyzed through a JDR lens, emphasizing (1) the benefits to the judicial system; (2) the benefits to the parties; and (3) the benefits to the judge that follows in our second chart.

Quality statement cluster	Constitutive elements
INDIVIDUAL SATISFACTION	1. Process is fast 2. Parties felt heard 3. Parties felt the outcome is fair 4. Outcomes are actually obtained 5. Parties comply with the solution 6. The process had a positive effect (or at least no negative one) on the relationship of the parties 7. Creative outcomes have been obtained 8. The "solution pie" was expanded 9. The parties articulated their interests and needs to the other party 10. The parties felt their time was appreciated 11. The process was inexpensive 12. The process was fast
INDIVIDUAL AUTONOMY	1. The parties participated in a decision that affected them 2. The parties felt empowered 3. The parties felt their dignity was acknowledged by the other party 4. The parties exercised control over the process 5. The parties exercised control over the outcome
SOCIAL CONTROL	1. The process manages social conflict 2. The process and outcome serves political interests 3. The process atomized disputes
SOCIAL JUSTICE	1. The process gives no advantage to disputants 2. The process manages power imbalances 3. The process does not harm poor parties 4. The process encourages one to be aware of one's own biases and blind spots 5. The process limits the state control on parties 6. Injured parties receive compensation expediently
SOCIAL SOLIDARITY	1. The process articulates collaborative norms for resolution 2. The process creates shared narratives 3. The process has the potential to create or improve communities 4. The outcome is guided by the rules of law (bargaining and mediating in the shadow of the law)
PERSONAL TRANSFORMATION	1. The process helps parties improve their emotional, intellectual and communicative skills 2. The process helps parties enhance their empathy and understanding of the situation of the other 3. The process stimulates truth, honesty, active listening, openness and creativity 4. The process creates an outlet for channeling emotions

JDR offers benefits not listed in Bush's descriptions. For instance: those seeking reality-testing get the judge's evaluation of how their claims are likely to be seen in court; the judge's "social" standing contributes to the credibility of the mediation effort; and the background and knowledge of the judge (acting as mediator), as well as his or her trial experience, provide a balance between interests-talk and rights-talk when the latter is necessary. In the BJDR experience of the mediating judges with whom we spoke, even cases headed toward a binding judge's decision consistently settled consensually prior to the judge offering a binding ruling. These judges rarely had to write a final decision aside from instances in which the parties asked the judge to provide a ruling on an interim point of law or issue a formal (i.e., binding) decision. In the majority of JDR cases, however, just knowing that the end was in sight—with a judge leading the discussion—was enough to inspire the parties to reach a voluntary agreement. As will become clear in later chapters when we discuss the details of specific cases, many JDRs are initiated after cases have been through multiple appeals over extended periods of time. Having an imminent conclusion provides an incentive for both sides to settle.

Qualitative advantages of JDR	*Description*
BENEFITS TO THE JUDICIAL SYSTEM	• Reduction of court backlogs • Time and resource management (protect from crushing overload of cases) • Aim to fulfill the judicial system purpose • Prevention of future conflicts • Minimization of enforcement problems • Avoidance of supervision • Dispute resolution pedagogy • Easier to implement online JDR system than online trial system
BENEFITS TO THE PARTIES	• If an agreement reached, likely to be complied • If an agreement reached, likely to be an enduring one • Saves money (legal fees and negotiated outcomes) • Saves time • Parties taking ownership of their conflicts • Subjective satisfaction • Participation in the decision that affects them • Preserves or enhances the relationship • Judicial participation controlling inequality in bargaining power • Judicial participation drawing hardlines to protect the rights of the weak party • Creative solutions not available through trial • A reality test or lowering of unrealistic expectations • De-escalation of social conflict • Alerts defendants to the fact that they could lose the case • Confidentiality • Avoids uncertainty of trials

(Continued)

(Continued)

Qualitative advantages of JDR	Description
	• Cooperation • Design the process • Grants a "day in court" • Provides an external evaluation of the case • Self-transformation and empowerment • Empathy • Less stress • Perceived fairness (the procedure is perceived as fairer if parties can decide the outcome)
BENEFITS TO THE JUDGE	• Self-fulfillment • Honed his or her listening, facilitative and mediation skills • Flexibility in role of a facilitator and evaluator • Empathy • Less stress • Availability of other options (i.e., apology, reference letters, etc.) • More fun than litigation • Process powers aimed to facilitate and reach an agreement (disclosures, binding orders, procedural direction, etc.) • Enforceability of the agreement • Overcoming counsel and litigant resistance • Providing a binding solution to end the dispute • More information to decide or facilitate • Understanding and getting to know more about the disputants • Exploring options and solutions outside of the box • Sustainability of the outcomes of their work • Democratization of the law (excluding legalese) • Using a lifetime of experience and knowledge in disputes that need more than rule-following and rule-application

Adjudication is complex, formal, protracted, and worst of all, uncontrollable. When we asked our interviewees about the quality of litigation and its outcomes, as we did about the quality of ADR and JDR, their answers were muddy. Production and quality should both matter in assessing the outcome of a legal action or the ongoing work of a court. The main question of how the outcome in each instance of litigation compares to what might have happened otherwise, is unanswerable: not only does the substance of the decision need to be assessed against some expert measure of best practice, but so does the subsequent relationships among the parties and the implementation or enforcement of the agreement. If the outcome is not implemented because the loser felt they were treated unfairly, should we determine that the process was inadequate? Finally, we especially need to assess the work of courts generally, not just the results of particular cases. Does the system of dispute handling being used help the society improve relationships and results over time? Is there any way to determine whether the means of dispute handling or dispute resolution is helping everyone improve their individual and collective capacity to deal with their differences? Is the society becoming more efficient and more just?

Chapter 5

ADR v. JDR

While ADR is part of the legal system in a growing number of countries, there are only a few that rely on JDR by mediating judges. The best way to illustrate the special features of JDR, as well as the way it overlaps ADR but differs from litigation, is to share the details of a JDR case. Until now, that was not possible due to JDR's confidentiality mandate, which prohibits publishing accounts of the process and the parties' reactions.

With permission from the Alberta Court of Queen's Bench, we were able to interview the judges, lawyers and parties in nine JDRs, ranging across a number of civil law cases. The names of the parties are changed, as well as a few of the facts to preserve confidentiality, but the accounts offer the first clear picture of how JDR works, how it differs from other forms of ADR (especially mediation offered by independent professional mediators), and how parties behave differently in JDR as compared to more traditional litigation procedures. The first case we will describe is *The Contaminated Land Case*, which appears in its entirety in Appendix 1.

Summary of *The Contaminated Land Case*

Two friends, Edward and David, invested in industrial land that they thought had great development potential, only to later find out that the land was contaminated. Edward sold out and David tried to keep the land and went to great lengths to pay off his debts to the mortgage lender, ultimately handing over his family's country home. Nonetheless, the lender felt it did not get back all of its interest and principal. Several lawsuits followed and the case was ultimately settled at JDR with both sides moving on, paying nothing to each other, and walking away from all their claims.

The Deal

The friends purchased the land through a newly incorporated company, 270 Incorporated (270 Inc.), in which they were equal shareholders. Each agreed to finance half of the $750,000 purchase price. Edward financed his half with a vendor-takeback loan from the seller, who was his sister. David obtained and personally guaranteed a mortgage loan from a third party, Forte Banking Corporation (Forte Banking), which had previously provided David and his wife a mortgage for their country home.

The Surprise

A month later, David's counsel (who incorporated 270 Inc. for the friends) told him that the land had a caveat on behalf of Coal Creek Oil and Gas due to contaminated waste beneath the soil. David and Edward had a difficult time making mortgage payments and otherwise advancing their development project.

Edward sold his 50 percent share in 270 Inc. to the sole shareholder of Forte Banking, and his sister transferred the mortgage to Forte Banking. It would eventually come to light that Edward and his sister engaged in a series of related party transactions for increasingly greater amounts that inflated the land's value and looked like a classic straw buyer mortgage fraud.

David still felt there was development potential and tried to hang onto the land, making further agreements with Forte Banking to help with the payments over several years. Eventually, Forte Banking lent David additional funds securitized by a mortgage on David's private home in the city, and also received David's 50 percent shares in 270 Inc. as security for his debt.

The Bank Took the Home

Nothing improved for David. The industrial land was not suitable for development in large part due to the contaminated subsurface and surface. With no cash flow and further financial difficulties, David and his wife turned over their entire country home to Forte Banking with the understanding that this would cover the overdue interest and some of the principal on his outstanding Forte Banking debt. Believing this transaction covered his entire debt, he demanded that his 50 percent shares in 270 Inc. be returned to him so he could develop the land.

The Bank Keeps the Shares

David did not get his shares back from Forte Banking, its individual shareholder and the shareholder's family (who became involved in the lawsuit). Their refusal was based in part on what they had put into the land financially and that David allegedly ran a rent-free business on the property. Again, several lawsuits ensued including Forte Banking moving to foreclose and David eventually claiming damages against Forte Banking totaling around $1 million for breach of contract, breach of good faith, fraud and unjust enrichment.

Forte Banking not only defended on the basis of paying the taxes and utilities, it also claimed for its role in the rezoning costs, appraisals, environmental studies and negotiating remediating costs with Coal Creek Oil and Gas. Forte Banking counterclaimed for the remaining unpaid mortgage and the bills it had paid for David, totaling around $300,000. The provincial environmental regulator was also involved and required cleanup of the hazardous waste.

How and Why Did JDR Work in *The Contaminated Land Case*?

Our interviews with the parties revealed how and why the case settled. In contrast to litigation, JDR gave the parties an opportunity to step back from their adversarial positions and consider their shared interests and realistic alternatives. JDR's track record, the condensed time frame offered by the JDR judge, and the relatively low cost to the litigants and the court made it a much more favorable option for the parties than trial or private ADR.

The defendants' attorney described Alberta's mandatory ADR requirement as "smart." He explained that in his experience, when ADR was not required, there was often a negative impact on the case, mainly a delay in getting to trial. He favored JDR for two reasons. First, JDR is free, compared to private mediation which can be extremely expensive: a one-day mediation including preparation time with one of the most sought-after private mediators—a former judge of the Ontario Supreme Court—could cost $30,000 to $40,000. Second, JDR takes parties and litigants "behind the curtain," sharing a judge's impressions of the case. An experienced JDR judge may also offer insights regarding how other judges on the bench might view or value the case.

The judge in this case pointed out JDR's advantage of enforceability over private ADR. Private ADR results in a private agreement, while JDR can result in a court order which is enforceable through normal processes, including contempt of court where the same judge will review contempt applications. Compliance is rarely an issue in JDR, especially when experienced attorneys work to ensure that agreements are followed. A judge may or may not sign a court order in a JDR; the judge can issue a court order containing a general clause specifying that parties agree to file discontinuances and legal documents, transfer funds, and so on, to give effect to the agreement as soon as possible.

After consultation with the judge, each party agreed to file a discontinuance of action and end the lawsuit, and as is the usual practice of the judge, neither side received a cost award. There was no reason to insert additional terms into the judge's order; his order by consent simply dismissed all claims and counterclaims. The parties, in essence, walked away at the end of the JDR; a simple ending to a problematic series of lawsuits and counterclaims. The defendants did not receive any damages, nor did they have to pay any. The plaintiff did not get back his 50 percent of the shares in 270 Inc, but he avoided responsibility for the costly land cleanup. There were no issues regarding implementation or compliance.

The judge in this case drew on his extensive background in environmental law and was able to explain the contamination issues and cleanup costs, and provide insight into the regulator's perspective. The judge recalled being sympathetic to the plaintiff's case at the outset and would likely have transferred the shares back to the plaintiff if he were adjudicating the claims.

The judge's hybrid approach—of facilitative and evaluative mediation—stands out as a unique option in JDR that would not have been possible in a litigation setting. His range of mediation skills allowed him to customize his method to this case, leaning a bit more on a facilitative approach, asking the right questions, actively listening, quickly grasping the core issues and expressing equal empathy toward both sides.

From this case, we see that JDR is completely judge-centric in contrast to ADR and litigation. We are not certain that all JDR judges are fully aware of the specific ways they can interpret their JDR role since they are not allowed to communicate with each other about any case work they do, and that includes all their JDRs. Newly-appointed judges are so busy, it's not likely they even think about the discretionary choices they have to make in their initial JDR assignments. In the words of Associate Chief Justice Rooke:

> JDR stands in contradistinction from the court's traditional exclusively adjudicative role. JDR is not focused on truth, [such as the rigorous cross-examination under oath model] but on the result. The objective of the process still, however, presupposes crucial elements that we have always associated with "justice"—fairness and finality. The focus of JDR is to allow the parties to move back to their regular lives without the costs, delay and stress of traditional, adversarial adjudication. In other words, the objective is a process that achieves justice, but in a manner by which the *interests* of the parties are as important as the legality of their *rights*, and where, in the process, there is a wise balance of a fair and just, but speedy, inexpensive and efficient procedure for achieving finality for such disputes (Rooke 2010).

JDR (and in particular BJDR) allows for questioning of parties and experts, so in this sense it is like traditional cross-examination. In JDR, however, it is only the judge who may ask for reports from relevant experts and cross-examine them if he or she feels that will help the parties reach an informed agreement. Experienced JDR judges report that they seek to balance fairness with efforts to achieve an efficient result. Associate Chief Justice Rooke says that to be effective, JDR has to be uniquely adaptable in each case, including separating parties for caucuses with the judge (Rooke 2010).

There are some clear and compelling reasons why this emotional and complex case was resolved through JDR. The judge's choice to begin with private meetings to hear settlement proposals allowed him to determine that there probably was a Zone of Possible Agreement (ZOPA). Thus, he felt that mediation could succeed. The same caucuses also helped the judge determine how to structure an agenda for the mediation. He emphasized caucusing because it was immediately clear that the relationships among the parties had seriously deteriorated and that breakdown would probably preclude them from cooperating or even being in the same room during the mediation. Both sides informed the judge in the initial, confidential meeting that repairing the relationship was not a key interest for either of them. Nevertheless, the judge's awareness of the relationship status between the two parties helped him decide how to structure the settlement process. During the mediation, somewhat surprisingly, the parties asked the judge whether he would agree to make the JDR binding—not what they or their lawyers had requested at the outset. The judge concurred.

What happened in this case is significantly different from what would have happened in court-annexed ADR. Rooke says "in his court [the Court of Queen's Bench], all JDR's are performed by justices of the court, something quite unusual in court systems. In most court systems, court retained (in-house or on a list) non-judicial mediators and/or judicial officers are used. A few use both, e. g., the District Court of Northern California where then-Magistrate Judge Brazil presided" (Rooke 2005).

As long as judges are trained and experienced in mediation, as the Queen's Bench Judges are, they have a variety of tools to resolve even the most difficult cases. The parties in this case were confident in this judge's status, and they endorsed his perceived fairness by requesting a binding decision. This is not a possibility in ADR administered by an independent non-judge mediator, even if suggested by the court.

This judge's mediation skills were critical to the outcome. He identified and implemented appropriate key process choices, including requesting confidential settlement proposals from both parties at the start, using multiple rounds of confidential caucusing, and agreeing to make the JDR binding.

The parties felt his empathy was genuine as he listened to their stories. The defendants' attorney thought the judge may have told the plaintiff that his case was relatively weak and noted this was an example of a more evaluative approach, which the attorney believes contributed to the case resolving in a fair and efficient manner. The judge's environmental expertise also proved pivotal for addressing the contamination issues interwoven through the case. The judge recalled being sympathetic to the plaintiff's case and believes there was a shift to resolution when he pointed out the significant cleanup costs that would be imposed by the environmental regulator. This move stands out as something unique to JDR that would not have been possible in a more traditional litigation.

The defendants' attorney noted that the opportunity to change from non-binding to binding JDR was important to the parties reaching a settlement. He characterized BJDR as binding arbitration, where the judge is empowered to settle the file for the parties if they cannot reach agreement on their own. This contrasts with non-binding mediation, and in the defendants' attorney's opinion, had the effect of incentivizing the side with a relatively weak case to agree to a settlement. The judge explained that his BJDR mediation approach is the same as his approach to non-binding JDRs, and that, in fact, he has never had to make a decision for the parties in a BJDR. Just the notion that a judge can and will, at the request of the parties, impose a decision can be enough to nudge the parties toward a settlement that they construct themselves.

The judge moved this JDR request to Alberta's Special Resolution Project (SPECS), Under the SPECS program, judges have settled many previously scheduled three- to four-week trials in just two or three days. Alberta's court rules preclude parties from booking trial time until they first participate in ADR (including JDR or private mediation). This requirement holds almost all the time, although it is possible to secure a court exemption under very limited circumstances (e.g., class action, small dollar value claims, and some rare family matters).

JDR is unique. When it works, the result is largely dependent on the skills, attitude and experience of the mediating judge. It also hinges on the perceptions of the parties— and especially their lawyers—which we will analyze in the chapters that follow.

Chapter 6

JDR PRODUCES SATISFACTORY RESULTS

The Divorce Case

Several studies suggest that ADR produces levels of satisfaction not achievable through other forms of dispute resolution (Sander 1996; Susskind 1995). This is likely due to ADR's lower cost and more rapid results. Mediation, in particular, engages the parties directly and gives them control over the outcome—something litigation does not do, in part because parties must speak through their counsel and cannot have a normal conversation with the judge. Private caucuses in JDR allow parties to speak directly and confidentially with the judge and with each other.

JDR usually moves the judge and the parties out of the courtroom to another part of the courthouse. It shuts down most fault-finding and avoids the airing of private grievances in a public setting (which often triggers escalation). JDRs are off the record, unlike normal courtroom proceedings which are taped or transcribed. Avoiding the trauma of cross-examination on almost every personal detail, including one's ability to parent, increases the odds of restoring family unity. Our JDR case studies show how voluntary agreements can arise from highly emotional contexts. We now look closely at a family law case, originally battled in court, but finally resolved through JDR.

Summary of *The Divorce Case*

The couple with two children were in a marriage that began to unravel. Dad filed first for divorce only a few years into the marriage, and mom filed soon thereafter, each seeking judicial resolution to settle several matters. Claims presented in affidavits and court filings sought a declaration of divorce, child support, clarity about parenting time, and a division of matrimonial property.

The parties received an interim court order calling for shared custody of their son, who would be with dad every other week. That worked until dad's work schedule changed, requiring him to commit to two weeks on and two weeks off. For a while, the parties managed to live within the new schedule; inevitably, though, disagreements arose. With nowhere else to go for help, the parties headed back to court.

Mom wanted to return to the terms of their initial court-ordered agreement, abandoning the informal arrangement they made when dad's schedule changed. In response, dad filed an application in court to officially amend the order to reflect his new schedule. His application included a complaint that his wife was working every other Saturday, leaving their son with a babysitter; dad wanted to be with his son, and did not want to contribute childcare costs to a third party.

Mom firmly disagreed; she did not want her son to be away from her for two weeks at a time. First, she raised doubts about dad's ability to ensure the health, education and social wellbeing of the children (they also had an older daughter) for two-week blocks of time. Second, she alleged their son did not want to spend more than a week at a time with the dad. Third, she proposed that her work schedule would allow her Friday and Saturday off every other week and she could care for her son during that time. She also raised financial issues, contending that the real reason dad wanted more parenting time was to avoid paying child support.

On top of this, she now raised the issue of retroactive child support for their children. And for the first time, she raised the question of alimony because of the extra costs and living expenses she has been incurring for the children as well as herself. Finally, mom alleged that dad was hiding assets and income behind a company front. To her, it seemed that his reported income was substantially lower than the industry average.

Facing old and new issues and allegations, increased court time and related legal fees, the parties opted to try to work things out in JDR.

Before the informal JDR took place, the attorneys exchanged settlement proposals. They both believed this would be a good place to begin their negotiations with the judge. They also initiated a discussion of possible child and spousal support payments and division of property.

The parties met with the judge and set the JDR for two days, with the first day set aside for discussion of child and spousal support and parenting time. They hoped the second day could be used to mediate the division of matrimonial property. The judge stated that if all went well, at the end of the second day, he would immediately divorce the parties, sparing them the extra time it would otherwise take to get back on the court's busy divorce docket.

During the initial plenary session, the judge told the parties that he believed every family law case was resolvable, as long as the parties were honest, creative, listening without arguing, and of course, patient. The judge noted that the only exception is if there was violence or allegations of violence, which would move the case to a quasi-criminal category, but that was not a factor in this case.

In conducting the JDR, the judge stepped down from the bench and used conference rooms for confidential caucuses with each party separately. The two days went as planned and the JDR concluded successfully. The issues that were resolved included the allocation of property, the terms of child and spousal support, and most importantly, assigned parenting time. The judge also granted the divorce. All in all, the parties were very satisfied.

Why did it Work?

In our view, the JDR was successful because the judge listened carefully to the parties' proposals before offering any suggestions of his own. The parties believed the judge's evaluative skills allowed him to correct some of their misconceptions. They did not feel they were forced into anything; rather, with the judge's help, they worked to generate a mutually beneficial agreement.

One of the attorneys felt it was important that the judge had the discretion to award court costs in the event that one party was being unreasonable—a form of judicial authority not available to a professional mediator. Another positive factor was that judge had set up the JDR fairly quickly, saving everyone the time and money involved in waiting for a scheduled court date. The JDR process aims to be fairly quick, but without institutional endorsement and allowing judges to take time off the bench to do JDR, it would be slower and, perhaps, less satisfactorily for the disputants.

The parties stopped quarreling and were able to take a breath and truly listen to each other without interruption or re-stating legal claims. The judge noted that the parties listened respectfully to proposals from the other side, and even asked if an apology from one or the other of them might move things along. The judge's offer to immediately grant a divorce if they reached agreement on everything else seemed to set a conciliatory tone. Granting an immediate divorce where happy parties take the stand after completing a successful mediation is not something that would happen in a traditional family court setting. On top of that, once the mediated agreement was reached, the judge included a memorandum of settlement in a consent order ensuring that the terms of the agreement would be implemented immediately.

When the mom first became aware of the possibility of JDR, her attorney described it as an experimental way to resolve family law cases. She was excited about a "non-litigation" option because the case had already gone on for almost two years while legal fees piled up. Like the dad, she wanted more control over the outcome. When the JDR was over, the mom said she would ".... choose JDR over litigation if she ever had to go to court again."

The JDR transformed the role of the parties from antagonists to problem-solvers, shifting the situation from one in which the parties had no control over the outcome to one in which they had substantial self-determination. In retrospect, the judge noted that attorneys might have been less favorable toward JDR than their clients because a quick end to the conflict meant that they would collect lower fees. This was not, however, something the lawyers confirmed.

The judge also stated that some family litigation is prosecuted to a judicial conclusion by attorneys in an unrelenting way because they believe the result might set a valuable precedent. This is rarely a goal shared by the court; being involved in a case that finds its way into the law books is not a high priority for most judges. Similarly, the parties just want the litigation to end so they can let go of it and spend their money on something else.

Settling family law disputes outside a courtroom is important for other reasons. In the area of family law, "[f]eelings are often so intense that we may justifiably question whether the normal legal processes will be effective" (Sander 1983). Further, as Professor Frank Sander notes, judges must "... often deal with individuals who have serious personality pathologies . . . Another important characteristic of family disputes is that the very nature of family relations means that we often are dealing with continuing relationships. This is true even where the family is seeking to dissolve, as in the case of divorce" (Sander 1983).

Mediation in family law is necessary because, again as Professor Sander notes, the solutions that can be reached are more flexible than those that can be generated relying on litigation. Mediation does not require that there be a winner and a loser, and it allows a wide-ranging inquiry into whatever the parties want to talk about. Although mediation is not therapy, it can have a therapeutic benefit. There is also evidence to suggest that people who go through mediation may well learn something they can use in the future. This is valuable if they are going to have continuing relationships (Sander 1983).

All the parties in this case agreed that their conflicts might well have been resolved in the course of further litigation, but not with the long-term benefits offered by JDR. The mom's attorney felt that they came to an agreement because both parties wanted the mediation process to succeed and the litigation to end—they were in a mood to make compromises. Evaluating the judge after the fact, the mom felt he was an effective listener. She also indicated there was a certain power in having a judge with his authority pay undivided attention to the litigants. She maintained it was the informality of the JDR process that relaxed the parties and " … enabled them to cooperatively come to an agreement." As is so often the case, the attorneys mentioned how important they felt it was for the parties to hear the judge's opinion on key points as they decided whether and how to proceed.

The dad's attorney believed the case settled because the parties wanted to settle. She noted how diligently her client worked with the mom to accommodate her needs. She also favored a draft settlement proposal as a JDR starting point so that the parties had a vision of where they might end up. She felt the judge's evaluative style was another crucial element in the success of the process—the parties listened to the judge's opinions about what was and was not reasonable. She tends to react favorably when a JDR judge says, "If I were hearing this at trial, this is what I would do." The judge, however, said that he rarely makes such evaluative statements, and if he does, only well into the JDR process, never at the outset.

The mom was quite happy at the end of the process, saying the JDR was " … an unmitigated success." For her, saving time was the main draw and she was surprised a court case could be resolved in just two days. She repeated her concern that they had waited for almost two years, paying attorneys' fees along the way. Her attorney said, "[Mom] reported that sitting in a room with someone you were disputing was transformational after years of talking only through attorneys and legal briefs; [the parents] were finally able to hear each other's perspectives and respond immediately. In court, by contrast, [Mom] might have never had an opportunity to speak."

She also felt this particular JDR judge was integral to the resolution of their case, saying that he had a "down to earth" demeanor that put her at ease immediately; he just listened, without judgment of them or their relationship. She felt that another person in the same role, such as an outside mediator, might have done this with success, but that her husband had responded well to the JDR because " … the judge brought such credibility." The mom also appreciated not feeling pressured to reach an agreement.

Empowerment was particularly important to this couple. They both felt that they could control the direction and outcome of the process.

Given that we interviewed the parties sometime after they had reached a settlement, they reported that they had been able to successfully have civil interactions and accommodate each other's varying parenting time requests. They found they could also disagree without fighting or threatening to run to a lawyer as they had done in the past. The mom did not believe that they would have had such a cooperative relationship if they had pursued the litigation to the bitter end. Her new relationship with her ex-husband surprised her—even after the JDR's conclusion, they continued to talk without fighting.

The attorneys agreed with the parents' positive assessment. They noted that while their clients did not get everything they wanted, they were so relieved to finalize the divorce that the

" ... details became less significant." Had the litigation continued, the details would probably have remained more central to the mom. In the words of the researcher who interviewed everyone in this case:

Ultimately, the JDR resolved the issues of property, child and spousal support, and parenting time, which likely would have been resolved—one way or another—in a trial. However, the mom felt that only JDR could have allowed a respectful dialogue that enabled her and the dad to move forward and have a productive coparenting relationship. Further, while a court order endorsing the JDR resolution was put on the record, the parties in this case were so happy with the outcome, they subsequently complied with the agreement and did not need further written memoranda or court orders to keep them in line ... The parties left the JDR with not only a finalized divorce—significant to them both—but also with the possibility to resolve conflict between them without the intervention of a third party.

Were the Results in This Case Unusual?

Does research in other contexts validate these findings? It seems that the answer is yes; both litigants and attorneys found mediation to be fair and satisfactory with little doubt as to its effectiveness in disposing of a substantial number of contested custody and visitation cases.

In addition to producing agreements during sessions, several evaluations found that mediation has often sequenced into more voluntary agreement-making and less judicial decision-making (National Symposium on Court-Connected Dispute Resolution Research 1994). Is it surprising that mediation with a family—or any other type of dispute—empowers the parties in such an emotional and compelling way? Not really. Or at least we should not be surprised given the three reasons most often cited to justify mediation in the Model Standards of Practice for Family and Divorce Mediation:

1. Increase[s] the self-determination of participants and their ability to communicate
2. Promote[s] the best interests of children, and
3. Reduce[s] the economic and emotional costs associated with the resolution of family disputes (Model Standards of Practice for Family and Divorce Mediation 2001).

The parties in *The Divorce Case* were happy with the outcome, but how did they get to that point? They had had enough litigation and needed to get out from under the continuing court battle and its rising costs. They were prepared to bet on the judge's mediation skills. They also wanted to talk directly to a judge who understood their particular problems. Judy Wallerstein notes, "If one were to set out to design a system poorly adapted to the resolution of family conflict or for safeguarding the children, one would, with a little luck, invent the adversarial system presided over by a perplexed, frustrated judge whose background in law and politics have no conceivable bearing on the issues before him or her" (Sander 1979).

A trained judge in a family law dispute will try to find the real reason for the dispute, but that's not easy to undertake through formal court filings or official exchanges only through the lawyers. He or she will try to tamp down the emotional exchanges when the parties are present, keeping the focus on the facts. A mediating judge, however, will focus on the parties' stories of the conflict, engage them in problem-solving, and help them build working relationships for the future. The JDR judge needs to be a patient listener who can park the legal arguments to the side, at least until the outlines of a set-tlement emerge. In the process, he or she "alters the power dynamic and seeks to bring peace to the room" (Bowling and Hoffman 2000).

We will take up questions about the judicial temperament of JDR judges in Chapter 9. For now, we highlight the important connection between judicial temperament and achieving a satisfactory outcome in the eyes of the JDR participants:

> The two indices that were best able to predict both the settlement and willingness to recommend the process were users' perceptions of the mediators' ability to facilitate communication, and of the mediators' ability to provide them with a better understanding of their own feelings and those of their children and ex-spouse. (National Symposium on Court-Connected Dispute Resolution Research 1994)

All of this underscores the significance of the training JDR judges receive before they are allowed to mediate. Given the trends in family law of moving toward media-tion and collaborative participation, the training of judges may need to include more emphasis on mediation and techniques for processing the highly emotional content of family and child custody disputes. With children sometimes being used as a wedge in family law cases, counsel must be able to manage the exchanges between the parties, move toward possible settlement, and allow the emotional content to emerge without overwhelming the children if they are present. JDR judges need to know how to do this, as the *ADR Handbook for Judges* indicates:

> In what is a remarkably short time for legal institutions, the paradigm for resolution of child custody disputes has shifted from sole custody and adversary courtroom combat to mediation, education, and self-determination that aims to involve both parents in the post—divorce life of their children consistent with safety. The adversary system paradigm assumes that one parent is more important to the child's future than another and that a court can identify that parent through courtroom combat. These assumptions do not meet the needs of parents and children in an era of mass divorce and separation, gender equality,

research establishing the importance of both parents in the life of the child, the harm to children of continued conflict, and overcrowded courts.

ADR programs, in contrast, assume that parents—not judges or mental health experts—should, if at all possible, determine how a child of divorce is parented, that both parents are important to the child's future, and that carefully structured interventions can encourage parents to place their children's interests above their anger and pain. These assumptions have, in general, been validated by the available empirical evidence and experience since coming into public consciousness. They are also more morally attractive than the assumptions of the adversary system and the sole custody paradigm because they appeal to the better instincts of people (Stiensra and Yates 2004).

In a JDR 2003 symposium summary report we find the following conclusion:

> The judges also noted a number of issues that reflect positively on JDR. For instance, in the area of family law, JDR has been transformational. In cases of custody and access, 90% have been resolved around the table. It has promoted a shift from an adversarial to a child—centered model. JDR has demonstrated that it offers the potential for creative solutions, that it can resolve cases earlier, in a simpler fashion, with a wider range of solutions, at lower cost. (Brenner and Baird 2003)

Judges know the litigation statistics. Less than 5 percent of all cases are ever completely tried from beginning to end. Given these numbers, why not proceed on the assumption that lawsuits, once filed, will be settled, especially where children are involved? Years ago, an experienced attorney and mediator said litigation is a "myth":

> "In the last few years, arising out of the principle of appropriate dispute resolution, I have discovered a concept that seems to resonate for a number of lawyers, judges and mediators. I refer to this as the 'myth of litigation.'
> The fact is that 98% of all civil lawsuits in North America are resolved, one way or another, prior to trial. That leaves approximately 2 percent that are actually tried. Many litigants simply 'give up' due to the costs associated with continuing. Most are eventually settled, later than sooner. Yet we continue to create settlement processes that are alternatives to litigation. This is the 'myth of litigation.' It's as if we are all in some kind of societal 'trance' in which we continue to agree that we are involved in a System of Litigation. The objective reality is that we are engaged in a settlement system in which settlement occurs too late and, more often than not, ineffectually and inefficiently. The truth is litigation is the alternative to settlement, and we continue to engage in the world 'as if' it is the opposite" (Fogel 2002).

Conclusion

Ultimately, satisfaction in JDR is a product of the parties gaining control over the outcome of the mediation process and reaching a mutually acceptable result. This applies particularly to divorcing couples who must decide how children will be cared for and property divided. Self-empowerment, as this case shows, is equally important. It hinges on the ability of the parties to be heard directly and to make quick decisions. Because the JDR judge asks parties to speak to him or her, not through counsel, the process can move quickly. Counsel gives advice all along, of course, and ensures that their clients' legal rights are protected, but in a JDR the parties do the speaking. The parties and their lawyers decide together what documents to show the judge. All of this is psychologically important:

> A number of advocates of mediation emphasize the empowerment it brings to the disputants and even to the communities in which it is practiced. Empowerment has been described as including all the steps by which the parties can be encouraged to take responsibility for finding their own solutions, negotiating their own agreement and implementing it.
>
> The rationale behind mediation is that the parties have to take control over their own lives, not hand their lives over to the state. They must accept the consequences of their own decisions because they control the outcome. It is not imposed on them. This is generally regarded as being psychologically advantageous. The parties can also withdraw from the process at any time if they wish.
>
> Certainly, in theory, the parties also control the litigation process, but this is not so in practice. Once parties enter the litigation process they hand over control of the conduct of their dispute. The client comes to see his actions as dictated by the requirements of procedures. He sees the lawyer's actions as representing, not the clients' own choices, but rather features of autonomous proceedings (Clark and Davies 1991).

Settlement of family law disputes is particularly satisfying for judges. Compared with other civil lawsuits—where the issue might be the reallocation of money or property from one side to another—family law typically involves children. It is painful and sometimes heartbreaking for a judge to order that one parent have sole custody of a child. Thus, it is one of a judge's most satisfying moments when decisions of this sort are made by the parents rather than by someone who knows very little about the family and has had no hand in raising the children.

Chapter 7

ADVANTAGES AND
DISADVANTAGES OF JDR

We have made the case that JDR works, especially in a family law context, and will now look more generally at the pros and cons of JDR; first, as compared to litigation and then as compared to other forms of ADR.

Associate Chief Justice Rooke has written the following based on his own survey:

> … 96% of the lawyers doing JDRs are repeat users, with over 80% of both lawyers and clients (the latter heavily weighted by insurance adjusters) having done more than five JDRs. Moreover, as [his research shows] 80-96% of the JDRs held were recommended by the lawyers involved, with as high as 34% being recommended by the clients themselves (again, mostly insurance adjusters)—meaning that often JDR is a logical joint choice of both the lawyers and clients in a case. Another significant measure of success of the JDR program is the willingness to recommend JDR in the future—very high at 93% (Rooke 2010).

JDR settlement rates at above 90 percent means it works as a method of dispute resolution. That doesn't mean, however, that it is always the right approach.

Advantages

Canadian courts of Appeal point to several advantages of JDR, especially, as we have discussed, in the highly litigated area of family law:

> The judicial mediation process best serves the interests of children in the sense that it can be readily expedited and offers a flexible, adaptable, informal venue where the most current information can be exchanged and discussed at ground level in reasoned, solution-oriented fashion. The bane of all parenting disputes—dysfunctional communication—can be addressed head on. Participation in high conflict mediation can be facilitated. Meaningful information can be obtained from the parents without all the filtering, editing and reframing that the preparation of court documents so often entails. Innovative outcomes can be explored with the full and active assistance of an experienced judicial intermediary. (Canadian Court of Appeal 2016).

In *The Contaminated Land Case* presented in Chapter 5, the defense council considered JDR's main advantages over ADR to be the limited cost and the judge's ability to share the probable trial outcome. More, since JDR is readily available in Alberta, it was easy to take that case into Alberta's SPEC program. The rest of Canada, as noted in Chapters 2 and 3, has slightly different forms of JDR. Again, Associate Chief Justice Rooke points out:

From this view, which I share, it is clear that these dispute resolution processes are now within our system of dispute resolution in the court, in a normative, institutionalized and ordered way, alongside the previous norm of adjudication only (Rooke 2010).

Reflecting on the idea of "fitting the forum to the fuss," Justice Rooke offered this observation:

> This is exactly the institutionalized, normative result that I now see in the dispute resolution regime in the [sic] Alberta with private ADR outside the court, and the JDR program, along with the traditional adjudication, in the court. This is consistent with the view that "it is important to dispel the ideals that there is or ought to be any one particular settlement conference mode, model or style that should or needs to be embraced or implemented to ensure a successful settlement outcome." One size does not fit all, and the parties can choose. While adjudication is unilateral at the instigation of one party (the plaintiff), both ADR (privately or Court annexed) and JDR (within the court currently) are based on the consent—indeed, the agreement—of all parties to the dispute. Therefore, I believe that this new institutionalized normative ordering has been established—adjudication and JDR (with its broad range of services) within the court. Accordingly, as others have done, I declare that the "multi-door Courthouse" is open in Alberta. ... This closes the circle (Rooke 2010).

Disadvantages

Judges need training, and this may be the biggest problem of JDR. They cannot just walk out of court and into JDR, and frankly, until recently they have rarely been trained sufficiently in mediation—either to provide it or know when to suggest it. Judges are not settlement trained mainly because JDR was not part of a judge's designated or historical role. The traditional judicial role was outlined by the Supreme Court of Canada in the case of *Re Therrien*:

> The judicial function is absolutely unique. Our society assigns important powers and responsibilities to the members of its judiciary. Apart from the traditional role of an arbiter which settles disputes and adjudicates between the rights of the parties, judges are also responsible for preserving the balance of constitutional powers between the two levels of government in our federal state. Furthermore, following the enactment of the Canadian Charter, they have become one of the foremost defenders of individual freedoms and human rights and guardians of the values it embodies. Accordingly, from the point of view of the individual who appears before them, judges are first and foremost the ones who state the law, grant the person rights or impose obligations on him or her.
>
> If we then look beyond the jurist to whom we assign responsibility for resolving conflicts between parties, judges also play a fundamental role in the eyes of the external observer of the judicial system. The judge is the pillar of our entire justice system, and of the rights and freedoms which that system is designed to promote and protect. Thus, to the public, judges not only swear by taking their oath to serve the ideals of Justice and Truth on which the rule of law in Canada and the foundations of our democracy are built, but they are asked to embody them (Supreme Court of Canada 2001).

Bluntly put, judges are not always inclined toward settlement. In the federal judges' school in Canada there is little said about JDR or the skills needed to mediate. The daily role of the judge, understandably, is to interpret legislation and apply the law to a certain set of facts. Judges rule on motions before and during trial, instruct juries on the law, hear appeals of lower courts, and exercise jurisdiction, such as issuing orders of contempt when appropriate. Attorneys' written submissions to judges always take the form of legal briefs, noting relevant statutory provisions and court precedents; nothing that is presented is aimed at resolving a dispute. A judge "in robes" is supposed to make the final decision, but never to go beyond the filed briefs. Thus, a fair criticism and strongly held view among some jurists is that a judge should never leave the dais to sit at a conference table with the parties for any reason. In this view, the settlement of cases is in the hands of counsel and outside mediators or arbitrators, but not sitting judges.

Another disadvantage lies in the implementation of JDR outcomes. If the entire JDR process is confidential with no written agreement or court ordered reports, how can challenges to implementation be adjudicated? How is the result recorded and what if it is challenged? As far as subsequent lawsuits (i.e., regarding challenges to the terms or implementation efforts) are concerned, judges cannot be called to testify about what happened during a JDR. So, whose version of the facts, if disputed, should a subsequent court accept? This dilemma was posed almost thirty years ago in the words of the Saskatchewan appeal court:

> The evolution of these Rules brought about something of a change in the role of the judges, a matter of some controversy (…) The controversy is not apt to abate soon, and the present Rules are likely to spawn issues of vires, meaning, and scope quite beyond anything associated with the former Rules.
>
> … the current Rules are to be taken in the first instance as mandating obligatory mediation to be conducted by judges, as judicial-mediators, empowered to take a leading, active, and even decisive part in settling the action if possible, but who are immune, should a dispute arise over what occurred, from being called upon to testify about what was said or done. If that be so, and since these conferences are to be conducted off the record, the present Rules are likely to give rise to some vexing questions.
>
> For example, if such mediation is to result in contracts of settlement, but the discussions preceding their making are inadmissible in all subsequent proceedings, as the current Rules provide, and no record is maintained and the judges are so immune, then how is the Court of Queen's Bench to handle actions on such contracts? Actions, for example, to enforce them in the face of ambiguity or to rectify them in the case of alleged mistake, where extrinsic evidence of the circumstances giving rise to the contract must often be adduced. Or actions to rescind them on the basis, let us say, of alleged misrepresentation or duress or undue influence, as in the case, to use an obvious example, of matrimonial property settlements, where the same evidentiary considerations apply. And how is the exercise of the powers afforded the judges, including for instance the power to impose sanctions by way of costs, to be reviewed on appeal in the absence of a record or other effective means of determining what occurred?
>
> Judges deciding disputes have long been immune from compulsion to testify with respect to their decisions. That is clear, and the immunity is absolute (Saskatchewan Court 1993).

The above referenced statement further underscores the need for judges to be properly trained, not only so they can perform dispute resolution functions during JDR, but so they can take steps to ensure that the parties (and their attorneys) keep copies of pre-JDR process descriptions, statements submitted during the JDR, and all negotiated agreements (initialed by the judge). In recent years, individual courts have required mediation and dispute-resolution training of judges asked to provide JDR. This typically involves court-based educational JDR instruction and has occurred through the National Judicial Institute. In Alberta, there is an internal online-training module available with a forward from the Chief Justice; a presentation of JDR examples; tips; review of a data base of JDR forms and documents; and other BJDR materials.

Returning to the general arguments for and against ADR and JDR, courts have recently upheld JDR agreements and processes, including judicial decisions agreed upon in binding JDRs (Alberta Court of Appeal 2005).

Since Owen Fiss published *Against Settlement*, mentioned in Chapter 4, one of the critiques of ADR in general, and JDR in particular, has focused on the notion that judges cannot be working to privately settle disputes—as ADR and JDR require—while also giving "force to the values embodied in authoritative texts such as the Constitution and statutes: to interpret those values and to bring reality into accord with them" (Fiss 1984). In this view, the role of judges and courts is not to bring peace, but rather to bring justice, making critics of ADR and JDR argue that society gets "less" when parties settle because there is no cathartic engagement or public venting of the values at stake. More, since JDR does not create judicial precedents, an argument can be made that the process misses an opportunity to inform society how to orient their behavior based on previous handling of disputes. Settlement brings with it still another risk: that the inherent power dynamics among the disputants will leave the weaker or poorer parties no choice but to renounce their rights in exchange for satisfaction of some of their needs or to sacrifice their rights because they have less capacity to predict what will happen in court (Fiss 1984; Delgado et al. 1985). There is also the chance that some parties who are more empathetic and relational might be inclined to sacrifice what is best for them for the well-being of other dispute stakeholders (Grillo 1990).

The disadvantages of ADR in general must be distinguished from those of JDR and the unique features of each form of JDR: binding and not binding JDR, pre-trial conferences and settlement conferences.

We have identified ten specific criticisms of JDR. (Some also apply to ADR.) They are as follows: (1) the legal question; (2) concerns about truth-seeking; (3) the non-binding nature of some forms of ADR; (4) possible coercion to mediate; (5) the lack of evidence to support claims of ADR efficiency; (6) concerns about the ungenuine quality of mediated conversations; (7) the anti-pedagogical role of the lawyers and the judge; (8) the downsides of confidentiality; (9) what we will call the "dirty laundry" criticism; and finally (10) what might be named the "lost in the woods" criticism.

The *legal question* assumes there is a dichotomy between questions of fact and questions regarding legal interpretation in a dispute. Questions like whether a particular legal principle applies in a case or whether a specific precedent is relevant in a case, are matters of interpretation, not fact. Such interpretation clearly ought to be based on legal knowledge and experience. Presumably, the same knowledge and experience are not necessary to assess whether facts are being presented correctly. According to Moore, "where cases involve pure questions of law, e.g., constitutional law questions, or where there are conflicting lines of authorities and the law is not settled or clear, the mini-trial [or other forms of ADR] may be of limited value" (Moore 1995). The point of this criticism is that if a case relies heavily on questions of legal interpretation, ADR variants may not be appropriate. Why, though, should we assume that such a dichotomy always exists and thus cases (involving facts and interests) are fine to go to ADR, but cases involving legal interpretation should not? In JDR, the dichotomy is not relevant since the mediator is a sitting judge.

In all forms of JDR, the judge has the knowledge and the capacity to present and explain the legal interpretations at stake—an advantage over other forms of ADR. Even though the JDR judge may try to shift the conversation from rights-based talk to interest-based talk when appropriate, this does not keep the judge from reminding the parties what the law might potentially have to say. In other words, with regard to legal questions, while it might apply to other forms of ADR, it does not apply to any form of JDR in which a sitting judge is the mediator. Further, even in ADR—in the U.S. at least—many participating independent mediators are retired judges or law professors who can explain the legal issues to both parties and even offer a well-informed evaluative interpretation of what might happen if the case proceeds to court.

The *truth-seeking criticism* charges that ADR, including JDR, is not a process for finding truth, but rather a setting for listening and healing (often through storytelling and merely promoting dialogue). The discovery of the truth is presumably dependent on the use of adversarial tools like cross-examination and testifying under oath, which are not available in JDR (Landerkin and Pirie 2003). "The benefits traditionally attributed to the adversarial system are often outcome focused - - discovery of the truth, protection of individual rights." (Bowal 1995). ADR and JDR, by contrast, are process-focused. They do not put a premium on determining the truth; rather, they allow the parties to hold different truths while still reach agreement regarding what should happen next.

The *non-binding nature* of ADR and some forms of JDR means that they are not conclusive. According to this criticism, ADR and non-binding JDR do not guarantee closure (which, presumably, can only be imposed by a third party). Since JDR can be binding (which participants may opt for and at any point in the process, as we saw in the cases we reviewed earlier), this criticism does not apply. If parties to ADR know they want closure, they can agree to BJDR or even private arbitration. For principled reasons, if parties want closure on the basis of the law, and believe that the only person who can provide this is a judge, they can choose BJDR.

BJDR and settlement conferences—chosen by the parties because they want a binding decision if they are unable (with the help of the judge) to reach a settlement on their own—are similar to a form of ADR known as med-arb (i.e., a combination of mediation and arbitration) where parties choose the same neutral for the facilitated negotiation and, if it fails, the neutral will conduct the adjudicative process.

The roots of this hybrid process date back to indigenous communities led by a village elder who acted as facilitator and, if parties did not solve their differences, played the decider role for the sake of the whole community (Auerbach 1983). The ethical conundrums that surround med-arb are based on the assumption that the facilitator's morality is distinct from the decider's morality (Menkel-Meadow 2020). This morality tension, however, might be trumped by the parties' free decision to be part of a mediated setting, knowing that the neutral (or judge) will have knowledge of the information shared if the case requires a binding decision. If the parties feel that only a judge—with the power to tell them during the mediation what is likely to happen if they pursue litigation—can help them, then binding arbitration offers med-arb with an acting judge. BJDR grants parties ownership and accountability of the dispute handling process (since the first goal is for the parties to generate a mutually acceptable agreement) but also ensures them a conclusive and enforceable result.

The *coercion to mediate criticism* is the by-product of the way some jurisdictions have adopted ADR. Mediation was and still is mandatory in some places. The parties cannot book time with the court until they can show they have made a good faith effort to reach a settlement. Usually private mediators, not JDR judges, are the key to mandatory mediation. Unfortunately, if parties are forced to mediate or participate in a form of ADR, they sometimes feel they are wasting their time and resources, which intensifies their emotional distress. As Landerkin and Pirie write: "parties may resent being forced to mediate. The parties may not agree and feel they have wasted valuable resources. They may think the judicial mediator unfairly pressured them to agree or took sides in the mediation" (Landerkin and Pirie 2003).

There is no guarantee that both parties in a mandatory mediation will enter the process with an inclination to work toward a mutually acceptable agreement. Nevertheless, many ADR practitioners and scholars have defended mandatory mediation, arguing that the parties will only discover that mediation can help them if they try it. In our view, however, mandatory mediation is an oxymoron. In the context of efforts to manage growing caseloads, mandatory mediation might seem worth a try from the court's perspective. But, it ignores the importance of ADR's voluntary nature; parties should be free to enter ADR and JDR and walk away at any time, even without a settlement. Our opinion is that's one reason it works. JDR is not mandatory anywhere in Canada (except Alberta's requirement) and it needs to be reviewed more carefully to realize there are exceptions in law and in practice.

In Chapter 3, we set out the Court Rules for Alberta passed in 2010. These Rules, a small portion of which we now discuss, require ADR (which includes JDR). This Rule is mandatory but has exemptions as follows:

[Alberta's Rules of Court] Dispute resolution processes

4.16(1)   The responsibility of the parties to manage their dispute includes good faith participation in one or more of the following dispute resolution processes with respect to all or any part of the action:

(a) a dispute resolution process in the private or government sectors involving an impartial third person;

(b) a Court annexed dispute resolution process;

(c) a judicial dispute resolution process described in rules 4.17 to 4.21;

(d) any program or process designated by the Court for the purpose of this rule.

(2) On application, the Court may waive the responsibility of the parties under this rule, but only if

(a) before the action started the parties engaged in a dispute resolution process and the parties and the Court believe that a further dispute resolution process would not be beneficial,

(b) the nature of the claim is not one, in all the circumstances, that will or is likely to result in an agreement between the parties,

(c) there is a compelling reason why a dispute resolution process should not be attempted by the parties,

(d) the Court is satisfied that engaging in a dispute resolution process would be futile, or

(e) the claim is of such a nature that a decision by the Court is necessary or desirable … (emphasis added)

That Court of Queen's Bench suspended this mandatory rule in 2016, three years after passing it, and did so because of the busy docket and shortage of federal judges to hear JDRs which, due to its popularity, had started to have longer lead times. In 2018, JDRs were still popular in Alberta and the Court proposed to lift the suspension, which it did in 2019. One judge's experience is that making it mandatory made no difference as to why people chose JDR; they did so because they wanted a judicial mediation. This is important because a concern we raise with making J/ADR mandatory is that to do so in the face of busy court dockets risks parties using it for free judicial mediation just to meet a court rule. That is not the Queen's Bench experience, but it is a real possibility. Apart from that, the opinion of certain Canada-wide judges is that: "… mandatory mediation does not make sense." And while there are counter arguments, judges generally do not like JDR being imposed. The following statement echoes the feeling of Canadian judges: "Still, in general, [judges have] a preference for non-mandatory mediation" (Brenner and Baird 2003). Thus, the *coercion to mediate criticism* does not apply to JDR.

The *lack of evidence to support ADR efficiency criticism* is attributed to Marc Galanter, a legal scholar who argued that eliminating trials (through the use of ADR) was not necessarily a good thing, even if it increased the speed and the number of cases a court can handle. While there is disagreement about why the number of verdicts issued by courts in the U.S. has continued to decline, he did not like what he saw as "the vanishing trial" (Galanter 1985; Lande 2006). He was worried about access to and the quality of justice in situations that did not follow full trial procedure. In Galanter's view, the efficiency of the court system is not the only important objective. There are, in fact, very few studies that have presented evidence to show that court efficiency is worth pursuing if it produces less "justice" for some segments of the population. We have not found published comments from Galanter on JDR as a form of ADR in the Canadian context and whether he feels the same way about JDR as he does ADR. While JDR eliminates trials in the usual sense—because it's provided by sitting judges and can become bind-ing under the judge's aegis—he and other critics may not be as concerned about JDR displacing trials as they are about ADR.

The confidential nature of the JDR process, the lack of official transcripts or records, and its fragmentary application makes it difficult to do a comprehensive assessment of the benefits and costs of JDR. However, there have been task forces and studies that have tried to weigh the overall pros and cons of JDR. The Canadian Forum on Civil Justice report, among others, offers an overall assessment of JDR's contributions to improved court efficiency (Farrow 2017; Canadian Judicial Council 2008; Canadian Forum on Civil Justice 2010, 2012). This is a partial rebuttal to Galanter's criticism of the lack of evidence for claiming efficiency benefits of ADR and, particularly, for benefits beyond efficiency, like the fact the facilitator is a sitting judge who knows the rights of the parties and what they can expect from a trial.

The *unreal conversation criticism* suggests that ADR and JDR often encourage parties to consider unrealistic offers. These critics claim that ADR (and JDR if the judge does not assert his or her expertise) allows the parties to indulge in unrealistic claims of what they are legally entitled to. According to Agrios, this is the main disadvantage of JDR. He quotes a private memorandum from a judge who says:

> My most recent experiences with JDR tell me that the majority of JDRs involve unrealistic positions by one of the parties. Some claims are utterly fanciful. Too often I see counsel who have little ability to evaluate their file. I see them and their clients coming to the judge in hopes of getting a negotiated or mediated settlement without having to face the legal frail-ties of their claim (Agrios 2004).

This judge may not be alone in his belief that JDR allows parties to consider unre-alistic positions and, even worse, that their counsel are unprepared to put an end to outlandish demands. This view means JDR makes the judge's job even harder by making them responsible for educating parties about their rights, setting counsel straight on potential trial outcomes, and shifting some of the discussions from fiction to reality.

Neither Agrios nor the judge who wrote the memorandum present anything more than their hunches or intuition about what happens in JDR. They may just be revealing their blind spot: perhaps what we need more of is not lawyers who are better prepared for trial, but rather lawyers better prepared to make a non-adversarial and non-adjudi-catory dispute resolution effort.

The *anti-pedagogical criticism* is closely related to the previous one, building on the comment from the anonymous judge. He believes JDR encourages lawyers to be less prepared for trial and thus unprepared for settlements, needing a mediating judge to help them frame the dispute, forecast the likely litigation outcome and clarify their parties' interests. In his words:

> My view is that we have raised a generation of lawyers on JDRs, too many of whom have little or no ability to prepare for trial. They prepare for the JDR. If they are lucky enough

to get a judge who will deal with interests, they do okay, and they return. By engaging in interests, we are creating a new industry in soft legal claims which is bad for the judges, the bar and the litigants. Judges get more work, some of which ought to be weeded out by counsel well before seeing a judge (Agrios 2004).

This is a strong criticism, but it relies on the assumption that the role of lawyers in JDR should be to know the legal issues at stake and how best to negotiate in a zero-sum, win/lose fashion. Perhaps JDR will indeed shift legal education and push lawyers to do a better job of listening to one another and translating their clients concerns into clear statements of interests that can be the basis of mutually advantageous agreements. If you don't believe that lawyers should help to heal conflicts, manage disputes and support parties in their efforts to resolve their disagreements as quickly, painlessly and inexpensively as possible, then you will probably blame JDR for leading lawyers in the wrong direction. (We talk more about helping attorneys participate effectively in JDR in Chapter 13.)

Let's turn to the *strategic confidentiality criticism*. JDR imposes strong rules of confidentiality (as do other ADR methods), in an effort to ensure that anything the parties share cannot be used subsequently if a case goes to trial. However, in practice, some counsel use JDR and other forms of ADR to gain access to confidential information and the other side's view of their case in the hope of turning this to their client's advantage if the case continues to litigation. And, they may well be assuming from the beginning that the case will be litigated. This criticism is also channeled by Agrios: "counsel should be aware that in proceeding with a JDR, there is a risk that information disclosed during the JDR process may be used in this fashion" (Agrios 2004). In other words, some parties might proceed to trial with access to privileged information which, if the JDR had not taken place, would not have been disclosed.

This may be a problem, but it is a small one. In Alberta, with decades of experience, more than 80 percent of all JDRs settle. For the cases that do not, some will proceed with one or both sides enjoying privileged information that was disclosed in good faith during the course of the JDR—something counsel need to be aware of during a JDR.

Still, this line of criticism is weakened since confidential information can never be quoted at trial. Independent of ADR or JDR, there is a risk that any conversation where parties disclosed confidential information to each other—or sometimes in the presence of a jury—will have to be "struck from their minds." Sometimes even legal responses, like non-disclosure agreements, are not enough to eliminate this risk. Lawyers need to think carefully about the information they reveal in the presence of the other side in a JDR and what they are prepared to present only to the mediating judge in private session. If they tell the JDR judge that something is confidential, it is unlikely to reach the other side.

The *dirty laundry criticism* goes back to one of Fiss's attacks on ADR as a system that deprives courts of interpretations that can ignite a public conversation or that can promote social change. According to him, "[t]o be against settlement is only to suggest that when the parties settle, society gets less than what appears, and for a price, it does not know it is paying" (Fiss 1984). But what is society actually getting less of? There is no doubt that society has dirty laundry to wash; there are great inequities in the way our social, economic, environmental and other systems work. But who benefits when litigation makes these conflicts more visible and raises them to a higher level on the public agenda? It is rare that litigation spurs systemic changes that reallocate gains and losses in a meaningful way, especially for the litigants themselves. Litigation, in fact, might transform parties into tools for societal benefits and cause them to disregard their own moral worth and fundamental need to manage their dispute. JDR and other ADR forms, by contrast, hold out the prospect of immediate improvement for those involved, albeit without the societal catharsis.

Agrios believes that the dirty laundry criticism cuts both ways: "Most parties prefer to keep the details of their dirty laundry out of the public courtroom. But we need to be aware also of the merits of an open and accountable public justice system." Fiss's criticism touches on a real disadvantage of ADR/JDR, but it is a disadvantage more in theory than in practice. It is difficult to see how society loses something when two neighbors settle their differences amicably, avoid court and commit to living together peacefully. ADR/JDR also brings social benefit, but to see it a change of perspective is required: it generates real social change from below instead of betting on a possible and general social change from above.

In our view, Fiss misses an important point when he writes that even if "parties are prepared to live under the terms they bargained for, and although such peaceful coexistence may be a necessary precondition of justice, and itself a state of affairs to be valued, it is not justice itself" (Fiss 1984). Fiss's lack of pragmatism makes him blind to the virtues of ADR/JDR. It is not clear that litigation is always going to lead to a public airing of social injustices in a way that will help to remedy the underlying problem. For those who find mutually agreeable ways of resolving their differences, Fiss would make what he considers "the best" the enemy of "the good." For those who would benefit directly from JDR, they would much rather have their mediated agreement than wait for society-at-large to make reforms or take action that will eventually benefit them, following the airing of their case. And even if what they want is to air their case and use it as a platform for strategic litigation, the channel is open to them and the JDR door will not fetter that possibility. Fiss actually says, "[t]o settle for something means to accept less than some ideal." (Fiss 1984) Indeed, that's one definition of compromise or settlement: sacrificing an ideal to deal with our differences as best as we can.

Claiming that justice in itself is preserved through litigation is a hard sell. Claiming, instead, that settlement might be a window to see how justice in a specific dispute limits forward movement, might be a more practical endeavor. Perhaps, we should "be judged by our compromises more than by our ideals and norms. Ideals may tell us something important about what we would like to be. But compromises [and settlements] tell us who we are" (Margalit 2010).

Finally, the last criticism of ADR (and JDR in particular) is perhaps the strongest: the *lost in the woods criticism*. This name fits because JDR in Canada is not guided by many regulations or even an agreed upon roadmap that explains exactly what it is and what each party is expected to do at each stage of the process. As Landerkin and Pirie note: "Judicial dispute resolution may also be problematic if the judge lacks the necessary skills to engage in JDR activities. Outside the court, serious attention has been given to the qualifications needed by individuals working in the ADR field, particularly mediators" but almost none have been given the training and qualifications needed by judges conducting JDR (Landerkin and Pirie 2003). The lack of serious and sustained JDR training is a significant criticism. Part of this training should probably include a clearer roadmap (even if multiple options are preserved at various points in the process). With more substantial training, JDR judges will be better equipped to find their way out of the woods in especially complex cases. In 2018, Zariski identified a roadblock to ADR/JDR implementation: "lawyers and judges are largely left without guidance concerning the 'non-legal' elements of disputes, commonly called 'interests'" (Zariski 2018). However, he also identified some responses to this lack of formal guidance in the published work of numerous ADR and JDR scholars (Denlow 2010).

The path to improved JDR implementation is steep. Lawyers are not taught about JDR in law school. The public learns of JDR almost only from their lawyers since all the cases and results are confidential. JDR initiatives still operate under different names such as settlement conferences and BJDR. The differences between ADR in the U.S. and JDR in Canada can be confusing, as can the differences among provincial court systems. There is more than enough evidence, though, to justify formalizing some JDR ground rules and definitions across Canada, and letting the public know that it has a dispute resolution option that ensures user autonomy, a definitive outcome and access to a judge.

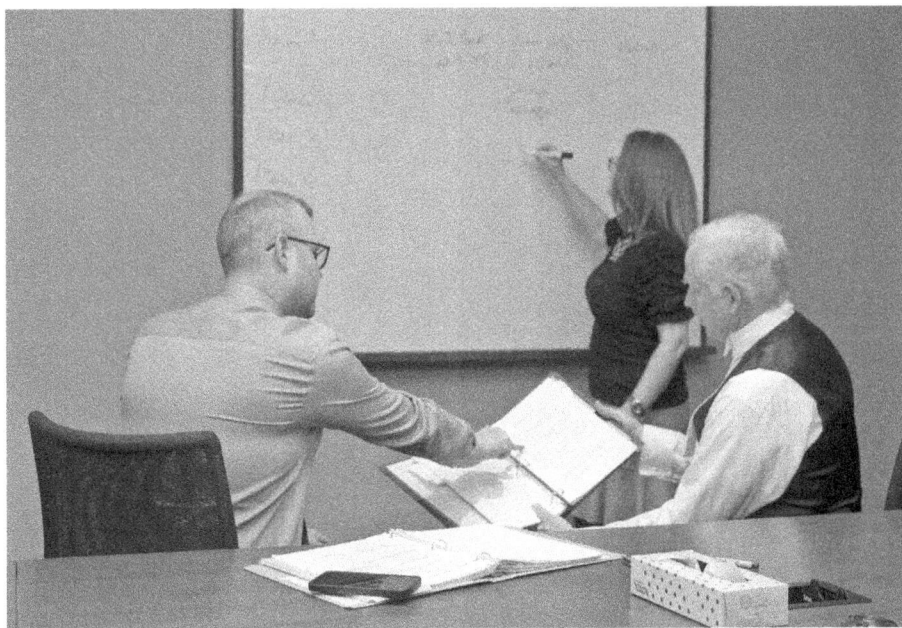

Photo 1 Parties leave the court with Justice Tilleman, who asks them to identify their issues and options, so the judge can help the parties create value and reach a final settlement.

Photo 2 Sr. and Supervising Justice Tilleman leaving the Dais to begin a JDR in the Boardroom where he can directly engage with parties and counsel.

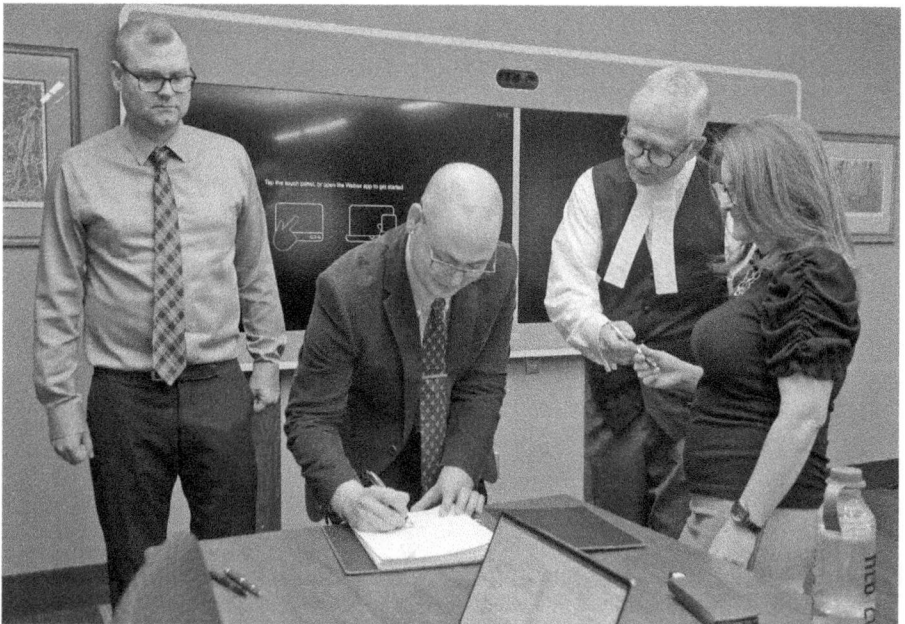

Photo 3 Case settled. Parties signing Consent Judgment approving the settlement and discontinuing lawsuits. Counsel looking on.

Chapter 8

JUSTICE AND FAIRNESS IN JDR

The Motor Vehicle Accident with Pedestrian Case

Is JDR Fair? Is it Just?

If we see that someone was robbed or killed without the perpetrator punished or the victim compensated, we say, "this is unjust." And yet, when we are asked to define or explain the essence of fairness or justice, we find it hard to answer. We are unsure whether notions of justice are unique to individual actions or apply equally to institutions, laws, policies, or all of the above.

To answer the question of whether JDR is fair or just, we need to first grapple with its competing definitions. We will then couple a theoretical view of justice with the views of the parties in one of the actual JDR cases described in the appendix, *The Motor Vehicle Accident with Pedestrian Case* (*The Motor Vehicle Case*). Our goal is to show what justice looks like in practical terms.

The first distinction we want to make is between justice in the narrowest sense and justice in a broader sense. In the narrowest sense, it is a characterization of a decision made through the legal system—read litigation—following established rules and procedures. For people who define justice in this way, it is impossible to think of it being determined outside the legal system. For them, ADR or JDR could not possibly be a means for determining justice; they see justice as only what a court generates through a particular kind of battle. In ADR and JDR, the assumptions are different: the justice system is not a battleground where a pre-appointed judge makes a unilateral decision. JDR, specifically, opens a space for the disputing parties to generate a resolution of their differences with the assistance of a mediating judge. Whether the JDR process is fair or not, justice in the narrowest sense cannot be the product of a JDR process.

Justice in the broad sense, though, need not be linked to the judicial system. Broadly, it is the product of actions, institutions, policies and laws in a wide variety of contexts. It is not determined universally; it is generated contextually. As an illustration, "just" might be applied to a public policy decision aimed at allocating resources to different segments of the community *(distributive justice)*. Or, it might be a way of characterizing an act of government aimed at punishing those who have harmed others *(corrective justice or retributive justice)* (Aristotle 1962, 2000). Since the end of WWII, the notion of justice has been applied to decisions about the transition from an authoritarian regime or a war-scenario to a democratic and peaceful society *(transitional justice)* (Murphy 2017). More recently, the idea of justice (applied institutionally) has been used to character-ize narratives aimed at helping us see our contributions to larger, ongoing unfairness *(narrative justice)* (Winslade 2000). And finally, the idea of justice has been used to assess non-state responses to violence aimed at healing communities and restoring human relationships *(restorative justice)* (Braithwaite 1999). If we ask whether JDR has produced a just or a fair outcome, we need to apply notions of justice in the broader sense.

It is also important to focus on another distinction: between *procedural justice* and *substantive justice*. Procedural justice refers to the means by which decisions are reached, and benefits and burdens distributed or imposed on people (Miller 2017). In other words, procedural justice "refers to the fairness of (the) process by which a decision is reached" (Hollander-Blumoff and Tyler 2011). Substantive justice, on the other hand, refers to the outcome itself, the distribution of benefits and burdens, goods and sanctions. For example, communities must often make resource allocation decisions that benefit some at the expense of others. There are several ways to make these decisions: they can take a vote, rely on a lottery, or perhaps more creatively, ask everyone to participate in a survey indicating how and why they rank various processes for making the decision. These various procedures value majority rule, impartiality, full group involvement, or other considerations differently. For some, the trustworthiness (and just nature) of the final decision is primarily a function of the procedures used to make a decision. So, procedural justice depends on the means used to make a decision and assumptions about the best procedures to use. Substantive justice focuses not the process or how the decision was made, but rather on whether the results of the decision respond to a priori assumptions about how fair or how appropriate the outcome is.

For some members of a community that have to make a tough decision, if the final choice does not allocate gains and losses equally among all of them (justice as equality), they will not consider the result to be just. For others, if the decision does not allocate gains and losses to those who deserve them the most or the least (justice as merit), the result will not be viewed as fair. Still others would argue that the final decision should allocate gains and losses in a way that gives the most to those with the greatest need (justice as need), or they will not see the results as fair. For many, the criteria they use to judge the fairness of substantive outcomes are a product of their upbringing or their religious beliefs. For others, they are part of their political or ideological beliefs. Whatever their source, their criteria for judging fairness or justice of the outcome are independent of the process by which the final decision was made.

Our argument finds that procedural rather than substantive justice should be measured in determining whether JDR produces just results. Moreover, since the court system and not just individual judges use JDR to settle disputes, a broader, institutional rather than a narrower view of justice should apply. Let's look more closely at *The Motor Vehicle Case to* see whether and how broader and procedural justice concerns were met.

The Motor Vehicle Case

Mr. Barton parked his car on the side of the TransCanada Highway and ran across the road toward a city mall. While crossing the road, he was hit by a GMC truck, driven by Mr. Driggs. Barton sued Driggs for failing to observe him or honk the horn, and sought around $1 million in damages. Driggs argued that Barton was negligent and did not observe the highway warning signs while crossing and provoked the collision. The parties filed their pleadings. Barton hired a law firm and Driggs was represented by his insurance company.

It was not an easy decision: pain and loss on one side, personal liability counterarguments, on the other. Yet, Driggs, his counsel and insurer, and Barton participated in a JDR. The outcome: Barton received $150,000 and all claims were dismissed. Was that a just outcome? Was it fair?

Procedural Justice

In his most important work, *A Theory of Justice,* John Rawls contrasted three types of procedural justice: perfect procedural justice, imperfect procedural justice and pure procedural justice (Rawls 1971, 1999). *Perfect procedural justice,* according to Rawls, consists of designing a procedure that guarantees a just outcome. One theoretical example we can all relate to is when several people are sharing a cake and the person cutting the cake takes the last piece. Such a procedure guarantees a just and fair outcome because the last person served is sure to split the cake as equitably as possible for everyone else; the maximization of interests of the person cutting the cake guarantees that everyone will receive more or less the same amount. *Imperfect procedural justice,* by contrast, does *not* guarantee a just outcome, though it is likely that justice will be produced. This is illustrated best by a criminal trial in which the process is designed to uncover the truth, convict criminals and acquit innocents. "A trial," as John Rawls explained, "is an instance of imperfect procedural justice. Even though the law is carefully followed, and the proceedings fairly and properly conducted, it may reach the wrong outcome. An innocent person may be found guilty, a guilty person may be set free" (Rawls 1971). It is imperfect justice because the process does not always produce a just outcome. The third and final type of procedural justice is what Rawls calls *pure procedural justice.* Unlike the other two, there is no independent way of determining whether the process was successful or not. In Rawls's words, "[a] fair procedure translates its fairness to the outcome only when it is actually carried out" (Rawls 1971). A coin-toss is an example of a fair procedure; there is no way to assess whether the result is fair other than carrying out the coin-toss fairly. Gambling, under certain circumstances, is another form of pure procedural justice, in the sense that the outcome is fair if the specific gambling procedure was followed fairly without any cheating (Miller 2017). The fact that one player wins everything is beside the point.

JDR is a means of providing *pure procedural justice.* The outcome of gambling is fair provided that bets were made voluntarily; no one cheated; everyone had an equal opportunity to win considering their initial endowments; and so on. Similarly, in JDR, the last distribution is fair and just if: the agreement was reached voluntarily; the facilitator was neutral and did not favor one side; the process was known and understood by all the parties; all the parties were treated with equal respect; the parties were all heard and their participation counted as part of the decision-making process; and the decision-maker(s) articulated trustworthy motives and grounds for the final decisions. This means that in JDR there is no independent criterion by which we can determine that the result was just, other than the process itself. In other words, JDR is less concerned about the outcome of the process than it is about the means through which the outcome is achieved (Thibaut 1974; Tyler 2003).

The key elements of procedural justice turn out to be primarily social-psychological:

- *Transparency*: Promoting understanding of the process
- *Neutrality*: Perceived neutrality of decision-making
- *Respect:* Respect or treatment with dignity and concern for rights
- *Voice:* An opportunity for each party to tell its side of the story and be heard
- *Trust:* Faith in the motives of the authorities (LaGratta 2017; Lind and Tyler 1988)

These five elements have been identified by psychologists who study the levels of satisfaction people feel when they participate in what they perceive to be a fair process, which is different from the satisfaction they feel with a good outcome.

Understanding the process, neutrality, respect, voice/participation and trustworthiness are the principles that, if applied correctly, will lead to the conclusion that JDR was just and, therefore, the outcome was as well. In *The Motor Vehicle Case,* what made the JDR process a just or unjust procedure was not whether Barton received one million or one hundred thousand dollars. What mattered is whether the procedures used to arrive at the final agreement, namely, voluntary negotiation guided by a mediating judge, were indeed fair. What does this mean exactly? If Barton and Driggs were treated respectfully by a neutral judge who did not favor either of them—allowing them to actively participate, tell their side and to take control over the final decision—then the outcome was just.

In JDR, parties are guided by a neutral mediating judge who must appear to the parties to be unbiased. The judge must also provide the parties with consistent and transparent explanations and grant them some level of control over the design of the process—depending, of course, on whether it is binding or non-binding. During the process, the judge guarantees that every participant is treated with respect and dignity.

Promoting Understanding of the Process during the Pre-JDR Conference

How was the process designed and trust in the judge built in *The Motor Vehicle Case?* Once the lawyers agreed on which judge would conduct the JDR, the judge provided each counsel with an overview of the process—a key part of pure procedural justice. It is like giving the parties and their counsel a map of where they will go first, what they will do next, when they will stop, for how long, and so on. This ensures transparency. In this case, the justice's assistant sent a letter to both parties requesting: (1) a pre-JDR conference call between the judge and the lawyers to set the atmosphere and clarify the nature of JDR; (2) a short brief from each party which guaranteed that both parties felt heard from the outset and gave the justice a broader overview of the dispute and (3) supporting materials including medical reports, case law, independent reports and the family physician's notes.

During the pre-JDR conference, the justice got a sense of what the case was about, and the lawyers on both sides got to hear how the process would be conducted. Here are some of the questions and topics usually discussed during pre-JDR conferences to enhance procedural justice:

- What is JDR about?
- What are the phases of JDR?
- What is expected in a joint session and caucuses?
- Are there deadlines to settle the case?
- What is the case about?
- What are likely stumbling blocks?
- Have there been any offers made already? What were they? Why were they rejected?
- Are there any disabilities involved? Language barriers?
- Why has the case not settled?
- Why do the parties want JDR now?
- What are the strengths and weaknesses of each side's view of the case?

During the pre-JDR conference with the parties in this case, the judge offered what she called his "JDR intro spiel" to explain what JDR entails. "No party can be called to trial to testify to the content of the JDR," he said, and he "would not keep any notes on the case or have any part in the trial if the parties do not reach an agreement." Then the justice described how the JDR would be structured, beginning with a plenary session where the clients state their accounts. She reminded the lawyers to make sure their clients were prepared. Next, three or four private caucuses with each party would take place until their 4:30 pm deadline—not a standardized procedure, but how this justice likes to structure the JDR. Every judge has their own approach; JDR's flexibility allows each judge in consultation with the parties to take a different route, adjust the phases, or establish deadlines to keep the parties on track. Some justices, like the one facilitating *The Motor Vehicle Case,* find that an efficient process is key. She explained to the parties that "everyone would need to cut to the chase, there would be no time for posturing ..." She later explained, "If you do not give people a time deadline, they will always have a reason to have another round."

Beyond laying out the plan and procedures, the pre-JDR conference shows the parties that the justice cares about them, and particularly about helping them feel comfortable with the process. Most importantly, the pre-JDR conference fulfills one of the key elements of procedural justice: it promotes understanding of the process while building trust between the parties, their counsels and the judge.

Neutrality of Decision-making

Neutrality implies a number of things. It is not limited to letting both parties speak for the same amount of time, not favoring one side, or not deciding who is right or wrong.

Being neutral during a JDR requires the judge to be impartial, showing no bias toward either side. It also requires an ability to consider all relevant information and, if needed, use it to make appropriate procedural decisions, like extending provisional negotiation deadlines, calling for unscheduled caucuses when unexpected obstacles emerge, and reality-testing claims on either side about what might happen if the case goes to trial. A neutral judge must be consistent in the application of all decision-making rules (Hollander-Blumoff and Tyler 2011).

In a JDR, whether binding or non-binding, procedural neutrality requires:

- Providing equal time to both sides during caucuses
- Providing equal time to the parties during their initial exposition of the case
- Identifying the elements of the dispute that are suitable for JDR
- Requesting and assessing information that might clarify each party's position and demands
- Retaining a receptive attitude toward what is shared
- Adjusting the procedure if a request is made by both parties and it might facilitate a resolution of the dispute
- Restricting evaluations of offers to private caucuses

In *The Motor Vehicle Case*, the judge talked about a rule-of-thumb she used to help ensure her neutrality. She is willing to tell a party she thinks they are lying, but she is careful not to embarrass anyone in front of the opposing side. A desire to maintain neutrality led the judge to restrict probing questions that might expose a party's weakness to caucus. Gestures like these enhance the procedural justice of the JDR, as well as the parties' satisfaction with the process.

Respect or Treatment with Dignity and Concern for Rights

Being treated with courtesy matters. To preserve someone's dignity requires not treating them in ways that degrade, insult, disrespect, or express contempt against them (Rosen 2012). To respect someone's dignity means not using them as a tool to achieve some other purpose. Like neutrality, it involves numerous actions in the context of JDR.

First, it means attaching adequate value to each person's perspective on the dispute. It is not enough to let parties voice their concerns; the mediating judge must actively listen. Second, the judge needs to check his or her own biases throughout the JDR. Third, the parties should not be used by the judge to achieve any sort of end. They should not be manipulated (Tyler and Bies 1990). And finally, the parties' rights must be protected. Although in JDR it is possible that a party might give up their right to sue to help reach agreement, the mediating judge needs to be sure that parties understand the implications of what they are doing.

In *The Motor Vehicle Case*, the justice stated at the outset that she had read all the papers the lawyers sent and that she wanted to ask some questions about them, adding, "I hope you don't mind." She addressed the plaintiff, Barton, and framed the JDR by saying to him, "They can give you money but can't make you better. This is just about compensation." This a very good example of how a JDR judge can frame the case in a way that treats the harmed party respectfully. By making it clear that the victim could not be made whole again and shifting the discussion to fair compensation, the judge was letting both parties know that the goal of JDR was not about determining guilt or innocence, but rather about reaching an agreement that allowed both sides to feel they were treated fairly.

And yet, the case was not just about fair compensation; Barton needed a chance to be heard. Indeed, during the JDR, he felt empathy from both the judge and the defendant's counsel. He definitely did not want to go to trial and risk being contradicted or embarrassed on the stand; he wanted to move on from a horrific accident and put his life back together. And he wanted to be treated with respect.

Voice and Participation

As long as there is an opportunity to share one's story and shape the final outcome, procedural fairness is provided. Researchers call this the "voice effect" in procedural justice (Folger et al. 1979). "The presumption is that in ADR given an opportunity to express their views, the chance to speak will give parties a measure of control over the outcome. Their arguments might persuade a litigating judge to provide a better outcome … These expectations lead to higher procedural fairness judgments" (Folger et al. 1979). The voice effect works a bit differently in JDR where parties have complete control over the outcome of the process (unless it is a BJDR). What counts in JDR is not the fact that the people believe their voice will allow them to control the outcome by convincing the other side to accept their arguments, but rather the fact that expressing their views will increase the fairness of the procedure.

Barton got to share his story directly with an empathetic judge and opposing counsel. Being heard and making his own story count heightened Barton's perception of a fair process. Even the defendant's counsel acknowledged the value of having a judge who required a recitation of the case's facts and let both parties share their views.

Trust in the Motives of Authorities

Legitimacy is one area in which JDR differs from others forms of ADR. Theoretically, legitimacy is the belief that those in power deserve to rule and make decisions that shape the lives of others. Legitimacy implies trust on the part of those whose lives are being affected. Generally, people trust judges, their knowledge of the law and legal procedures, and that they will make fair decisions. When judges are conducting a JDR, that same trustworthiness applies. The parties and their counsel are still inclined to see the judge as an authority figure with the capacity to accurately predict what will likely happen if the case is not settled. Parties and their counsel trust mediating judges to be fair, but this is not always the case with private mediators. Even if the mediators are retired judges, they do not carry the same "aura" or standing as active judges. This is why the legitimacy of private mediation suffers (whether fairly or not), along with the procedural justice of the process.

Trust in authorities managing dispute resolution procedures is key to perceptions of procedural justice. Trust hinges on an assumption that the authority or the mediating judge in the case of JDR, is "sincerely trying to do what (is) right and (is) motivated to do what (is) good for the people involved" (Hollander-Blumoff and Tyler 2011). Neutrality follows closely. It is almost impossible to trust someone we perceive to be biased against us. Trust is a product of neutrality and neutrality is a major contributor to trust.

In *The Motor Vehicle Case*, counsels expressed their trust in the expertise and unbiased opinions of the judge presiding over the JDR. They felt the judge played a major role in ensuring the JDR's effectiveness precisely because the parties wanted to know "what the courts would do," and the judge had the knowledge required to provide a fair prediction. For instance, the insurance adjuster wanted to know what they owed according to the court, and the defendant wanted to know what compensation they would get at trial. The judge provided unique insights into how a court would probably rule in their case, and the parties trusted her prediction because they felt she was motivated by good intentions. From the outset, the judge had three goals: letting the parties and their counsel know that she was neutral, that she was familiar with the facts of their case, and that she empathized with the difficult situation they were facing. This was enough to establish her trustworthiness.

In JDR, parties sometimes have a higher level of trust in the judge than in their lawyers. As the plaintiff's counsel put it, "some people just need to hear [the predictions of what they will get in trial] from a judge." A judge's neutrality, expertise and, above all, good intentions may certainly be more compelling than a lawyer merely telling a party what they want to hear.

The Motor Vehicle Case ended with the parties agreeing to settle as the courthouse closed for the day. They walked to one of the counsel's homes to draft the agreement and finally put the issues behind them. Both parties were satisfied with the draft, in part, because the process was perceived as fair.

Now, let's turn to substantive justice, which addresses a whole different question: was the agreement between Barton and Driggs (through his insurer) fair and just?

Substantive Justice

Substantive justice asks about the final allocation of resources or, in the case of JDR, about the final decision or agreement. Is it just that Barton received $150,000 and all claims were dismissed? Well, if the sum is similar to what Barton might have gotten at trial, then it might be just, but this is only one possible answer. Another might be that the agreement is only just if, from a distributive justice perspective, resources were distributed between the parties according to their needs or merit. Or, as we have already noted, it might only be just if the agreement restores (and heals) whatever harm was done to Barton. Perhaps it matters whether the agreement restores the relationship between Barton and Driggs. All these possible answers to the initial question depend on the criteria used to determine what justice requires in general, as well as in this case.

The reason questions of substantive justice are not a central focus from the standpoint of a JDR judge is simple: the judge is not responsible for deciding the case, unless, of course, it is a BJDR, and even then it depends on the terms the parties agree should frame the resolution of their differences. If a party accepts an apology and renounces his or her claim to compensation, the JDR judge should not intercede or try to persuade a party to ask for more. The judge is not the arbiter of the substantive justice of the final agreement; control over the final decision and how the dispute is best resolved rests with the parties.

Distributive Justice

The specific principles of distributive justice are *equality*, which means to distribute benefits or burdens on an equal basis or, colloquially speaking, everyone takes the same share; *proportionality*, which means benefits and burdens are distributed with reference to an independent standard or measure (i.e., in proportion to one side's negligence or their contribution to the harm generated); *fair compensation*, which means resources are allocated in response to loss, harm, or disadvantage (this will be explained from a different angle in the next section on corrective justice); and finally, *need*, which means benefits or burdens are allocated based on the needs of the individuals involved (Druckman and Lynn 2016).

When a case is brought to JDR there is a grievance at stake: an accident, a medical malpractice, a breach of contract, property damage and so on. The grievance, if events actually occurred as claimed, implies an allocation of benefits and burdens to the parties in the dispute. Distributive justice demands that a revised allocation, or a "reallocation" of benefits and burdens be imposed. In short, in JDR, distributive justice asks how benefits and burdens should be reallocated to return things to a time before the grievance ever happened. The law determines how benefits and burdens should be reallocated depending on whether the grievance occurred, and whether the claims can be proven in a trial. And sometimes, if they can be proven, the answer to the question of who was responsible might still be blurry. Therefore, JDR provides a space to discuss a fair distribution of the benefits and burdens before tackling all the other questions— many of which could be difficult to answer because of legal technicalities.

In *The Motor Vehicle Case*, the justice noted that though Barton had contributed to his injuries by not crossing at an intersection, he was almost all the way across the road when he was struck by Driggs. This meant that Barton's liability was low, but it opened a new set of questions. Assume that total resources to be allocated for the accident amount to $300,000. What is the appropriate distribution of this much money? And why? Here are some further considerations: (1) Barton did not cross the road at an intersection; (2) Driggs did not honk or manage to warn Barton; (3) Driggs did hit and severely harm Barton; (4) Barton does not have a solid work history to prove future lost income; and (5) what would Canadian law establish as the amount of money owed to Barton if the case went to trial (because of past precedent)? Should compensation be proportional to the liability of the parties? To their future work capacity? Or should the compensation—that is, the potential resources available for compensation—be distributed equally insofar as both parties have good arguments supporting their claims?

Corrective Justice

Officially, corrective justice "concerns a bilateral relationship between a wrongdoer and his victim, and demands that the fault be cancelled by restoring the victim to the position she would have been in had the wrongful behavior not occurred; it may also require that the wrongdoer not benefit from his faulty behavior" (Miller 2017) and, sometimes, requires punishing the wrongdoer. Corrective justice is mostly about compensating the victim and making an evaluative judgment about the wrongs of the offender. One approach, retributive justice, suggests that the offender should pay a price (not just financial compensation) if the original action achieved the level of high moral outrage; if, for example, the wrongdoing was intentional. Or, it might just call for compensation when the level of moral outrage is low because the action was merely negligent. And if the action was undertaken without fault, then no punishment or compensation is usually called for (Darley and Pittman 2003).

Compensation requires restoring the victim's life to what it was before the harm was done. In *The Motor Vehicle Case*, that would be impossible. As the justice confessed to Barton, compensation could never restore his health and way of life to what it was before the accident; it could only compensate him financially for what cannot be restored.

But often the impulse to compensate will not suffice when the wrongdoer has inflicted harm intentionally and a desire for retribution arises. Correcting a harm might imply a form of retribution demanding punishment or some burden to the wrongdoer proportional to the harm he or she inflicted. The punishment is, thus, the expression of a moral judgment that articulates the views of the victim and likely of the community. In JDR it is important to take into account the impulse for retribution even though, strictly speaking, no punishment is discussed. Recognizing the desire of retribution is part of what constitutes substantive justice.

The notion is that compensation and punishment are integral parts of corrective justice branches out from a general principle of responsibility. "Corrective justice must lie in the principle that each person must take responsibility for his own conduct, and if he fails to respect the legitimate interests of others by causing injury, he must make good the harm" (Miller 2017). Unlike distributive justice where the question is how to allocate benefits and burdens by determining who gets what, how much, and why, corrective justice approaches the problem in a different way: is punishment deserved? Is compensation enough? If so, how should the victim be compensated to restore what life was like before the harm was done?

From a corrective justice standpoint, JDR in civil cases focuses primarily on compensation, not punishment. Even when one of the parties feels the other deserves to be punished, he or she is more interested in getting life back on track. In *The Motor Vehicle Case*, the justice began the JDR process by clarifying that even though she had read the case, she had some questions to ask the plaintiff related to his work history, education, goals and health before the accident. Did the plaintiff have any preexisting disabilities? Were there any effects on his education and work opportunities? Was his ability to work reduced? Had he always wanted to be a plumber? These questions all pointed to the same corrective justice concern: what was the victim's situation before the accident and how had the accident altered his plans? Only by hearing his answers, could the judge reflect on appropriate compensation if asked to do so.

Final Remark

In JDR, the judge plays an important role in ensuring that neither side takes advantage of the other. From a purely procedural justice standpoint, the judge should first confirm the parties understand what to expect from a JDR. Outlining the phases of the process, allocating time to each party and determining fixed deadlines will help parties overcome their fear of uncertainty. A pre-trial conference is one way to do this, but there are other possibilities like offering a brief explanation during a hearing about the JDR option and what that would entail. The judge must be and appear neutral and as transparent as possible about the basis for any predictions about what could happen in a trial. The judge should listen attentively to both parties and treat them with respect and dignity throughout the process. By doing so, the judge will not only build rapport but also trust. The judge should protect and enhance, when possible, his or her legitimacy. This means using their authoritative role sparingly, and sharing the legal knowledge that leads them to certain conclusions. Many outsiders might urge the parties in a case to settle, but, as one counsel in *The Motor Vehicle Case* put it, unless they "hear from a judge," they are not likely to take such advice seriously.

From a substantive justice perspective, although the mediating judge is not the one deciding the outcome, he or she can influence the way the parties perceive the dispute and frame potential settlement options. The judge can choose to emphasize distributive or corrective considerations. Questions like, "Who gets what? How much? Why?" are simple ways of unlocking what the parties think would be just outcomes in distributive terms. On the other hand, the judge can also ask how the victim's compensation ought to be calculated, or whether there is a concern about retribution threaded through the case, and if so, why. The judge should help the parties gain a clearer sense of whether and how a distributive versus a corrective notion of justice should be prioritized in their case.

The Motor Vehicle Case was settled. The JDR process produced an agreement that might not have otherwise occurred. The outcome of the case was not just if we define justice in the narrowest sense. There was no trial with a verdict rendered by a judge or jury. But the process was fair from a procedural point of view, given that transparency, neutrality, respect, voice and trust were all guaranteed, and just from a substantive point of view.

Chapter 9

TYPES OF JUDGES

Skill, Temperament and Attitude in JDR
Temperament in an Estate Dispute Case

What types of judges should or should not be asked to deliver JDR services? If we think of judges primarily as rule-followers, then those who know how JDR is supposed to work ought to be able to do the job. Should we assume that all judges who have had basic mediation and facilitation training will be successful JDR judges? Or, are temperament and attitude toward ADR as important as legal background and a rule-following orientation? In our view, only some judges have the appropriate temperament, attitude and necessary skills to conduct successful JDRs. Both knowledge about JDR and learned skills are essential, but so are the right temperament and attitude.

Why Talk about Types of Judges?

A "type" refers to a group that shares one or more common characteristics. Since JDR is a complex activity requiring active listening, considerable empathy, open-mindedness and a positive attitude toward empowering parties to settle their own disputes, we can divide judges into three groups vis a vis JDR: those who do not have either the necessary skills or the right temperament to practice JDR; those sufficiently skillful and temperamentally suited to provide JDR; and those who are appropriately skillful and temperamentally suited, but not interested in providing JDR. We think it is important for senior judges, court administrators and ADR trainers to know which judges are in which category. Just offering additional training to judges of the first and third types won't guarantee that they can deliver JDR services effectively.

This doesn't mean that JDR skills can't be taught, but skill training won't transform a judge with the wrong temperament or no interest in delivering JDR services. As Carrie Menkel-Meadow once put it more generally with regard to lawyering skills, "we aim to improve lawyering, yet, in doing so, we must take into account what lawyers are actually doing" (Menkel-Meadow 1993). We can extrapolate this to JDR: the aim is to improve the administration of justice, not just reduce the workload of the court. That means that judges must be able to mediate effectively in each JDR case that comes before them. But before that is possible, we must be sure that the right types of judges are assigned in the first place.

Types of Judges

If JDR is highly dependent on the people leading it, then our focus should be on what qualities those leaders need to be effective. What skills, temperament and attitudes are necessary? We will analyze types of judges based on:

- their skills (*skill-type*)
- their temperament (*temperament-type*)
- their attitude toward JDR (*attitude-type*)

The skills judges need to conduct a successful JDR are:

- dispute framing
- active listening
- empathetic inquiry
- problem-solving (including paraphrasing)

The temperament judges usually display in a JDR are:

- adversarial or cooperative
- facilitative or evaluative

The attitudes a judge might have toward JDR can be:

- pro-JDR
- anti-JDR

In this chapter, we will describe types of judges based on a combinations of skills, temperaments and attitudes who are most likely to deliver JDR services effectively. It is possible, for example, for a judge to be skilled, collaborative and pro-JDR or lacking skills, authoritative and pro-JDR. We will draw from the examples we have seen or heard to showcase what happens when some of these combinations are in play.

Skills

We say that a JDR judge needs a combination of skills because particular cases might call for one skill rather than another. Thus, we recommend that JDR judges be trained in all of them so they are prepared when the need arises. These are the core skills from which others that we are not emphasizing might be derived. For instance, we focus on framing, but not storytelling. We think a good mediating judge can hold several versions of the same story in their head at the same time; that is, they can imagine multiple frames that fit the same fact pattern. Being able to narrate those multiple frames (i.e., tell several compelling stories) derives from effective framing. It is a separate skill, but derivative and not on our list of core skills.

Framing

Framing makes it possible for one of several alternative versions of a story to be more compelling than another, depending on how it is presented and organized (Malhotra 2016). Metaphorically speaking, framing is the position in which you locate yourself when you offer or take a picture of reality. Frames are rhetorical devices that illuminate some parts of the picture while keeping others in the shadow. Because dispute resolution is a collaborative effort, the parties need to agree on a shared version of the dispute they are trying to address (and a rationale for how it ought to be settled). A skilled mediator helps the parties focus on the key elements of the dispute in which they are immersed, as well as shared interests and possible elements of a negotiated agreement.

Temperament in an Estate Case (The Estate Case) **and its Framing**

On November 8, 2019, before the Court of Queen's Bench of Alberta, two siblings, Tom and Elsa, discussed how to distribute their deceased parents' estate. Their father had died three years before their mother and both had left them an estate which included a residence where Elsa lived, personal investments and a cabin. The dispute, however, was not limited to distributional issues. Who got what and in what proportion was, of course, part of it. The bigger issue was that both siblings were grieving in their own ways. The judge knew he had to turn their attention to their shared loss instead of focusing first on their divergent views on how to distribute their parents' assets. As Tom's counsel later acknowledged: "the judge found a clever way to plant a seed of collaboration."

Although some details of the case are still pending at the time of this writing, the way the case was framed fostered collaboration between Elsa and Tom that led to a provisional agreement. They have agreed largely on how to divide most of the assets, but the sale of the property where Elsa lives or what she will owe if she keeps it are still unresolved. The parties are waiting for a final session with the judge to make a binding decision on this last issue.

Instead of asking about the assets, the judge opened the session by asking Tom and Elsa about the headstone of their parents' grave because he knew they could not even agree on what should be written on it. The justice was receptive to the uniqueness and the emotional background of the dispute, and realized that if they agreed on one thing like the language on the headstone, it would be easier to agree on others. This is a good example of how, by framing the dispute as one of common grief instead of asset division, the judge focused the parties' attention on their commonality of experiencing grief, and not antagonism about dividing their parents' estate.

Active Listening

Active listening requires us to listen constructively and pay attention not only to what is said, but to how it is said, and to notice the mood of the speaker. By listening actively, the listener can interact with the speaker in a way that does not provoke a defensive reaction. Active listening is not a step in the process of persuasion. Rather, it is about gaining a more complete understanding of the speaker's perspective (Royce 2005). In short, active listening requires the capacity to put oneself in the other person's shoes, to see from their perspective, and to let the speaker know that the listener understands what they are trying to say—even if they may not agree with it.

Active listening serves cognitive, emotional and practical needs. The cognitive goal is to better understand the desires, interests and perspectives of the parties. The emotional goal is to defuse anger and move disputants from passionate dogmatism to rational openness. And, the practical goal of active listening is to build rapport, even trust, among the participants in the mediation process.

The Estate Case and Active Listening

The story about the headstone was recalled differently by Elsa's counsel. The problem was not about the inscription, but rather that Elsa had not had a chance to articulate her feelings about the death of their parents. It was an issue of anger and emotional release, not about the content of their communication, or how the opening of the JDR was being framed. "She needed some catharsis," her lawyer insisted. "What was important to my client was to express her feelings in a safe environment where she could honor her parents. The justice provided great respect for my client … She felt listened to."

By listening actively to Elsa's story, the judge opened a channel for the parties to communicate how they were feeling about the dispute. This led to a much clearer view of each side's perspective. But stopping there would have gotten the judge only to the cognitive level. He needed to listen in a way that allowed both parties to feel heard and respected. That then gave the judge connections to both parties at the emotional, cognitive and practical levels.

Empathetic Inquiry

Inquiring involves being curious about what someone else is thinking as well as the reasoning behind their views. This requires open-mindedness as well as an awareness of one's own ignorance regarding others' thoughts and feelings. An inquiry hinges on open-ended and clarifying questions. Open-ended questions are general enough to give others leeway to speak about a topic in a way that is most comfortable for them. The goal is to avoid narrowing the topic so much that the other party loses interest in or doesn't see room to share their perspective. The traditional examples of open-ended questions are: "Can you say more about that? Could you tell me more about this?" (Stone et al. 2010). Such questions aim to shed light on parts of the preceding conversation where the party's meaning or reasoning was unclear. Follow-up, clarifying questions will then make sense and arise from actively listening.

The Estate Case and Empathetic Inquiry

JDR has a better chance of succeeding if the parties and the judge understand that being right or wrong is not especially important. Elsa's counsel specifically noted that understanding the other side's perspective was key. A successful JDR requires a judge's open-minded inquiries—not pre-judgment. And more importantly, the judge must understand the parties' perspectives in the context of their worldviews.

For instance, if the judge had initiated the JDR between Elsa and Tom in a less empathetic way, he would have started by listing the assets. He resisted the temptation and instead worked to understand where they were coming from and why they were struggling. By inquiring with an open mind, he released their thoughts and feelings.

Problem-Solving and Paraphrasing

Problem-solving often involves putting the pieces of a puzzle together in an ingenious way. The pieces can't be re-made—they are what they are—but they can be assembled differently. In JDR, new pieces can be added and some existing pieces can be left out. Often, there are many ways to solve a multi-faceted problem. So, effective problem-solving in a JDR context requires (1) inventorying the pieces of the puzzle; (2) finding out which pieces are the least and most important to each party, and why; (3) inventing or discovering new pieces that could be added; 4) generating multiple "packages" or solutions that incorporate the most important pieces from the collective standpoint of the parties before deciding which is best; and (5) all parties agreeing on objective standards or criteria to use in choosing among the options or alternatives they have developed. It is relatively easy to follow this formula if there is just one person doing the problem-solving (and asking at the end whether the other parties endorse the solution). It is much harder to help all the parties go through all these steps together.

One sub-skill we want to focus on is paraphrasing; it is an essential ingredient in collaborative problem-solving. A judge saying in his or her own words what they think they have just heard one party (or both parties) say, allows parties to feel heard; hearing their words come back to them signals both comprehension and respect (Rogers 2003).

The guidelines for good paraphrasing are: (1) repeat what you heard in your own words; (2) emphasize the idea or emotion you think is most important to the party; (3) use a tone of voice that matches the emotion of the original utterance; and (4) ask for confirmation to be sure the way you have phrased it reflects what the party meant.

The Negligent Land Transfer Case

In *The Negligent Land Transfer Case*, the role of the judge was critical to a smooth resolution; particularly, the judge's ability to listen, be empathetic and make sure he and the other party understood the information that was being conveyed. Both attorneys noted the judge's ability to do this; "This judge was a perfect JDR judge. He's firm, he listens, he's empathetic, he's an all-around terrific person. He's just so good at his job," said the respondent's attorneys. The plaintiff's attorney also appreciated the judge's ability to "guide and broker" the settlement, but felt that the real value was in gathering information from him about how far the other side was from agreeing. What made the difference was the judge's ability to listen, respect the emotions and experiences of the parties, and act as a "conduit between parties who were unable to hear one another." The judge relied on paraphrasing what the parties were saying; you cannot help parties communicate better if you don't understand what they are saying and confirmed that they have expressed their views as they intended.

Skills Grid

Below is a grid that can help keep track of what skills one has to grasp at a conceptual, practical, or habitual level. Judges have a combination of skills at different mastery levels. The chart can be helpful for trainers who have limited time to train judges and who want to focus on what their trainees need the most.

	Framing	*Active listening*	*Empathetic inquiry*	*Problem-solving (including paraphrasing)*
Conceptual level (The judge knows the concept.)	Yes No	Yes No	Yes No	Yes No
Practical level (The judge applies the concept in JDR sessions.)	Always Sometimes Never	Always Sometimes Never	Always Sometimes Never	Always Sometimes Never
Habitual level (The judge's habits are grounded in the skill.)	Always Sometimes Never	Always Sometimes Never	Always Sometimes Never	Always Sometimes Never

The question of what type of judges should do JDR does not have a singular answer. However, the skills listed in the chart above might help to identify what sort of capabilities judges need to be effective.

Types of judges based on their temperament

The notion of temperament comes from William James's *Pragmatism,* one of the foundational texts of classical American philosophy. His opening lines are powerful: "I know that you, ladies and gentlemen, have a philosophy, each and all of you, and that the most interesting and important thing about you is the way in which it determines the perspective in your several worlds (…) For the philosophy which is so important in each of us is not a technical matter (…) it is our individual way of just seeing and feeling the total push and pressure of the cosmos" (James 2018).

The way of seeing and feeling what surrounds us is one way of defining temperament. For James, our disagreements and conflicts are grounded in our temperament.

But we tend to neglect the impact of temperament on what we do and how well we do it.

In JDR, we can see how there might be a clash of temperaments—some call it a clash of mindsets (Mnookin 2004). Some judges are intrinsically adversarial in their orientation toward the law while others are collaborative. Some are facilitative in their orientation toward mediation while others are evaluative. Most judges are not exclusively of one temperament, and a judge's temperament is not fixed for life; it can be modified with training, practice, mentoring and habituation.

Our temperaments frame the way we feel, see and understand the conflicts we try to manage, mitigate, or resolve. Our practices follow our skills, but we cannot learn how to mirror or paraphrase just by knowing the concept. We have to apply such skills on an ongoing basis. If we repeat such skills and reflect on what happens, we might become habituated to them. Even if we develop habits, though, we still have to modify the temperaments that guide what we do, almost automatically.

In our interviews, for example, some counsels used the term "temperament" to refer to the way the judge conducted their JDR session. In *The Estate Case*, one counsel indicated the reason why JDR worked well was because the judge displayed an "appropriate temperament" and had a "cultivated sensibility."

The temperaments we have outlined below correspond to the adversarial, cooperative and evaluative temperaments of most JDR judges. A judge doesn't always reflect the same exact temperament, and some judges are quite purposeful in matching one of several alternative temperaments to the situation in which they find themselves. But with most judges, there is a pattern or a predisposition in the way they operate in their mediating role.

Adversarial temperament

In a nutshell, an adversarial temperament in all negotiating contexts is defined as: whatever is good for the other side cannot be good for me. Too many people see negotiating partners as adversaries (Susskind 2014). This impedes their ability to see an opportunity in every dispute; a chance to create value by identifying mutually advantageous trades. Further, an inability to see the other side as a collaborator is the essence of an adversarial temperament. How does this apply to JDR judges?

A judge with an adversarial temperament determines how they will size up a dispute. An adversarial judge will see a dispute mostly in distributional terms involving a zero-sum allocation of scarce resources. In *The Estate Case*, an adversarial judge might have asked initially for a list of the assets of the parties' deceased parents instead of initiating the conversation with a focus on matters that might be less distributional like the wording of the gravestone epitaph.

An adversarial judge might consider every statement from a party as if it comes from a person focused solely on maximizing his or her interest. So, it will be difficult for them to take a party's claim seriously if they are offering the best option for all the disputants. In short, an adversarial judge will see JDR as just another battlefield where two or more parties are contestants fighting for limited resources who cannot possibly trust one another.

An adversarial judge will focus primarily on the "true" facts of the case, assume the parties are exaggerating their demands, and concentrate on the likely outcome if the case proceeds to litigation.

Collaborative temperament

A collaborative temperament emphasizes that disputes are opportunities for parties to engage in problem-solving together. Indeed, the parties need each other to reach agreement if they want to control the outcome. The judge with a collaborative mind-set guides parties in their problem-solving efforts and works to adjust the setting—and the information that is shared by the parties—as they work to deal with their differences.

The collaborative judge will help the parties continue to add to their options. If necessary, the judge will intervene to guarantee fairness (that all parties are being heard) or work to ensure that clear and valid information is shared (Schwarz 2017). He or she will work to protect free and informed choices by the parties. If necessary, the judge will provide a dose of reality-testing, evaluative estimates, so that all parties understand the probable outcome if they return to litigation. For instance, as it happened in *The Medical Malpractice* case, the judge said to one of the parties who was inclined to start with trial: "I have a sense from the ten minutes that we talked that you find it difficult to go through dates and times and places." The judge then cautioned the party that remembering dates would be crucial when testifying in trial. Such an intervention provides parties with clear information about the potential adversarial setting of trial, and can draw them more actively into collaboration.

Besides guaranteeing a fair procedure, clear information flow, free and informed consent from both parties, internal commitments and greater empathy between the parties, a collaborative judge might use precedent to shift the parties' and their counsels' mindset more toward collaboration. In *The Estate Case,* the judge persuaded the parties to try JDR by describing to them a similar dispute that lasted many years in litigation without any progress and was ultimately resolved through JDR.

Another tool some judges use to fuel a cooperative engagement between the parties is the use of opening remarks in the JDR. For instance, the same judge who used precedent told us that sometimes he initiates his JDR sessions by drawing a diagram of two separate circles with no intersection, and saying to the parties: "This is how you might think about the dispute and your positions; no common ground, no shared interests, no commonality whatsoever." Then he draws a two overlapping circles and says: "unlike these circles, you, at the very least, have four things in common. First, you want to resolve this dispute as soon as possible. Second, you want to resolve it at minimum cost. Third, you want to reduce any litigation risk. And finally, you both want to live a happier life." He reminds them that he often "asks people involved in litigation if there is one day that they haven't thought about their dispute. The answer is clear: "There isn't one day ... and it doesn't make me happy."

Collaborative judges may also use a pre-trial JDR meeting to explain the process to the parties and help them understand what they should expect. For instance, some judges interviewed for this book demand that the parties submit a joint statement of facts and issues before the JDR begins. This way the judge knows the facts the parties agree on and what they expect from the JDR. In fact, some judges require that the parties and their counsel meet before the JDR so they can start working together on issues not likely to require the attention of the judge. This can frame the perceptions of the parties in a collaborative way: they are working together on a task required by the judge.

Evaluative temperament

A judge with an evaluative temperament is primarily interested in providing a decisive judgment, using normative criteria to determine what a good or a bad settlement would contain. Evaluative judges tend to extrapolate from their litigation experience to the JDR settings in which they find themselves. They are quick to ask themselves who should get what and why, instead of letting the parties generate their own justice criteria. Evaluative judges are also quick to make predictions about how another court might respond if the dispute is not resolved in JDR.

Even if a judge is well trained in the skills needed to conduct a JDR process, too much evaluation can distort the purpose of JDR by making it about meeting external normative criteria rather than enabling the parties to control the outcome.

Types of judges based on their attitude toward JDR

Our final way of classifying judges with regard to the practice of JDR is based on their overall attitude toward ADR and JDR. Some judges are eager to provide JDR services and truly believe in their usefulness. We consider this a pro-JDR attitude. In contrast, some judges are not at all interested in providing JDR services themselves or, they simply do not believe in JDR's benefits. We call this an anti-JDR attitude.

In classifying a judge's attitude toward JDR, we look at two things: whether the judge believes that JDR can help solve disputes more efficiently or satisfactorily (in the eyes of the parties), and whether, provided they believe in it, they are motivated to suggest JDR if it means having to do this work themselves. If judges are not willing to do JDR, then even if they have the skills and collaborative temperament required, their use of JDR will be limited. In fact, in many provinces in Canada—such as Ontario, Nova Scotia and British Columbia—if a judge is not inclined to provide JDR, they do not have to do so. For this reason, it is crucial to train lawyers and judges from the outset of their legal education in a way that encourages them to advocate for JDR. Judge's believing in JDR is as important as parties believing in it.

In *The Estate Case* arriving at JDR was due to both the willingness of one side to suggest JDR or a similar collaborative dispute resolution procedure, and the direction of the judge, who skillfully sensed the parties were leaning toward a collaborative approach and explained the contours of JDR and what they should expect from it. One of the siblings' lawyers saw the case file and realized the trial would entail substantial cost to her client and, more importantly, saw that relationship issues needed to be addressed. In her first intervention in the case, she told the judge: "In everything I read of this case, it struck me that there were issues, feelings and finances, and that it would lend itself to either a collaborative approach to resolution or some other alternative dispute resolution mechanism. I think there should be an effort to resolve this in a way that would not require the court's intervention." The lawyer from the other side was skeptical, and insisted his client wanted a final resolution, implying ADR would not provide a definitive solution. The justice hearing the case was inclined toward JDR and responded to the skeptical lawyer: "You can still do a JDR." And since he knew the key was not about persuading the parties to do JDR but letting them know that it could work, he explained that a BJDR would satisfy both parties: it would be collaborative and, if a settlement was not reached, it guaranteed a final decision. Then, the judge ordered a break so the lawyers could talk to their clients and make a decision.

This case shows how important it is for a judge to believe that JDR is an appropriate process, at least for some disputes, and to be willing to provide JDR services if asked. In this case, the judge's pro-JDR attitude took the form of explaining to the parties the benefits of the process—an example of how such a favorable attitude is translated in the JDR process is the following statement by a pro-JDR judge:

(1) The parties want to resolve the dispute as soon as possible. (2) They want probably to be heard by a judge at some point. (3) The dispute has been going on for some time and given the nature of the dispute, there are interpersonal difficulties that need to be dealt with. To be sure, the reallocation of finances or property rights are drivers in many civil and family cases. But an overlooked critical component in lawsuits is the relationship between the Plaintiff and Defendant. Apologies are often needed and with the assistance of a judge, can be given. As a judge gets to know the issues and parties, he will realize the role of compassion and love; he will understand the fears of losing a relationship and crying or tears with the recognition that it can be healed, in part or in whole. This sporadically happens but it does occur by the end of a JDR.

In short, a favorable attitude toward JDR requires a judge to believe in it and to explain to the parties why it might be a good option for them. If the judge lacks a favorable attitude toward JDR, either the judge will not suggest it, or the parties will not be persuaded. And if they are dissuaded, it will not matter whether the judge has the appropriate temperament or skillset.

Conclusion

Skills are necessary to provide effective JDR services. Skill-building should consistently be offered to judges. Framing disputes, listening actively, inquiring empathetically about parties' perspectives, and helping them engage in problem solving through paraphrasing and other related strategies can all be taught. Every judge can benefit from additional instruction and practice. But skills are not the only thing judges need to cultivate. They also need to forge a temperament; ideally, a collaborative temperament aimed at empowering parties to resolve their differences, guiding them through a fair process that makes them feel respected. An evaluative intervention—offering a forecast of how a particular argument is likely to be viewed by the court—sometimes provides a reality test that leads parties to reach their own agreement or ask their JDR provider to offer a binding judgment.

Unlike skills, temperaments do not tell us what to do in a particular moment during a JDR, but they shape the environment in which the parties do or do not achieve a settlement. And yet temperaments are not sufficient. In order to work, JDR needs the participants, especially the judge, to adopt a belief and volition that a dispute may be resolved. Without these two components, a Herculean judge for JDR with the appropriate temperament and a conglomeration of skills will not facilitate dispute resolution.

One of the lawyers we interviewed made us aware that choosing a JDR judge is not so simple. Advocates of JDR and other ADR methods often emphasize the importance of the forum and forget that the result depends on the effectiveness of the mediating judge. Counsels agreed that JDR works because some judges have the right sensibility, temperament and a willingness to listen empathetically and respectfully to the parties. Without these, the institutional setting (i.e., court) may not be enough to generate agreement. This is why the question of what types of judges should and should not lead JDR is so important.

Chapter 10

CONFIDENTIALITY AND PRIVACY IN JDR

Much has been written about confidentiality in ADR (Kovach 2005; Chatterjee and Lefcovitch 2008; Shiravi and Javad 2017). It is the bedrock of successful, informal problem-solving and fosters open discussion. Confidentiality is critical in JDR for a number of reasons, some of which we discovered in our research cases. In *The Falling Rocks Case*, we found that both attorneys and parties rely on confidentiality going into a JDR: ".… Confidentiality, always a priority for the attorneys, was of primary importance for the insurance company's counsel: if the case went to trial, the claim would be publicly disclosed and it would likely provide a potential benchmark for future insurance claims. That scenario would not be in their best interest, so their counsels had a strong incentive to settle."

Confidentiality in JDR eliminates precedents and that impacts judges, as well. Judges routinely rely on precedents in applying the law to their decisions and even finding the goalposts for assistance in JDRs. Wearing their settlement hat as a JDR judge, they may not seek advice or talk to anyone—including their colleagues—because they could later serve as trial judges if the case does not settle at the JDR. This isolation is important for the preservation of privacy reasons discussed in this chapter and referenced in *The Motor Vehicle Case*: "Confidentiality was a significant factor in this case. It meant that the justice could not be as transparent as she might have liked when strategizing with other justices about the best way to approach this JDR. Nonetheless, she preserved the conditions necessary for the parties to move forward with a fair trial and impartial justice."

Although confidentiality brings challenges—including the constriction of legal precedent—it serves a vital role in helping parties come to resolution. Again, referring to *The Motor Vehicle Accident Case*, we identify the obstacles to confidentiality but more importantly, we learn why it brings about settlement opportunities when judges and parties are free from the encumbrances of precedent:

> Confidentiality also contributes to a lack of precedent. Given that so many personal injury claims settle, it becomes more difficult for justices and lawyers to review standards and advocate for fair results. However, confidentiality may have been key in ensuring the dignity of the parties and in pushing them to settle; trial can be embarrassing, and the process can undermine relationships and injure reputations. This JDR allowed the justice to privately question and expose the weaknesses in Mr. Barton's case and assess the sincerity of the insurance company.

Not having a precedent affects the judge's process in the JDR—as well as other judges who will never have the case as a precedent (as they would have from a trial).

But ironically, it can have a positive impact on litigation, as detailed in *The Motor Vehicle Accident Case*:

> .... the lack of recorded precedents complicated the justice's ability to provide accurate assessments of the value of the case. She commented on the challenge of accurately predicting what any given justice might do because of the constant changeover in the bench. It is possible that a lack of precedent makes lawyers and parties less confident in their own assessments and more interested in the JDR judge's assessment. The lack of recorded precedent may also allow JDR judges to be more persuasive. Perhaps this is why such a large percentage of JDR cases settle.
>
> One of the lawyers commented on another way that precedent in JDR can be particularly effective: many personal injury plaintiffs know of similar claims and their settlements without being aware of the distinguishing facts. A plaintiff might say, "My cousin had a truck accident, and he got $3 million. So, there's no way I'll take less than that." Unfortunately, the cousin's case ended in a settlement without a written precedent, and it is difficult to show a client that the facts in the earlier case were very different, and that their expectations are unreasonable. JDR provides a solution by letting misguided clients hear from a justice what their lawyers (should) have been telling them.

When we remind ourselves that the goal of the court system is to bring peace to the community, discarding precedents in favor of the greater good of settling lawsuits achieves justice in tangible and intangible ways: from parties' satisfaction and a freedom to move on with their lives, to the elimination of wasted costs and court time.

Mediation is dependent on parties freely expressing themselves and the JDR setting needs to encourage this candor (especially in considering possible agreements). Though a courthouse is one of the last places anyone is likely to feel relaxed, measures are taken to do just that: most JDR judges step down from the bench before they begin and meet with the parties in separate conference rooms. A JDR judge's explicit guarantee of privacy (i.e., no public observers) and confidentiality (i.e., no record is kept and nothing that is said will be subsequently used at trial or in any other way) is essential in creating the right mood and setting. Absent confidentiality, a court-wise party might try to use mediation/JDR as a way to informally depose an unwary party (Goldberg et al. 2020). A mediating judge can head off such a possibility by laying out clear ground rules for the proceedings and promises regarding their own behavior.

Confidentiality has many components: the mediating judge's obligation to maintain confidentiality; strict limits on what parties can disclose or take advantage of after a JDR is completed; and a question of what can be disclosed in subsequent legal proceedings under various sets of circumstances.

Significant scholarly writing about JDR describes four main reasons to keep information confidential during the mediation:

> First, the assurance of confidentiality correlates with a greater likelihood of the parties being willing to enter into the process. Parties may be especially desirous to protect details of business dealings or matters that might attract regulatory attention.

Second, confidentiality is thought to enhance the effectiveness of the process. It is plain, however, that the parties will not make admissions or conciliatory gestures, dilute their claims, or venture out of their entrenched positions unless they are confident that their concessions and admissions cannot be used as weapons against them if conciliation fails and full-blooded litigation follows. Encouraging parties to speak openly and honestly is integral to the concept both of private caucusing and joint sessions. Failure to respect confidentiality might cause the parties to doubt the mediator's neutrality and impartiality.

Third, knowing that the mediation must remain confidential constrains parties from entering into the process primarily (or solely) as a "fishing" expedition for information that they can subsequently use in litigation.

Fourth, mediators might be unwilling to act if they could be required to disclose what they had said or been told during the mediation (Astor and Chinkin 2002).

Understandably, there are exceptions to the rule of confidentiality:

Information disclosed in mediation may be subject to discovery if there is an independent ground for discovery. A few of the statutes have an exception for discovery in actions between the mediator and a party to the mediation or damages arising out of the mediation. In others, confidentiality may be subject to policy-based exceptions, such as where child abuse (Washington DC, Texas and Colorado) or abuse of the elderly (Texas) is disclosed, where any statute requires disclosure (Arizona), where violence occurs or is threatened (Arizona), where the information reveals an intent to commit a felony (Colorado), or criminal or illegal act likely to result in death or serious bodily harm (New Jersey) or where public interest requires disclosure (New Jersey) (Brown and Marriott 1999).

These examples are from the U.S. In Canada, the rules are a bit different.

The Case Law in Canada

Inevitably, the issue of confidentiality in mediation will lead to the question of mediation *privilege*: does such a privilege exist? A three-member appeals panel of an Ontario Superior Court faced this question head-on in a case where the parties reached a settlement but at least one party felt it necessary to enforce the decision. That party sought and received a court order compelling the mediator to be examined as a witness. The appeal court disagreed with the lower court, arguing that mediation falls within confidential relationships in society (Ontario Superior Court of Justice 2006). It is also true that common law principles have recognized a privilege for confidential communications in certain important societal relationships. In *Slavutych v. Baker*, the Supreme Court of Canada held that the four considerations should be applied to determine whether communications are privileged:

(1) The communications must originate in a confidence that they will not be disclosed.
(2) The element of confidentiality must be essential to the maintenance of the relationship in which the communications arose.

(3) The relationship must be one which, in the opinion of the community, ought to be "sedulously fostered."

(4) The injury caused to the relationship by disclosure of the communications must be greater than the benefit gained for the correct disposal of the litigation. ...

The Court went on to say:

> The communications at mediation have been held to be privileged unless there were over-arching interests in disclosure—for example, to protect children at risk from criminal activity (Ontario Superior Court of Justice 2006).

And, finally, the Court said:

> The parties to this mediation signed a confidentiality agreement, which expressly stated that the communications at the mediation were to be confidential. More importantly, the parties agreed that the mediator's notes and recollections could not be subpoenaed in this litigation.
> ...confidentiality of communications during the mediation is essential to the functioning of the mediation process in which the parties were engaged. In order for mediation to succeed, parties must be assured of confidentiality, so that discussions can be free and frank (Ontario Superior Court of Justice 2006).

As the Court pointed out, the Rules of Civil Procedure require mandatory mediation of many civil disputes in order to assist the parties in arriving at settlement and thus reduce the costs of litigation. There is clearly a significant public interest in protecting the confidentiality of discussions at mediation in order to make the process as effective as possible.

It is true that the mediator's evidence might be of some assistance in determining the terms of the settlement. However, it is not the only evidence available on the scope of the parties' agreement. Both the parties and their counsel can give evidence of the agreement's details. Indeed, it is the intention of the parties that is key to the resolution of the motion for rectification.

> Weighing against disclosure is the fact that the parties entered into a confidentiality agreement in which they agreed not to make the mediator a witness. This is not a case where the parties, by their confidentiality agreement, seek to block a third party's access to information that is important for the resolution of a case. Here, the parties agreed on the rules for the mediation, which included confidentiality and non-compellability of the mediator. Absent an overriding public interest in disclosure, their agreement should be respected (Ontario Superior Court of Justice 2006).

Other Canadian courts have held that these privileges cannot be easily overridden even by freedom of information (FOIA) guarantees. The Alberta Court of Appeal said this in *Imperial oil v. Alberta:*

> The Commissioner was incorrect in concluding that the Remediation Agreement is not privileged. At common law mediations and the resulting settlements are privileged ...

Section 27(2) of the [FOIA] *Act* is in mandatory terms, and does not give the Commissioner any authority to override the settlement privilege by consideration of broader aspects of public policy, such as any perceived "public policy of openness". There is in addition no common law jurisdiction in the Commissioner to ignore or override legal privileges: ... Since the Remediation Agreement is privileged in law, that ends the debate (Alberta Court of Appeal 2014).

This is not to say mediators and JDR judges are not accountable. They are, but accountability is a function of the specific issues in a lawsuit and the parties at the table. As we have written elsewhere:

"To whom are mediators (i.e., professional neutrals) accountable?" The answer, usually, is "to the parties" with whom they are working. In the parlance of dispute resolution theory, "the parties to a dispute must own the resolution." The case for adherence to this principle is typically framed in strategic terms. Agreements will not be implemented (i.e., they will not be durable) if the parties feel they were strong-armed into accepting something that did not really meet their needs.

In the same way that lawyers are "officers of the court" and have certain obligations that extend beyond merely representing the interests of their clients, mediators have a responsibility to help make the case for mediation by ensuring that the outcomes in each instance are as beneficial as possible to all the relevant stakeholders. To do this, they may have to push the parties to go beyond the obvious solution. While outcomes unacceptable to the parties at the table cannot be imposed by a mediator, that still leaves a great deal of room for mediators to encourage the parties to "maximize joint gains" (Susskind 2004).

The question is, can accountability of the judge and the parties be ensured even with a guarantee of privacy and confidentiality? The best way to ensure that both occur, is for the parties to include in a final written agreement with each other (initialed by the JDR judge) exactly what they are promising, including guarantees of confidentiality. They could post a bond that would be lost if they violated the terms of their agreement. (We call that a "self-enforcing agreement.") But, even short of that, a written version of what both agreed to (initialed by the judge) should guarantee accountability while avoiding any need for the judge to file or retain a formal record of the JDR agreement.

Summary

JDR, like most mediation, needs to be conducted confidentially so that: (1) parties feel free to participate; (2) parties, their employers, families, and friends are not embarrassed; and (3) mediators can do their job without worrying that they might have to testify later. The Supreme Court of Canada wrapped all of these issues together when it decided the seminal case of *Union Carbide Canada Inc. v. Bombardier Inc* (The Supreme Court of Canada 2014):

A form of confidentiality is inherent in mediation in that the parties are typically discussing a settlement, which means that their communications are protected by the common law settlement privilege (Boulle and Kelly 1998). But mediation is also a "creature of contract" which means that parties can tailor their confidentiality requirements to exceed the scope of that privilege and, in the case of breach, avail themselves of a remedy in contract. (Glaholt and Rotterdam 2018).

...The reasons why parties might want to protect information exchanged in the mediation process are not limited to litigation strategy. When [the parties] have resorted to mediation in an attempt to settle pending or threatened litigation, they will be particularly alert to the possibility that information they reveal to others in mediation may later be used against them by those others in that, or other, litigation. "The parties may also be concerned that their communications might be used by other adversaries or potential adversaries, including public authorities, in other present or future conflicts. ... Parties may also be concerned that disclosure of information they reveal in the mediation process may prejudice them in commercial dealings or embarrass them in their personal lives" (Supreme Court of Canada 2014).

It is therefore no surprise that contracts often contain strongly worded confidentiality clauses that place limits on the disclosure of communications exchanged in the course of the mediation process. Such clauses have been upheld by courts, though not in a context in which the parties were trying to prove the existence of a settlement. In *Bloom Films 1998 inc. v. Christal Films Productions Inc.*, the Quebec Court of Appeal upheld a confidentiality clause in a case in which a party was seeking to introduce evidence arising out of a mediation process. The clause in question specifically prohibited the use of such evidence for any purpose other than homologation or judicial review (Quebec Court of Appeal 2011). *Stewart v. Stewart* is another case involving a confidentiality clause with respect to communications made in the course of a mediation process, albeit in a family law context, and the Alberta Court of Queen's Bench refused to admit evidence arising out of that process (Court of Queen's Bench of Alberta 2008).

In private mediation (outside the JDR context), a mediator can contract with the parties to promise confidentiality and privacy. That promise may or may not hold. In JDR, it is the judge (and thus the Court) that is promising to protect privacy and confidentiality, a notable difference that presumably reassures the parties. They also, however, have the option of exchanging a signed written summary of what they have promised each other—not part of the court record, but it is a contract—that may be initialed by the JDR judge, thereby ensuring both accountability of the parties to each other and guaranteeing the confidentiality and privacy of the JDR process.

Chapter 11

WHICH CASES ARE UNSUITABLE FOR JDR?

Years ago, we suggested that certain public disputes should not be mediated (Susskind and Madigan 1984). We pointed specifically to situations where:

1. Parties are too numerous, diverse, or hard to identify;
2. Access to dispute resolution services is difficult for some of the parties;
3. The outcome is dependent on controversial value judgments while a community mandate or consensus might be most useful;
4. The community at large clearly cares about the outcome;
5. Implementation of a negotiated agreement could be readily blocked by a dissatisfied party.

In these situations, it makes more sense to depend on adjudication through traditional regulatory or legal mechanisms. Nevertheless, that still leaves a great many public disputes that can be mediated (Susskind 2006). These cases would probably not make their way to court, and thus private mediation rather than JDR would be the most likely source of attempting resolution. However, if a public dispute (in which one party is a public agency) did make its way to court, and none of the five conditions listed above applied, we believe JDR could be used to resolve the matter just as well as private mediation.

In the family law area, as we pointed out in Chapter 6, certain classes of cases should not be mediated either (Clarke and Davies 1991).

1. [W]here the parties are hoping to gain some tactical or strategic advantage which is not related to the subject matter of the dispute, e.g., to delay proceedings, or as a fishing expedition to gain information.
2. Where domestic violence or fear of violence is suspected;
3. Cases involving child abuse or sexual abuse;
4. Where the parties are so conflict-ridden they are incapable of considering the dispute between them apart from their own feelings (i.e., the "all or nothing" dispute);
5. Where one of the disputants is so seriously deficient in information that any ensuing agreement would not be based on informed consent; or
6. If the disputants reach an agreement which the mediator believes is illegal, is damaging to a third party, is grossly inequitable to one of the parties, or is the result of bad faith bargaining, the mediator should terminate the mediation but might not have the power to do so.

So, one category of disputes that is not appropriate for JDR would be the kinds of family law cases listed above. The second would be those cases with a significant public-interest component, which require an open and public litigation since the ruling affects the general population, all of whom have a stake in the decision. This category might include a public-interest lawsuit such as an environmental case with far-reaching, even cross-border effects on the larger society (such as the listing or delisting of an endangered species). JDR is about reducing social costs, not encouraging private deals regarding the allocation of public resources or the making of public policy.

There is a third category of litigation that is also not appropriate for JDR. To put it in positive terms, we believe JDR is only appropriate when the jurisdiction of the court is well-founded. One example of poorly founded jurisdiction would be an international lawsuit requiring parties from a different state or country to appear, without first resolving the attornment issue and appropriate judicial standing. The corollary is that if litigation is improperly filed in the originating court, the next application would not be for mediation, but rather to strike the lawsuit. Failing to do so would be condoning judicial resolution of a matter that ought not be in court in the first place. This certainly would be antagonistic to the voluntary nature of JDR. It is difficult to rationalize sitting as a judge in a mediation in which it is not clear that the court has jurisdiction. That being said, a judge can proceed with any JDR if the parties (including counsel) voluntarily wish to take part. The benefit being that litigation can close the matter without further attorneys' fees, pending carefully drafted consent judgments entered in both jurisdictions.

JDR in criminal law cases deserves closer scrutiny. One might think criminal cases *prima facie* should be excluded from JDR, but we are not so sure. Judges in pre-trial conferences on criminal matters do talk to the prosecutor and defense about the possibilities of settlement, always acknowledging that the state, not the court, has control of the prosecution, and any plea bargaining must be done within parameters set by the government. Admittedly, we question the rightness of voluntary settlement in cases involving punishment. In many criminal cases, there needs to be a public opportunity for victims to present impact statements to the court, and the confidential nature of JDR would not allow this to happen; the typical criminal case could not be resolved through mediation involving just the prosecutor, the defense, and the judge sitting behind closed doors. Assuming a criminal case did go to JDR, what would happen if the judge, once the process is over, sees value in discussing possible punishment with the prosecutor and defense, *before* imposing the sentence, even if the parties didn't come to that conclusion?

In actual criminal cases, when a judge is about to sentence the accused to multiple years of incarceration, and after the accused has been given a chance to speak before sentencing (a legal requirement)—and with little said by the accused—the judge could initiate discussion of a negotiated agreement. Indeed, counsel on both sides often engage in plea bargaining before the judge offers a disposition decision. While the criminal sentencing process is not the same as JDR, there is some overlap, at least insofar as generating a voluntary agreement that all sides accept—including the judge.

Imagine the following scenario: before imposing a jail term at the end of a trial, a judge ponders whether there might be another possible outcome. The judge asks the prosecution and defense if they can agree on an alternative to incarceration. Knowing that a jail sentence would deprive the children of a parent, undercut financial support for the family, and probably mean a lost future for the accused, the judge asks counsel if there might be a way to honor required sentencing guidelines while helping to repair the underlying societal loss.

We know of one case like this in which the judge, for the first time, suggested an alternative sentence if the accused agreed to: (1) open his heart and help the court fully understand the problems this particular set of federal charges posed; (2) help the judge steer others away from this particular kind of criminal activity; and (3) help the judge do a better job of imposing sentences in trials like this one. The judge's proposal proffered less jail time and more freedom for the defendant—if he agreed to participate. The agreement allowed the accused to continue working and living at home with his family during the week and serve limited jail time each weekend, while remaining on probation. Everyone agreed, and the judge asked the accused (now convicted) to answer a series of questions in a letter, creating a precise narrative for the court explaining how he got into this criminal situation and suggesting how others could avoid such a path. He was asked to explain how his misdeeds and being caught had affected his life, and looking back, how they affected others around him. He was given two months to send the judge the letter, during which time he could keep his job, do intermittent jail time, and remain on probation.

The two months came and went and the deadline passed without a letter. The judge asked his assistant to set up another time to complete the case in the court's busy docket, call counsel, and so on. Another month passed and the judge, still believing in the accused, waited; he was not ready to have him hauled back into court.

The judge's hunch was right. A week or so later, his assistant came running into his office holding up a letter, exclaiming: "Guess what, he did send you a letter in time, but he sent it to the wrong court (state, not federal court), and it got lost in the system. Here is the letter, judge!" The letter follows (with typos included and some personal details excluded):

First and for most I would like to thank you for giving me this opportunity to write you this letter, it's not every day an uneducated man such as myself has the chance to write to a man of your stature. It was very humbling and uplifting when during my sentencing you asked me for this. Not as a punishment to me, but because you wanted to understand more about this issue plaguing our society. Thus in future cases you would have greater insight of the matter, for that your honor I commend you and want you to know I took the responsibility of writing you this seriously.

It is my belief your honor that I have a unique perspective on this matter, as I have been [he described his crime to the court]. With my experience I have the knowledge and insight to describe the lure of fast money [for the criminal] and the escapism [doing the crime]. Both of which paths ended in destruction and heartache for everyone I loved around me and myself.

My view on society especially the younger generations is that most of us want everything the easiest and fastest way possible. We have forgotten the great virtues of patience, dedication, and hard work. The old cliché that "Rome was not built in a day" is just something that our grandparents lived by now. For me this could not be more truthful. I was always a hard worker and had goals, but did not have the patience nor the dedication to accomplish the goals I had set. In my mind [doing this crime] would enable me to accomplish my egotistical goals that I had said at a much faster pace. At that junction in my life I had no respect for authority. I wanted what I wanted and I wanted it yesterday, the illusion of fast cars, money, vacations, and providing more for my family. It was too much for my young soul to resist and in the beginning that's exactly what that regrettable choice gave me. Unfortunately I lack the wisdom and experience to see the life – altering mistake I was making and where these choices would take me and the people I loved.

My [crime] is directly attributed to [the crime itself]. I was young and when an underdeveloped mind has more money than they can spend they will inevitably find something to spend it on. That disastrously was my path that I chose. You hear from many people that [crime] is easy money. On the contrary, imagine living your life in a world full of corruption, violence and always looking over your shoulder. Evidently, I could not handle the stress so I turned to [the crime]. Possibly to escape the stress and now as I look back maybe even the guilt I felt for [doing the crime] I knew were harmful to people for my own personal gain. The consequences of my actions would forever change the course of my life. I was arrested, lost all the money I had, was forced to sell the [house] I had raised my kids in and shortly after losing all the material things that I had craved so much. I lost the most important thing of all … my family!

The peculiar thing is after losing everything and everyone that meant so much to me; I had what they call […] a moment of clarity in which I knew I had to change my ways. It was at that time I made the conscious decision to do just that. However, without the support of my family and friends I wouldn't have known where to begin. My parents set me to go to a world-class [place to recover my life]. It was there that [I figured out] how to be myself again. My Ex [and I never reconciled] but I was able to be a part of my [children's] lives again and be the [parent] I knew I could be. That was the greatest gift of all.

Every so often when I am stressed and life is not going my way, for a brief moment I feel as though I want to go back where nothing mattered except for [the crime]. I am then quickly reminded that everything and everyone who mean the most to me went away. And the greatest high I ever felt was being with the people I love the most. That for me is my nuclear deterrent from falling back [into crime].

I have two very dear friends of mine [to this crime]. I believe they're two clear cut examples of why incarcerating [these criminals] only perpetuates the problem. Both died within days of release from jail. It is my conviction that only through [help] can people be saved. If we as society are willing to spend millions of dollars incarcerating [these criminals] because of our ignorance and lack of education on the subject I ask you your Honor when are we as a society going to make the collective conscious decision to do what's righteous and spend these millions of wasted dollars on [helping them]? From my personal experience it is the only option we have to solve this current [wave of crime] that has taken far too many lives.

In closing your Honor I would like to thank you for giving me this [privilege] to write to you. My assessment of you your Honor from the experience of my trial is that you are a fair, compassionate judge who is eager to be educated more on this topic...for that I applaud you your Honor. In high school I would always finish my English papers with a quote. So I leave you your Honor with my favorite quote of all from the late Lyndon B. Johnson. "Yesterday is not ours to recover, but tomorrow is ours to win or lose."

Sincerely,

Name omitted

This story suggests that there can be value-creating exceptions to the rule of not using mediation for criminal charges. Further, if mandatory sentencing minimums had been imposed by the legislature, a negotiated agreement of this sort would not have been possible.

Going back to the third category we identified, in the circumstance where jurisdiction may be lacking, a judge can proceed with JDR if all parties voluntarily wish to be there. JDR could close the matter without further litigation costs, pending carefully drafted consent judgments entered in both jurisdictions.

In the criminal law category, prosecutors and defense counsel could negotiate the resolution of criminal matters—even murder indictments—on a regular and frequent basis. The benefits of such negotiations are significant: the prosecutor who successfully negotiates an indictment downward can obtain a conviction and punishment—including input from the victims via their victim-impact statements—all without additional cost or, more importantly, the risk of trial in which a guilty party might walk free.

Putting aside the family law cases, public disputes, and jurisdictional cases where JDR should be used with great caution, there are a great many cases that remain to be settled. Criminal law, and especially sentencing, could involve greater collaboration between parties, and we discuss such situations next.

Restorative Justice

The goals of criminal law are to determine guilt or innocence and mete out appropriate punishment. But criminal acts take place within the context of human interaction, and punishment may not be sufficient to restore the balance society needs after a crime has been committed; the population must receive the right incentives to reinforce law-abiding behavior, and to help those affected by the crimes return to some kind of normalcy. This is where restorative justice comes in: it seeks to engage the offender and the victim(s) in a facilitated dialogue. As Andrew Pirie writes:

> The overarching principle of restorative justice, matched with purpose, is that the most important task of criminal justice should be the restoration of stable relationships. Because crime affects more than the individuals directly involved and the state, restorative justice seeks to re-establish healthy communities by treating governments and the wider communities as active partners with victims and wrongdoers in restoring relationships and in maintaining harmony and social stability. Additionally, restorative justice stresses that a consensus approach to justice is the most effective response to crime." (Pirie 2000)

From our standpoint, the idea of restorative justice overlaps with some of the goals of JDR, even though the usual assumption is that JDR focuses on civil, not criminal cases. Both models bring people together with the idea of having a collaborative decision instead of one imposed by a judge alone. The open-ended search for collaboration engrained in JDR and restorative justice overcomes any binary models like guilt/innocence or right/duty. And both models avoid relying on a precedent as a solid ground for the decision-making process. In short, JDR and restorative justice are models rooted in participation of the people who care about the dispute.

Non-adversarial justice brings parties into a room with ADR assistance as they seek alternatives to traditional forms of punishment such as circle methods that involve members of the community, offenders, and victims to promote dialogue and a healing process. In some cases, a talking token is passed around the circle to enable dynamics of active listening and frank expression. Sometimes these circles, like Manitoba's Hollow Water Community Holistic Healing Circle, are used to address traumatic problems in the community such as incest or sexual assault. The circles can be expanded gradually from individual meetings between victims and offenders, to circles where community members participate, and even expanding to court (King et al. 2009).

The police have at times used restorative justice as a way to address certain community crimes. One example is the Thames Valley Police Project that held a restorative conference "to hear the details of the harm that [offenders] have caused" (Brown and Marriott 1999). The outcome of the conference may have been arriving at an agreement about how to best repair the harm through apologies, financial compensation, or other form of redress. "Restorative justice, in their view, gives communities a voice and ensures that offenders are faced with the consequences of their behaviour. It provides a means for offenders to change their behavior, instead of facing what the Thames Valley Police brochure calls the "depersonalized, technical nature of the proceedings and the mitigation process in the community setting" (Brown and Marriott 1999).[1]

All of these projects, together, point away from the traditional adjudicative response to criminal law problems and instead toward a new restorative justice perspective:

> Restorative justice offers an understanding of justice that is grounded in the inescapable reality of our interconnectedness to one another through webs or networks of relationships. Through this relational lens on the world the extent of harm flowing from wrongdoing comes into view. Harm from wrongdoing is not limited to the direct victim but can affect those connected with the victim, the wrongdoer, and the communities of which they are a part. From this relational starting point, it becomes clear that justice requires a response when our social relationships are marked by inequality—that is when our equal moral worth as individuals is threatened or disregarded. Justice then requires response to wrongdoing that restores this idea of human relationship—that restores relationships to ones of social equality marked by the features of equal concern, respect and dignity (Murphy and Molinari 2009).

---

1. The results of the Thames project are promising: "It is interesting to note that although face-to-face meetings between victim and offender only took place in 10% of the cases in Fife, around 90% of the offenders felt that the project had helped their understanding of their behaviour and had changed their thinking about getting into trouble. 75% of the victims said that they would recommend participation in the project to other victims. Apart from direct meetings between victims and young offenders, the project had various other outcomes. These included written explanations and apologies (13%), reparative work for the victim (8 %), reparative work for the community (27%), and agreement not to approach or harass the victim (eight%) and a discussion program (20%). Many victims appreciate the young offender undertaking reparation work. Equally important and satisfying to the victims is that they have been consulted and allowed to express their views." (Brown and Marriott 1999)

Canada's parliament has amended its federal criminal law for sentencing to incorporate restorative justice and societal reparations in addition to the traditional punitive goals of deterrence and enunciation (Criminal Code of Canada 1985).

Part 718 of the revised Criminal code now says:

> The fundamental purpose of sentencing is to protect society and to contribute, along with crime prevention initiatives, to respect for the law and the maintenance of a just, peaceful and safe society by imposing just sanctions that have one or more of the following objectives:
>
> (a) to denounce unlawful conduct and the harm done to victims or to the community that is caused by unlawful conduct;
> (b) to deter the offender and other persons from committing offences;
> (c) to separate offenders from society, where necessary;
> (d) to assist in rehabilitating offenders;
> (e) to provide reparations for harm done to victims or to the community; and
> (f) to promote a sense of responsibility in offenders, and acknowledgment of the harm done to victims or to the community. (emphasis added)

Restorative justice seeks to promote a different kind of dispute resolution. It emphasizes empowering those involved to take an active part in shaping the outcome through respectful dialogue and cooperative decision-making, facilitated in a supportive environment. Although restorative justice's main focus has been on crime, its principles are increasingly applied in a broader range of contexts outside the criminal justice system. It seems to yield high levels of satisfaction for participating victims and offenders. For some it helps to avoid psychological problems arising from or associated with the offense. For a minority there may be little effect, and in a few instances there may be an adverse effect.

Aboriginal Rights, ADR and Reconciliation in Sentencing

Special sentencing considerations for Aboriginal offenders reached prominence with the amendments to Canada's federal Criminal Code in 1995. In part, these amendments added a critically important provision requiring judges to expand sentencing options for Aboriginal offenders: "All available sanctions, other than imprisonment, that are reasonable in the circumstances and consistent with the harm done to victims or to the community should be considered for all offenders, with particular attention to the circumstances of Aboriginal offenders" (Criminal Code of Canada Sec 718.2(e)).

Subsequently, the Supreme Court of Canada required that a more holistic approach be used in sentencing with more expansive options for Aboriginal offenders. Judges "must do a thorough analysis of all *alternative* sanctions in their sentencing of First Nation offenders whether they reside on- or off-reserve, in a large city or a rural area." The Royal Commission on Aboriginal Peoples observed that many Aboriginals living in urban areas are closely attached to their culture (Royal Commission on Aboriginal Peoples 1996). The Commission goes on to recommend:

> If an aboriginal community has a program or tradition of alternative sanctions, and support and supervision are available to the offender, it may be easier to find and impose an

alternative sentence. However, even if community support is not available, every effort should be made in appropriate circumstances to find a sensitive and helpful alternative. For all purposes, the term "community" must be defined broadly so as to include any network of support and interaction that might be available in an urban centre. At the same time, the residence of the aboriginal offender in an urban centre that lacks any network of support does not relieve the sentencing judge of the obligation to try to find an alternative to imprisonment" (Royal Commission on Aboriginal Peoples 1996).

Canada undertook a *Truth and Reconciliation* study from 2008 to 2015 to hear from Aboriginal survivors about the earlier government's establishment of residential schools for Aboriginal peoples. The point of reconciliation was to establish a process that can continue to develop and restore respectful relationships to all peoples and in particular First Nations, Inuit, and Métis. An excerpt regarding justice from Canada's Truth and Reconciliation Commission's final report:

> We call upon the federal government to amend the criminal code to allow trial judges, upon giving reasons, to depart from mandatory minimum sentences and restrictions on the use of conditional sentences.
>
> We call upon the federal, provincial and territorial governments to recognize as a high priority the need to address and prevent Fetal Alcohol Spectrum Disorder (FASD), and to develop, in collaboration with aboriginal people, FASD preventative programs that can be delivered in a culturally appropriate manner.
>
> We call upon the federal government to eliminate barriers to the creation of additional aboriginal healing lodges within the federal correctional system (Canada's Truth and Reconciliation Commission 2015).

So, in addition to reforms in the national sentencing system, the Truth and Reconciliation process put the burden on judges to find a way to emphasize reconciliation in the administration of justice involving First Nations. There were lots of options to work with; more holistic, reconciliation-oriented approaches had already operating in First Nation communities for several decades. These included: (1) Circle sentencing; (2) The elders' or community sentencing panel; 3) The sentence advisory committee; and 4) the community mediation committee (Green 1997).

The push for mediation and reconciliation with regard to First Nations has a lot in common with the rise of ADR and JDR: both models work through dialogical practices to restore relationships as a forward-looking process. They focus on what can be accomplished together not only on "who did what," and they are flexible in addressing cultural issues and inviting in experts, elders, and other members of the community to heal the social fabric.

Although mediation is not concerned with the imposition of a criminal sentence, it does provide for the disposition and resolution of criminal actions by adults. The goals of mediation are varied. [One Professor] described the objectives of an Aboriginal mediation program operating in Alberta in 1981 as:

(i)   short-circuiting the lawbreaking-incarceration cycles of native offenders;
(ii) giving native people a better understanding of the criminal justice system;

(iii) increasing community participation in and "ownership" of the criminal justice system and;

(iv) minimizing the penetration of native people into the criminal justice system. (Green 1997).

Mediation and restorative justice initiatives including mediation, justice committees, and community-based restorative justice groups have now spread across all of Canada. (Tomporowski et al. 2011).

JDR has some of the same objectives as reconciliation: making the parties whole (including both offenders and victims) and ensuring that justice is served. Both build on the practice of mediation. First Nations and Aboriginal peoples have a history of pursuing these same objectives in their own way, and while JDR in Canada does not attribute its emergence to either First Nation practices or the rise of restorative (as opposed to retributive) justice, the overlaps are clear.

Our conclusions about when JDR should and should not be used are in flux. The rise of restorative justice and increasing attention to the needs and practices of First Nations suggest that the use of JDR could be expanded into new areas.

Chapter 12

JUGGLING COMPLEXITY IN JDR

The Falling Rocks Case

What makes a good judge a good JDR judge? We know training and temperament are important. The ability to handle complexity is also essential and can include reading stacks of material, sorting through challenging facts and maneuvering between difficult attorneys. We begin with *The Falling Rocks Case* to illustrate how a seasoned judge settled an unusually complicated, decades-old lawsuit. We then review several other cases to pinpoint how good JDR judges handle the complexity of the JDR process.

The Falling Rocks Case

This case study involves a large city building with elegantly designed glass panels, wind, blowing rocks and allegations of nuisance and multiple defenses, such as the claim that an act of God explains the situation. The litigants include the city, the building's owners, the consulting engineers, and eventually the architects who designed a beautiful glass-heavy building. The lawsuits included an allegation that lawyers never want to see: limitations of action. The parties and their attorneys represented the city, the insurers, the building owners, the consulting engineer and the architect.

A storm passed through the city and allegedly blew rocks off the roof of a private building onto the city hall, damaging several expensive class pyramids. A year and a half later, the city advised the building owners to take immediate action to keep it from happening again. A few years after that, another storm blew more rocks onto the city's glass pyramids, breaking over one hundred panels. The city more or less looked the other way, but ten months later, still another storm broke more glass panels. That triggered the first lawsuit.

After hiring an expert to investigate, the city charged negligence in the design, inspection and replacement of the roof. It also charged nuisance for allowing the rocks to accumulate and sought an injunction requiring the building owners to remove the blowing rocks or make repairs to avoid any damage to the city hall again.

The building owners were angry, asserting that the lawsuit was "embarrassing and vexatious." They denied all responsibility, claiming they had acted properly and alleged that the city either had purchased inferior glass panels or that the panels were installed improperly. Finally, claiming an act of God caused the damage, the owners asked the city to repair the owner's building if an injunction was issued.

The next year, the building owners brought still others into the lawsuit. They tried to indemnify themselves by involving the consulting engineers and building contractors, as well as the city hall architects for improperly designing the building.

The lawsuits escalated with predictable denials of liability all around and still more parties becoming involved. Discoveries and depositions occurred until the case was calendared for approximately a one-month trial. The expected cost of the trial, for all the parties involved, was estimated at several million dollars with fifteen experts scheduled to give evidence.

Fortunately, the case was diverted to JDR and it settled in one day. The city and its insurance company received $500,000—about half the amount they requested, including a small portion of their litigation costs.

Generating Trust and Building a Relationship

A good JDR judge will connect with the parties before the JDR begins, meeting to review procedure and understand each side's concerns. In this case, the judge had two initial meetings by phone, during which he talked about JDR logistics including how information would be shared and the allotted times for each party.

On the day of the JDR, the judge held a plenary session at which he assured the participants that the JDR would be confidential, and whatever either side told him in private caucus would not be shared. He solicited written summaries from each side and discussed what he saw as the strengths and weaknesses of their arguments. The fifteen days that had been set aside for a trial, he mentioned, would probably not be enough.

The judge then met privately with each side, shuttling back and forth from one room to another to get a sense of how they viewed their BATNAs, as well as the strengths and weaknesses of each side. Going between the rooms at least six times, he understood a bit more about the parties and their positions with each caucus. At the end of these exchanges, everyone gathered in a large boardroom to discuss a potential settlement suggested by the judge. The agreement covered the release and exchange of all documents and any last-minute additional funds the parties might be able to add to the pot. The case settled and there was no further litigation.

As we can see from this case, it is critical that a JDR judge spend time getting to know the parties, not just their lawyers. The judge may speak directly to the parties in private to understand their real motivations, build relationships and earn trust.

Applying Skills to JDR in Family Law

We talked in Chapter 6 about family law and JDR's satisfactory results in that context. As we made clear in that case, the judge built trust and ". . . never critiqued the parties, their decisions or their relationships." Further, he let them make their own choices using the information they gleaned from the JDR.

We now turn to another family law case (not in the Appendix), in which we knew the JDR judge. He read the briefs, listened to the parties, and, having a hunch the case might settle quickly, he came off the bench and began what turned out to be highly emotional interaction on the spot. In just a few hours, he managed to build a relationship with the divorcing parties. Here is how it happened in his own words:

I had a pre-trial special hearing scheduled. Among other things, I had to decide whether or not a psychologist should be appointed for the child, and if so, who that would be, and from what city they would come. Arguments over child support with the dad were chaotic because he had just started a new business and had little verifiable income. More importantly, he had yet to resolve parenting arrangements which would shape support payments. There was a brand-new mobility application from the mom. Such applications (moving with children) are always turbulent and emotional.

After introductions in court, counsel for the dad stood up and immediately started to make legal arguments. Politely, I stopped counsel and asked if she wanted to argue the case or resolve it. She and opposing counsel looked at me with somewhat of a stunned look, but not the parents—they perked up and were now keenly interested in what was happening. So, I told them I would be coming off the bench, switching my robes for a suit so we could all go to a boardroom and talk around a table. Before doing that, and to assuage the attorneys, I carefully read and summarized the statutory (case conference) rules that allowed me to proceed in this way. On reflection, the lawyers were okay with mediation. So, with everybody's consent, I came off the bench and headed to the boardroom where I could get to know the parents and their concerns a little better. This is how the JDR began.

After a couple of hours, we had made great progress. We had resolved everything except for two small issues that both counsel felt should be adjudicated. Given the lateness of the day I acquiesced. Accordingly, the two counsel and I were making arrangements for the next court hearing on these two small points, and once counsel and I had reached agreement on that, I asked them to draft an order that would encompass the settlement agreement and allocate one half-day to resolve the final two issues. Even with laptops, drafting an Order can take some time. I gave them about thirty minutes following which we would place the Order in the record and formally conclude for the day.

However, when I came back into the room (to sign the order)—with all counsel and parties present—the mom told me she did not understand why we needed to come back to the boardroom for the two small items because we had already resolved everything else. Since she now trusted me, she asked why we could not finish the last two items just like we had the rest—today, together. She went on to ask why judges and attorneys always preferred to come back to court for the end of the case. Her question amazed the lawyers who assumed they would be coming back to court for another day. That is, until their clients corrected them.

Speaking for herself and her husband, the mom told me that given the progress they had made, they knew they could settle the rest of the lawsuit now. They did not want to prolong the dispute. She said both parents wanted to put what money and time they had left towards their daughter, not lawyers and not court. I looked at the dad for a response and he said: "We have spent almost a decade arguing over this and now we've resolved almost all of it. There are only two items left, and we can clearly do this ourselves—without lawyers or the court."

With that in mind, and at the request of both parties, we all went back to the boardroom and resolved the last two items. With the full settlement in hand, both parents said they were happy putting the terms of the agreement into an order, as long as it covered one of their remaining concerns. I asked what their last concern was, and they said: "Neither of us wants to ever come back to court!" After some discussion, at their insistence, and following their counsels' review, I added a clause to the order that said, "No party can come back to court *for any reason* without prior leave granted by a judge in advance." Everybody shook hands, and actually smiled. It was late in the day, and I signed the Order. The Clerk and Sheriff closed the courthouse.

As I drove away, I noticed they were all still talking in the parking lot. I waved at them, and they waved back. I never heard from them again.

Hard Work

A good JDR judge consistently works after hours. He or she knows that it is impossible to converse with all the parties and understand their real concerns without reading all the submissions ahead of time, including as much evidence as possible, and personal statements, including what is in affidavits and depositions.

A truly qualified JDR judge knows that a mediation meeting with a judge is not at all like appearing *before* a judge in trial. During a trial, a judge will receive opening statements and then sit back and allow the attorneys to build their arguments, piece by piece. Everything the lawyers say is law centric. Fact and expert witnesses testify and are cross-examined, but the judge is rarely the person who asks questions. Neither do the parties—as opposed to counsel—get to talk to the judge. Once in court, parties have little control over how their case is presented. Unlike a trial, a JDR judge cannot sit back and let the case come to them. They have to know the case—all of it—before the JDR begins. And there is continuous interaction with both counsel and parties throughout the process.

Capacity to Listen and Be Creative

A JDR judge has to be a good listener, showing the parties that they are committed to resolving the dispute. Most JDR judges have a predisposition toward settlement as opposed to a win/lose adversarial practice. Returning to *The Falling Rocks Case*, the justice reported the following:

> "I am a big fan of JDR, and nothing in my mind changed when I became a judge," explained the justice, who had done a fair amount of mediation work during his tenure as a litigator. He considers himself to be a facilitative-style JDR justice. This resonated with one of the counsels who confirmed that in his experience JDR judges who were once litigators have strong opinions about how to run a JDR. Other counsels added that the justice's litigation experience brought a depth to the process and gave the parties a full understanding of JDR.
>
> This justice's impartial and diplomatic manner, his reputation for being an especially effective mediator, and positive experiences amongst the litigation industry in Alberta all won him the trust of counsels and put their minds at ease when they worked with him. "One of the risks when going to trial is you will never know who your judge is until the last minute, and that makes a huge difference in terms of preparing for the court," said one counsel. The justice's wide range of JDR experience allows him to diffuse difficult situations—or as he put it, "to shuttle the bomb away"—and to encourage stubborn parties who are "beginning to set traps" to instead work cooperatively.

The justice's approachable demeanor set a friendly tone during initial caucusing. "That made me have more respect for him," said one of the counsels. He added that the justice's conversational style helped clients open up, especially when he encouraged the plaintiff and defendants to share their feelings in the plenary session. Counsels confirmed that their clients needed the opportunity to have their say and be taken seriously. Sitting with the judge at the same table as other parties, as opposed to watching him or her rule from the dais, is a metaphor for access to justice.

The nature of JDR is such that when a judge becomes a mediator his or her words often carry more weight for the clients than that of their counsel. The justice in this case told the parties what his expectations would be if it were sent to trial, hoping each party would re-evaluate their BATNA.

Throughout the JDR process, the justice considers it essential that he recognize and react to how much authority each presenting party has, and said, "The process is very dynamic and moves all the time." For example, when a counsel has to phone clients during a session to clarify an issue, it complicates the mediation process. The justice would seldom weigh in, however, unless a particular action presented a serious roadblock.

This propensity to resolve litigation in a creative fashion is not unique to the justice in this case. Another case demanding a careful approach to managing complexity is *The Negligent Land Transfer Case*. Part of a report on the JDR judge is excerpted:

This JDR judge was well suited to the complexities of the dispute. A former defense attorney in legal malpractice cases, he ran a successful private mediation practice prior to becoming a judge. His judicial expertise as well as his mediation skills were both remarked upon favorably by the attorneys. The judge stated that he treats JDRs "very much like a mediation in most cases, with my ability to provide opinions from time to time." He said that sharing an authoritative evaluation of the case with the parties was "a service that the public wants. They really like the ability to hear what a judge thinks."

A judge can never completely stop being a judge. But good JDR judges must be able to think of themselves differently. Unlike their usual role when sitting on the dais, JDR judges do not make rulings on motions or evidence, grant injunctions, or order costs when they are mediating. Good JDR judges rarely think about right v. wrong or establishing a precedent. Lawyers might indeed suggest that the judge refer to a previously settled case as an informal precedent, but the judge and the other counsel will not have any knowledge of the case. A JDR judge will never expect a mediated case to set a precedent, nor will he or she expect a previous case (even if they were the JDR judge) to set a precedent for a current JDR.

A Fair Process of Problem Solving

Procedural fairness is always important to a courtroom judge and a JDR judge. JDR judges have been trained in procedural fairness because they sit in court every day and know these requirements. There are four procedural safeguards, in particular, that a good JDR judge needs to enforce. (All elements of procedural fairness in ADR and JDR were reviewed in Chapter 8, but these four are worth repeating in the context of balancing the complexity in the courtroom:

First, giving people a **voice**. Everyone needs to believe they have had a chance to express themselves. Second, parties need **respectful treatment** from the decision-maker. Everyone needs to feel that they were treated in a dignified fashion. Third, the parties will need even-handed treatment and **neutrality of forum**. In other words, both the structure and interactional nature of how the JDR judge works with the parties in resolving disputes has to be seen as neutral even if the outcomes may differ. Fourth, parties will want **trustworthy consideration** from the JDR judge. This element builds upon the previous three, meaning parties need to know they were listened to, understood and their issues sincerely considered. Parties certainly need to trust the JDR judge and the judge needs to be sensitive to cues in interactions with them that would indicate a fair process to reach the resolution (Sourdin and Zariski 2013).

Flexibility and Calm under Fire

Parties in JDR can get emotional, and a good JDR judge has to remain calm. They also have to be able to improvise as litigation dynamics change quickly.

In a case involving a multi-million-dollar oilfield, (not in the Appendix) two of the defendants settled during the JDR, but the third defendant refused. Regardless, all three defendants had signed a binding JDR (BJDR) agreement obviating the need for a long trial and sending the remaining defendant and plaintiff into the final JDR day with the judge. All went well until a couple of days before the final session when the defendant wrote a letter to the plaintiff telling him they would no longer appear at the BJDR. The plaintiff and defendant then wrote to the judge and filed affidavits and motions, essentially seeking costs of over $100,000 for a breakdown in communication. The issue was a single defendant remaining while the other defendants had settled, and who no doubt felt all of the pressure on their shoulders.

Wisely, the JDR judge ignored all of the new court filings and told his assistant to set aside all the affidavits and motions for safekeeping. The judge did not read them, and instead called the two remaining attorneys together, renegotiated the procedure and ratified the BJDR. The parties shook hands (virtually in this case), made some jokes about the coronavirus (not easy during a pandemic) and the case continued to a successful conclusion.

One last case (also not in the Appendix) illustrates how a judge remained very calm under fire. He was dealing with construction litigation that had divided two best friends and business partners and their families. A motions judge had been randomly assigned in the middle of litigation to give an interim ruling. He saw how the disagreement had escalated into tens of thousands of pages of discovery with no end in sight. He read what he could, separated the underlying issues from what was presented in the lawsuit, got the parties together, and began to explore ways of helping the parties resolve the disagreement that had torn two close families apart:

There were three different business parties who were at each other's throats for breach of trust, breach of contract, deceit, and other issues. As the judge went into the court on that particular day, the clerk gave him a heads up that there were new applications being filed that morning: one of the lawyers now alleged there were breaches of a lawyers' agreement. The judge would have to decide this issue—improper evidence—before the rest of the matters could be heard. Having received the file in advance, the judge knew it was large—several archive boxes full, in fact. The judge did not know how he could add this new argument to the day's hearing agenda. The litigation had gone on for years.

Before the heated arguments started, the judge proposed a resolution meeting (a case conference) and with everybody's agreement, he called all of the lawyers into a meeting room where the judge, surprisingly, was told he would have to make special arrangements for yet *another* lawyer who was standing by on the telephone—in an airport! The judge began by telling all of the parties this would be costly and lengthy litigation and the present motion would turn at least a one-day hearing into a two-day hearing, just to decide some interim issues and that there would be several more days of hearings just to get through these interim decisions, let alone the trial.

The judge asked them to park their misconduct allegations and look directly at the issues between the parties and whether they had ever thought about judicial dispute resolution. One of the three litigation parties strongly favoured the idea, but the other two were lukewarm. The judge asked them to contact their clients for instructions and said that he would wait for an answer regarding a possible JDR. After the phone calls, the clients requested JDR, and all the counsels said they would attend with the clients if this judge could personally preside at the JDR. He agreed.

When the mediation day arrived, the two key businessmen arrived but did not speak. The tension was high. The two men and half a dozen counsel filled the boardroom. The judge explained the JDR process, sought input regarding the procedure, and privately caucused with the individual parties and their counsel. Those meetings led to the two principal litigants breaking from all of their counsels' litigation plan. The two men (with lawyers standing by them) asked the judge if they could speak with each other privately. Before agreeing, the judge left the room so the clients and lawyers could talk about this. When the judge returned to the room, the counsel said they agreed to the meeting but worried that these bitter adversaries would actually get into a fist fight. The judge reminded the counsel that these men were best friends at one point and he believed in them. Still, with tensions running high, the judge told everyone he would give the two men just ten minutes to talk and, if necessary, the judge and sheriffs would deal with any fallout. The judge stood right outside the room and reminded everyone that if a fight started, the sheriffs were just down the hall, and somebody would be going to jail for contempt or charged with assault— or both. The meeting room, however, was quiet.

After the ten minutes, the judge peeked into the room and instead of finding two big men fighting, they had written some notes about a possible settlement on a white board. They asked the judge for a few more minutes, which he gave them. When he knocked on the door again, the two key parties told the judge they had settled and were now taking their lives in a different direction; they had a new decision to announce. The judge did not know what their decision was, but asked them to speak to counsel first, and then all parties and the judge could meet.

The judge called the meeting to order in the large boardroom. The two principals who were adversaries for five years, running up a half-million dollars in attorneys-fees, announced they were starting a new business, together! The judge suggested counsel look over this settlement agreement (ending the litigation and starting the new business). Once counsel and clients signed the agreement, the complex litigation was over and their new business began.

Training

Clearly, there is no substitute for training. Yet, for some, skill training is not enough. If a judge does not want to do JDR because they prefer to decide who is right and who is wrong, it is not easy to shift their mindset from adversarial to cooperative. Nevertheless, we believe training can help judges learn more than technical skills. With the right content and pedagogy, training can shift a judge's mindset—and even their attitude—toward JDR.

One of the judges interviewed in the course of our research thinks that the hardest part of a JDR process is finding parties and counsel willing to participate and then making sure that the JDR judge is properly trained. Think about it: judges are accustomed to giving directions and making substantive decisions all day. After years of practice and experience on the bench, they have learned the law and attended judges' school so they can interpret legislation, address constitutional questions, and call "balls and strikes" in applying the law to the facts.

Judges are not predisposed to walk into a courtroom and invite the parties to work out their differences on their own, at least not without intensive training. And even with the proper training, JDR requires a lot of preparation, an ability to improvise, and the capacity to manage the complexity of the courtroom. We cannot report that the JDR training for judges in Canada, at the present time, changes many minds, but we think that the more time new judges spend with experienced JDR judges (during training or in other settings), the more likely we will see more effective JDR judges.

Chapter 13

DIVERGENT INTERESTS OF ADVERSARIAL LAWYERS AND THEIR CLIENTS

The lawyer's job is to represent his or her client and to be the conduit through which the client receives information about the legal process. Lawyers play an instrumental role in ensuring that clients understand all the information they receive. They also give advice to their clients, especially with regard to the question central to JDR: "Should I settle this case?"

It is not always obvious what the attorney's interest is in promoting settlement. Is it the same as their client's? If the case settles, the lawyer might well be forgoing additional fees. If a case can immediately settle in mediation with a skilled attorney, why wasn't the agreement reached previously in trial? Why did it take so long and cost so much to get to that point?

There have always been lawyers who argue against mediating legal disputes. Some of the classic anti-mediation claims are: "We are big people, we can settle the darn thing, what do we need a third party for?" and "Why do our clients have to be there?" This is a bit reminiscent of the familiar argument, "We settle almost all cases anyway, what more do you want?"

The other reaction is an unspoken sentiment that runs through many cases. As one lawyer said, "Early settlement, in other words, settlement using court-connected mediation, perhaps kicks me squarely in the pocketbook. [The lawyer goes on to say] . . . If you are being entirely selfish just looking at the lawyers' interest, then why do I want this?" This statement—anonymous of course—reflects the anxiety that many lawyers feel looking at the phenomenon of the court-connected mediation, especially where it is mandatory and especially where it takes place early in the litigation process.

The third reaction—another "pushback"—is that mediation will produce a "watered-down legal system." This view proports that because mediation is not decided by a decision-maker according to recognized principles of law, legal principles are not imposed and required, and this is a dilution of what we think of as a justice system.

Another lawyer said: "I am personally concerned that if only 3 percent of cases actually go to trial; that means 97 percent of the time all of the pre-trial stuff is wasted to a large extent, so ... 97 percent of the money that I make is from wasted time?" (Murphy and Molinari 2009).

We do not think the time attorneys spend before a judge hears their client's JDR is wasted. In fact, it might be quite valuable because it identifies the facts that go into the JDR in the form of texts, emails, letters and discovery—and uncovers issues a judge will need to help the parties find resolution. ADR/JDR training is, however, absolutely crucial for all judges and attorneys. Knowledge of mediation in a courtroom context includes "knowing how to run a lawsuit" in terms of unfolding every aspect of a case and being familiar with all of the documents and reports that are typically generated. More importantly, it helps attorneys remain open-minded about settlement possibilities. Mediation teaches lawyers how to move from an adversarial win/lose point of view to problem solving and value creation.

Attorneys will have to transform themselves from officers of the court who examine and cross-examine witnesses during trial; entering JDR means helping the court and the parties *resolve* their dispute. To accomplish this, many lawyers will have to acknowledge that their law school training is not the training they need.

As Frank Sander has written:

> " ... having a law degree doesn't necessarily ensure that one has the needed skills. Some years ago, the *Yale Law Journal* (1976) did a study of *pro se* divorce. Students asked Connecticut lawyers why they thought lawyers were needed in divorce. The lawyers answered, "Well, to do the tax things and to attend to the interstate custody jurisdiction act." Then the lawyers asked the clients whether their lawyers did those things. Only in a very small percentage of cases was the answer yes. It means that we have to be very careful to get the people properly trained in the competencies that are necessary in financial divorce mediation, and not rely simply on professional labels.
>
> It can be argued that the best model is [Sander's] rectangular model ... if both lawyers were highly qualified, if both were eager to resolve a problem fairly and fully, and if both are relatively equal incompetence, then this model of two clients and two equal, highly-qualified lawyers would probably be the best—at least it would be better than the triangular model with the two disputants and a mediator, because it would solve the question of how one provides the disputants with the information and background that they need in order to make informed decisions and to prevent exploitation of one side by the other.
>
> The only problem is that things are not usually like that in the real world. One of the problems with the adversary process is that it is often more adversary than process. If one person has a high-powered lawyer and the other does not, or if one person wants to turn the process into a fight to the finish and the other just wants to reach a fair solution, then the adversary process is virtually impossible to use . . ." (Sander 1983).

Having said all of this, lawyers can play a crucial role in a successful JDR. As Judge Agrios notes:

> One of the toughest things about JDR is having to come up with the fair opinion in a brief period of time, give reasons, justify them, and in effect "sell" the settlement to the parties. This is very uncomfortable for most judges as they become part of the process instead of just making a decision. They are anxious not to fail . . .
>
> ... Sometimes wondrous things happen and lawyers make some very reasoned compromises, admitting the weaknesses of their case and proposing fair solutions. This is most likely to happen if, in the pre-JDR meeting, the judge has instilled in counsel the concept of a non-adversarial approach. I am not suggesting this is a foolproof answer, but it is a technique worth trying. Later ... after you have resolved a really tough part of the case, there are still some loose ends. Suggest to the lawyers that they try to work out the

rest. It will be good for their morale. You can ask them to call you back if they have been unsuccessful and further judicial assistance is needed.

The key to this approach is to get the lawyers out of the normal combative, adversarial mode and into a settlement mode of problem solvers instead of problem creators. There are a variety of ways for a judge to create this aura. As I have said earlier, I tell lawyers to take off their adversarial hats and come with their settlement hats. Sometimes I suggest the group problem-solving model "we have a problem to solve today, I cannot do it all by myself, I need the help of everyone. We jointly have to create a reasoned solution that is going to be mutually beneficial." Or, tell the lawyers, "I want you to come with solutions, not problems." Some judges believe it is helpful to have the clients engage in the discussion and be part of creating a solution.

At the end of the day, all I can say is, if you have good lawyers, they will often surprise you with the solutions they will create. Surely this approach makes sense. Lawyers become active, not passive participants in the process and can use the judge as a sounding board. It is even possible that lawyers might impress their clients by their reasoned and open approach (Agrios 2004).

JDR attorneys need to turn off their trial switch and flip on their resolution switch; the "we win, you lose," attitude will not help promote settlement. More, attorneys weaving legal arguments into opening statements miss the point of JDR. If they begin in this way, a wise JDR judge will have to move them in a different direction and might say, "it is understandable if you want to begin your opening comments with the belief that 'we should win, you should lose;' and instead, today's JDR operates on the premise that "we all should *settle.*"

In addition to a proper settlement mindset, there are several other qualities that attorneys can bring to JDR. First, they need to know their clients' underlying concerns and prepare them for the disclosure of what are sometimes very personal interests.

Second, attorneys have to bring the right clients to the table. It may seem obvious, but the person who comes to the JDR needs to have full authority to settle the case. If not, phone calls will have to be made during the JDR, creating delays and frustration on all sides. One example of this was in an insurance case where counsel brought a low-level adjuster, and not the senior representative with full authority to speak about the upper monetary limits of a possible settlement.

Third, timing is everything. Being open to resolution *as soon as possible* saves the clients' money (i.e., attorneys' fees). Whether the mediation is through a JDR or not, exploring ADR as soon as possible saves money, time and hopefully keeps relationships intact. For multiple party or multiple jurisdiction cases, and for longer and more complex JDRs (such as Alberta's SPEC cases) we believe JDRs should take place no later than six to nine months before a scheduled trial. This way, discoveries, expert reports and replies are likely in, while last minute witness preparation—and significant legal costs—can still be avoided.

Pressure created by the divergence between the attorney's interest in billable hours and the client's interest in resolving the case (and immediately eliminating any further fees) may creep into a JDR process. Clients almost always see resolution in a positive light. They are often exquisitely relieved to settle; many litigants report that prior to resolution there was not a single day they did not feel hurt and upset by the allegations in the lawsuit, embarrassed by depositions and cross-examinations, exhausted by trial preparation, or angry about increasing costs. Attorneys, on the other hand, may be of two minds: they obviously want to meet their clients' needs, but they continue to benefit the longer a case goes on.

One might think that judges are uniquely attuned to discrepancies between the interests of clients and the interests of their attorneys. Superior courts and common law jurisdictions operate under principles of law and equity. Equity is based on fairness to parties and thus, is a foundational principle used to settle cases. Equity is also the principle that encourages judges to break away from the strictness of the law. In Alberta, the Judicature Act is one of the most fundamental laws establishing and organizing the judiciary. It speaks of fairness and urges judges and parties to honor this perspective as they try to resolve tough cases:

> The Court in the exercise of its jurisdiction in every proceeding pending before it has power to grant and shall grant, either absolutely or on any reasonable terms and conditions that seem just to the Court, all remedies whatsoever to which any of the parties to the proceeding may appear to be entitled in respect of any and every legal or equitable claim properly brought forward by them in the proceeding, so that as far as possible all matters in controversy between the parties can be completely determined and all multiplicity of legal proceedings concerning those matters avoided.
>
> In all matters in which there is any conflict or variance between the rules of equity and common law with reference to the same matter, the rules of equity prevail (Alberta 2018).

Assume a JDR judge is settling a negligence case where the fair and equitable thing to do is to require the defendant to pay damages to the plaintiff. Imagine these damages are in the several hundred-thousand-dollar range or even higher. Most defendants, including corporations, do not have this much cash available, at least not immediately. The JDR judge knows this and understands that it makes it hard to reach consensus on the terms of a settlement. However, the judge also knows the defendants *can* pay large damages if they are given time to do so. That is where the Judicature Act helps. It gives the judge clear authority to structure settlements over time, and to even take account of taxes. It allows a judge to consider all these factors in reaching a fair outcome. How fairness is defined is at the court's discretion (Alberta 2018).[1]

---

1. On application by any party to a proceeding, the Court may order that damages awarded be paid in whole or in part by periodic payments, and where no party to a proceeding has made an application for periodic payments, the Court nevertheless

    (a) may, in the Court's discretion and on the terms that the Court thinks just, order that an award for damages be paid by periodic payments if the Court considers it to be in the best interests of the plaintiff, and

    (b) shall order that an award for damages be paid by periodic payments if the plaintiff requests that an amount be included in the award to compensate for income tax payable on income from investment of the award. (Alberta 2018).

A JDR judge probably won't say, even when the parties reach a mutually agreeable settlement, "you have now reached a result that is fair and equitable." From a judge's perspective, equity is linked to healing; because it could take a decade for a dispute to find its way to court, it will probably take the passage of that much time to realize the freedom and liberty that emotional closure gives to each party. More, only the passage of time will allow parties to realize the power and control they reclaim once the litigation is behind them. Judges realize all of this, but many counsel do not. Reaching settlement not only means that billable hours end, but the question will be asked: "Were all the attorney's previous efforts worth the cost?" As one mediator of commercial disputes put it:

> ... if mediation results in the settlement of a case, your fees for that case will be lower than they would otherwise have been. If that is a concern for you, a question you must ask yourself is whether the decision about whether to mediate should be made based on your interests or on your client's interest. If mediation makes sense for the client, do you not have a duty to recommend it?
>
> Further, if you earned a reputation as someone who settles cases, who gets good deals for your clients, who is an effective advocate at mediation, you may find a significant increase in the size of your practice (as has been the experience of a number of litigators who have embraced mediation).
>
> If you do mediate and the case does not settle, you can assure your client that you have made the attempt to settle, and it will be the client's decision to reject the other side's proposal and carry on with the litigation. The client may be less concerned about the cost of litigation knowing that you have made every effort to settle and avoid extra cost. If you settle through mediation, that will leave you more time to focus on the cases that do not settle and require the extra time to prepare for trial ... (Stitt 2003).

At least one judge we know has seen a settlement where the attorneys were upset they did not receive a large contingency fee. The client was overjoyed with the result, and the other side appeared equally happy, notwithstanding the large settlement the company had to pay. The attorneys, however, waiting for a larger settlement and contingent payment were disappointed.

We believe that judges are in the best position to deal with whatever divergence there might be between the clients' and attorneys' interests. Judges understand, and in some cases have to rule on contingency fees. Moreover, federal judges hear appeals from taxation officers regarding fees and therefore—over the course of a judge's federal or superior court time on the bench—they will have contributed to the common law and interpretation of statutes regarding not only costs but the obligations of attorneys (including their ethical obligations). Thus, JDR judges are quite sensitive to the potential for a difference emerging between attorney and client interests. Raising this ethical question in front of attorneys with their clients is of course inappropriate for a judge who must remain neutral regarding all the parties involved in a JDR.

Chapter 14

JDR AND THE ROLE OF PRECEDENT

The Medical Malpractice Case

This chapter discusses JDR's use of precedent and its occasional role in shaping an agreement, rather than providing a go-to standard as in conventional litigation. In general, we believe attorneys over-rely on precedent to justify the outcome of JDRs and in doing so, miss the entire point of getting parties together to settle their lawsuit.

History of Backing Away from Precedent

Why should JDR judges, given their legal training, ever seek to free themselves from their normal reliance on precedent? Legal precedents generally do not help to resolve judicial mediations. There is a long history supporting this view.

Modern-day arbitration can provide the best of both worlds: it allows one to remain out of the courts *and* to not be bound by judicial precedents, especially when the benefits of court intervention are not guaranteed. Arbitration has to be free from *stare decisis* because of the interests of the involved parties (American Arbitration Association 2003). In other words, reconciling the interests of the involved parties does not depend on legal warrants or entitlements, and thus there is no need for a judge or arbitrator to write a decision wrapped around legal principles, constricted by earlier court precedents. Instead, the resolution of lawsuits depends on the discovery of interests underscored by the facts of the case. This requires all parties to be open-minded about creating solutions to resolve their personal conflicts, instead of asking a judge to decide their lawsuit and provide written reasons that become a legal precedent for future use by courts and lawyers. A trained JDR judge does not use his or her juridical position to determine who is right or wrong; rather, they use it to help the parties resolve their differences in a manner consistent with procedural and substantive fairness—and that is justice (see Chapter 8). It is therefore in the interests of the parties in JDR to be open about the details of their dispute and work with the other side to invent a way of maximizing joint gains, and not be bound by what may or may not have been decided in published court cases in the past.

Different Kinds of Precedents

There are three ways precedents come into play in JDR: (1) judicial precedents written from the bench involving procedural or jurisdictional questions about JDR; (2) previous judicial precedents related to the particular issue or lawsuit cited by the parties or a judge in a JDR; and (3) JDR outcomes that become published and could therefore set a precedent to be cited by other parties in subsequent JDRs.

1.   *Judicial precedents from the bench about procedural or jurisdictional matters*

Canadian courts have addressed various questions about JDR. We now discuss some of these court decisions including their reasoning. The first has to do with whether judges are compellable as witnesses in future proceedings. An Alberta Queen's Bench decision by Justice Martin (now of the Supreme Court of Canada) who quoted the Quebec Court of Appeal, (*Kosko c. Bijimine*, 2006 QCCA 671) states that judges are not compellable:

> The Quebec Court of Appeal reasoned that as judges are not compellable witnesses, to allow another party to testify, once removed, as to what was said in a JDR would be doing indirectly what could not be done directly. A justice in a subsequent proceeding would be asked to decide whether or not comments were made by a colleague, without direct evidence of that colleague. The court ruled that such a process was likely to bring the administration of justice into disrepute, stating at para. 47:
>
> Since judges cannot be compelled to appear as witnesses and their duties of office do not permit them to testify voluntarily, we must not allow these principles to be circumvented by authorizing the parties to disclose the comments of trial judges (Alberta Court of Appeal 2010).

A second question was posed to the Canadian court: Do you have to agree to do JDRs—can they be forced upon you? The case *Luft v Zinkhover* (2017) determined what we consider an obvious answer: JDRs are consensual and neither party nor the judge can impose a JDR or BJDR unless parties agree to participate. The court made this comment about the value of JDRs and their consensual nature:

> The appellants argued at trial that the respondents should have proceeded with the binding JDR called for by the counsel agreement in order to mitigate their damages. The trial judge rejected this argument for a number of reasons:
>
> a)   If the respondents had "thought they could obtain what they needed from a binding JDR, they would have shown that by choosing that option".
> b)   Instead of proceeding to a binding JDR, the respondents "chose [the litigation route] to sue Mr. Zinkhofer".
> c)   Requiring the respondents to proceed in accordance with the counsel agreement they had never agreed to would be "unfair and extends the doctrines of causation or mitigation beyond their terms".
> d)   There are different opinions about whether a binding JDR is a good means to resolve disputes, and "personal choice plays a key role". The respondents did not want a JDR; they wanted [the litigation route of] a public trial" (Alberta Court of Appeal 2017).

So, in this case a BJDR decision that was not accepted by one of the parties at the time the judge offered it, did not set a precedent. That is, one side could not subsequently seek to have the terms of the BJDR enforced when the agreement had not been accepted voluntarily. According to the appellant in the case, JDR briefs are confidential, both during and after a JDR, and cannot be used in a subsequent action because "what happens in a JDR stays in the JDR" (Alberta Court of Appeal 2017).

And then there is the recurring question of whether a JDR judge can continue as the trial judge if the JDR does not settle. The generally accepted answer is no, as described by the majority of the Court of Appeal of Alberta:

> … the JDR process has become a valuable tool in expedited dispute resolution within the formal framework of the administration of justice. As such, its use and the practices and rules around it should develop with that purpose in mind, but without sacrificing the integrity of trial process. The principled exclusion of JDR judges from the trial role, premised upon the confidentiality of JDR discussions in furtherance of candour and transparency, enhances the efficacy of the process and facilitates the settlement of disputes. [We are] persuaded that trial judges should not be privy to such discussions, even with the consent of the parties, because to so permit diminishes the efficacy of JDRs and inevitably raises the spectre of an apprehension of bias in subsequent trial or contested chambers proceedings" (Alberta Court of Appeal 2007).

2. *The role of precedents related to an issue or lawsuit in a current JDR*

To what extent do judges rely on the precedents provided by JDR counsel to settle particular issues in a case? As illustrated in *The Medical Malpractice Case*, JDR judges depend on their own experience in settling cases, not the precedents that counsel bring to the table. True, there is some role for prior court decisions applicable to JDRs if those precedents aid a judge and parties toward resolution. Precedents in this sense, however, are highly bounded and do not impel a JDR judge to accept them.

In *The Medical Malpractice Case*, a medical procedure gave rise to an action and a successful JDR in Alberta, Canada. The plaintiff, Smith, had been suffering from impaired vision in one eye that was affecting his work as a laboratory technician. A licensed ophthalmologist recommended that he undergo vitrectomy surgery to his eye to improve his vision. Smith opted to have the ophthalmologist perform the surgery.

When Smith arrived for the procedure, the anesthesiologist administered a topical anesthetic and inserted a needle to the eye, causing Smith extreme pain. Stronger anesthetic was administered to his eye, Smith still alleged that his eye was not numb, and the ophthalmologist went ahead and began the surgery. Smith again experienced extreme pain and moved suddenly, causing the ophthalmologist's needle to perforate the globe of Smith's eye, resulting in vitreous and preretinal hemorrhage. Further medication was added to the eye, and the ophthalmologist completed the vitrectomy successfully. However, Smith had to undergo two more years of subsequent surgeries to correct his eye's perforated globe.

Smith sued the ophthalmologist and anesthesiologist for negligent medical care, alleging his right eye's vision had become even more impaired than when he initially sought care from the ophthalmologist. He claimed that this increased and permanent vision impairment further hindered his ability to do his laboratory work, which required analyzing details under a microscope, and led to loss of past and prospective income. He further claimed that he was unable to complete regular day-to-day tasks and required home care and other services. Finally, he asserted that he suffered depression as a result of his injuries and had begun taking medication. In total, he sought damages approaching $5 million. In response, neither of the defendants disputed the majority of factual events but did challenge the claim of any damage suffered by the plaintiff resulting from the doctors' negligence or other misconduct.

Like most judges, this JDR judge did not find herself bound by legal precedents. Instead, she started from scratch, asking about the legal issues in that lawsuit, such as whether there was a relevant standard of care that applied. The justice also worked with each party to make a list of other issues that would be important if the case went to trial, such as negligence and different types of damages. She asked the plaintiff's lawyer to give her "a summary of what you would say at trial about the relevant standard of care." She also asked the lawyer what they thought the strongest and weakest parts of their case would be at trial. Further, the justice did something in the JDR that a strict reliance on precedent would never have allowed: she noticed that an issue was particularly weak for one side after holding caucuses and shared her concerns with that party. Instead of imposing a legal precedent to push for parties to end up with a particular result, she focused on the respective offers and not the law.

As detailed in the case study:

> The justice expected the parties to work hard to come up with settlement offers, but she did not expect them to do so unaided. As the plaintiff's lawyer described, during each round of shuttle diplomacy, the justice worked diligently with each side to come up with a new offer that would bring the parties closer to settlement. Indeed, defense counsel indicated that the justice ensured that each offer was evidence-based and supported by "principled reasons." They went on to say that she pushed back against huge positional numbers and insignificant concessions that might aggravate the other side and stall the process. The justice was able to evaluate the fairness of each offer thanks to rigorous groundwork and assimilation of the facts, evidence, and relevant law in the case.

That is not to say the justice ignored precedent all together; like most judges she knew where the legal goal posts were, but that knowledge did not affect the way she conducted the JDR. The plaintiff's attorney told us that because the justice had experience litigating and adjudicating cases involving medical malpractice and insurance payouts, they had a general sense of the typical ballpark of damages for the specific injury that Smith suffered.

Precedents can play a part in JDRs (by interpreting rules and setting boundaries), but they are public and thus not the focal point for explicating and deciding an issue. Further, precedents raise practical and legal problems. The practical problem—at least for busy courts—is there are not enough hours in a judge's day for long trials and written decisions, even if the judge reserves some of them (e.g., takes them under advisement). This has a snowball effect, and the quality of decisions suffers as time passes from the hearing of evidence to the writing of decisions. The legal problem is how a judge uses precedent in a JDR if he or she does not quote from it, as is typically done in a court decision.

Fortunately, a JDR judge assigned even to long cases (called SPECs, as described in Chapter 17) can resolve the majority of them without quoting precedents or taking the court's time to write a decision for each trial and create further precedent. Not much is lost, however, without the establishment of a new precedent; it is wrong to assume that precedents—even from appeal courts—last and apply forever. As one author put it:

> If the number of adjudications increases, then worse craftsmanship, worse thinking, and worse law will likely result. From the standpoint of the public-life conception, bad adjudication is substantially worse than no adjudication: a settlement before judgment removes one opportunity for the law to work itself pure, but a bad adjudication reverberates until its precedent is overruled (Luban 1995).

The Well Fire Case similarly offers a word of caution with the use of precedent. The settlement was structured (but not forced) to conform with a recent opinion in the Alberta Court of Appeal that provided guidance for allocating liability for a series of negligent acts. The case, *Heller v. Martens*, outlined a "comparative blameworthiness" standard for allocating liability. That opinion grounded *The Well Fire Case* parties' discussion about how to go about structuring a settlement. It also provided a helpful standard of legitimacy against which they could assess whether the agreement was fair, compared to what they would have achieved in court (Alberta Court of Appeal 2002).

In *The Well Fire Case*, it seemed as if the justice did not dig deeply into the law and preferred a far more flexible approach to establishing legitimacy. He used the law as a framework but did not feel constrained or conscripted by the law (which can be rigid). Instead, he described himself as taking a "principled approach" to JDR mediation. This may have moved the conversation toward tying a settlement to a broadly acceptable standard of legitimacy. He even noted that not every case can be settled by looking to the law: "Sometimes you can do it on the law, and sometimes you can do it on the evidence." The facts put forth by a party may, at times, be compelling enough to spur a settlement that does not conform with past precedent. Parties who present a meaningful story in their opening statements or who otherwise win the sympathy of the judge, may be advantaged by this willingness to deviate from precedent. Other principles, such as fairness or compassion, can motivate the judge to employ a more flexible approach.

Parties need flexibility from a JDR judge and judges know that reliance on precedent can repress the search for creative resolutions. Instead of generating options, strict reliance on precedent numbs the inspiration of skilled negotiations.

In *The Negligent Land Transfer Case*, the justice stepped out of his normal decision-maker (precedent-setting) role to help the parties find a better solution. He was instrumental in generating creative options, describing "one of the beauties of JDR" as allowing him to "think outside of the box a little bit." In this case, that meant asking the defendants whether they had any other resources (land, specifically) they could offer to the plaintiff. Had this case been before the judge at trial, it was unlikely he would have ordered any land turned over pursuant to an agreement between the parties, and he would have lacked the authority to instruct them to give away parcels that were not at issue in the litigation. In his role as JDR judge, he could suggest almost anything that might settle the case. As he put it, "I was using more than money." The judge rightly assumed that as large landowners they would likely control several parcels, including some that could be subdivided and offered in the settlement. And he likely realized that at least one side would remain entrenched in the case if they did settle, potentially costing both reputational damage and additional legal fees. All the parties' interests were met by developing a novel solution that transferred land instead of money.

JDR judges know the law in particular legal areas such as contracts, torts, property, conflicts of law, remedies and so on. Even assuming that they did not know the relevant law in any given case, attorneys filing JDR briefs can outline what courts have done in deciding cases—especially recent ones—that are similar to their JDR facts. Yet, the whole basis for the JDR meeting is to resolve the case by fleshing out not only the facts but also the *values* of the parties (as opposed to a win/lose ruling of a court in a different case, for different parties, whose values and interests may have never been disclosed to the court).

3. *JDR decisions as judicial precedent in subsequent JDRs*

We strongly disagree with this practice, but it has happened. The case, *Re Blitz* (1997), involved a land reclamation decision imposed by an environmental regulator. The decision of the regulator was subsequently appealed and then mediated, not decided, by one of the Alberta Environmental Appeal Board's administrative law judges. The mediation precedent focused on nothing more than the fact that a mediation had occurred, and it resulted in the requirement that the company perform a vegetation assessment. If the assessment was completed, the Notice of Appeal by the complainant would be abandoned. Even if done by consent, publishing the private mediation result implied that another administrative law judge (or court perhaps) might be persuaded to reach the same result— a result that was, again, negotiated in a private mediation between the parties.

The publication of mediation precedents like this one are rare, given the confidentiality of JDR proceedings and the fact that future parties would not have access to what happened in the previous mediation. In our view, drawing on earlier JDR results as a kind of precedent should be strongly discouraged.

Chapter 15

THE IMPORTANCE OF A ROBUST
JDR INTAKE SYSTEM

Judges are extraordinarily busy, and perhaps due to a lack of time or because they take their titles too seriously, they sometimes walk into a JDR room and immediately begin mediating. Without an adequate intake interview, a judge not only risks misunderstanding the most important concerns of the parties but is disrespectful to the clients—unacceptable in today's expanding world of access to justice.

The British Columbia Court website provides a counter example, as well as resources to help clients prepare for mediation. It also allows the court to initiate an intake meeting—a vital component in the process that increases the odds that JDR judges will be properly prepared to mediate.

Intake is actually the first part of a JDR. It is a highly interpersonal meeting between the mediator and the parties; often the first moment at which we are able to begin to create that positive energy. When someone reaches out to you as a mediator, you begin to share who you are, your practice and the process. In exchange they share who they are, what they're experiencing in their lives at that moment, and what they hope, expect, or possibly fear will happen in mediation. When this important first dialogue is positive, you begin laying the foundation for what will hopefully be a successful mediation (Brill-Case 2015).

One mediator asks this of the intake experience: "How can they make the disputants comfortable, set out the process, start the disputants on the right track, and yet not take so much time that everyone becomes bored or frustrated?" (Stitt 2003).

The mediator must set the tone and create an atmosphere that is conducive to settlement. He or she must set the table figuratively as well as literally, creating a comfortable and positive tone for the disputants by proposing a structure that encourages them to participate.

This may be the first opportunity for the disputants to meet the mediator, who will try to earn the disputants' trust in both the mediator and the mediation process. The mediator will also attempt to calm the emotions and nerves of disputants who may be anxious about the process and outcome (Stitt 2003). Judges admit that while in court, when proceedings have started, they have a hard time assessing demeanor and body language. It is difficult to find out what the parties really want and need until there is an opportunity for a real conversation. An intake helps with these interpersonal challenges because:

> . . . listening to the intonation and words chosen by potential clients during intake can pro-
> vide you with insight into what to expect from them when they are in a room with you and

with each other . . . Getting a sense of the clients' demeanor can also alert you to whether they might be people that you cannot or might not want to work with. Do they push your personal buttons? Are they giving you an indication that they don't feel there is a lot of value in the process or are they underestimating the value of your time? You want these answers sooner rather than later and intake is the perfect opportunity to find out before you're in too far (Brill-Case 2015).

Intakes are not only necessary to discover the parties' views of the issues covered in the lawsuit; they also reveal a lot about the parties themselves. The ADR judge (or their assistant) will want to find out where the parties stand emotionally. They will try to discover whether the clients (1) feel they have been accepted as individuals and their personalities and values are not under attack (or no longer under attack); (2) feel they can maintain their dignity, or "face," as they move to resolution; (3) feel their core needs have been respected and addressed; (4) have enough time to gain perspective and experience healing; (5) feel that others are likely to accept their feelings as valid and values as legitimate; and (6) feel as if they are genuinely and nonjudgmentally heard (Mayer 2000).

Intakes are also the moment when JDR ground rules are shared. Some that are typically referenced:

- The mediator's neutral role and impartiality
- The procedure and timetable that will be followed
- The rules of confidentiality that will apply and the privileged nature of the discussions (making clear which aspects will not be privileged or confidential)
- The opportunities that will be provided for each side to outline their respective positions (in those processes where each opens with a presentation)
- The procedure for conducting separate meetings (caucuses), and the way in which these will be scheduled, in addition to joint meetings, where applicable; the special provisions regarding confidentiality of matters discussed during these private sessions may also be covered, and whether matters discussed in the separate meetings will be disclosed by the mediator to the other party or will be maintained confidentially.
- The right of each party to terminate the mediation
- The way in which the parties' respective lawyers can participate and assist in the process
- Any particular rules relating to the particular mediation, for example if the "agreements" reached are not to be binding but conditional upon some further event such as ... [getting advice or necessary approvals] (Brown and Marriott 1999).

Intake meetings are also important information-gathering opportunities. A typical list of items that might be shared include:

- Facts about the parties and the issues, including each party's views and submissions; these are usually obtained from an initial referral form or from written statements furnished by the parties.

- Relevant documents, including copies of pleadings or affidavits in situations where adversarial proceedings are already underway.
- Oral submissions and comments by each party; these can be provided at an initial joint meeting and/or in separate meetings with the mediator.
- The mediator or any party may raise questions as the JDR progresses; the parties may be asked to address these in writing. Supplementary information, oral or written, may be obtained in this way.
- Technical data and other information, which [subject to privilege] may include expert opinions, legal opinions, evaluations and assessments of damages and other specialized data; these can all be introduced through the respective lawyers, experts, or other professional advisors.
- Information of a formal nature will be supplemented by the mediator's observations during the course of the JDR. The dynamic between the parties, their attitudes to one another and to the issues and their underlying concerns are all part of the broader picture, and they may all be relevant to the resolution of the dispute (Brown and Marriot 1999).

Intake provides an important opportunity to deal with expectations—shaping the parties' understanding of what can and cannot be done. "For instance, the parties need to know that JDR will not punish someone who has, in the eyes of one of the parties, done "wrong"; it will not completely undo a harm that has been done, and it will not necessarily vindicate someone who feels that they are completely in the right" (Brill-Case 2015).

An intake is also an opportunity for JDR judges to educate clients about the judge's approach and to explain the differences between mediation, ADR and JDR. Many parties, and even some counsel, are not entirely clear about the mediator's or JDR judge's role, and how JDR differs from arbitration. "Intake is ... a good time to direct them to informational websites or other resources that can help them get educated about mediation" (Brill-Case 2015).

An intake can be completed as part of a pre-trial conference or settlement meeting. At the very least, it should be completed very early in the process. As one expert notes:

> A judge-hosted settlement conference may occur as early as the initial scheduling conference or as late as the final pre-trial conference, which in some courts occurs only a few days before trial. Early intervention . . . allows a judge to explore with the litigants the information they need to settle the case and to shape the discovery process . . . Some judges, however, are too burdened with pending cases to intervene early, or are reluctant to become involved in shaping the discovery process to contain litigation costs. For these judges, a settlement conference close to trial may be the most productive method of intervening.
>
> Whether it occurs early or late, a settlement conference can serve two important functions: it can help break down the psychological and strategic barriers that lie in the path of settlement negotiations; and, if this is not sufficient to produce results, the conference can provide the additional information the litigants need to settle the case. Judges cite both functions in describing the role a judge-hosted conference can play in promoting settlement (Provine 2000).

JDR judges, like all mediators, need to be aware of how getting to know the parties may affect them, and even unwittingly cause them to change their mediation style:

> . . . it is important to recognize that the personal qualities of the *parties* may influence the mediator, just as the mediator's personal qualities affect the parties. Trying to understand the effect of the mediator's presence, without considering the impact of the parties on the mediator... is to look at only half of the picture of the process, and the changes wrought by those interactions (Bowling and Hoffman 2000).

This doesn't apply to all JDR judges. Those with very little experience don't have a wide enough repertoire to make modifications in their style or approach.

How an intake system saved time in one federal judicial district

An intake system became vital for two judges who wanted to work with their staff and the local bar to reduce lead times in as many cases as possible. They also wanted to use JDR much earlier than typically docketed and developed an entry form for all new clients. They hoped the result would be that attorneys and clients would be more interested in judicial mediation and better prepared to participate in JDR.

They initiated this effort as a means of improving case management, but it ultimately served as an intake mechanism for all their JDR cases. In their outlying, backlogged federal districts in Alberta, delays were running about one year, and counsel repeatedly seemed satisfied to litigate for interim orders instead of closing files. These ongoing applications for interim orders never fully resolved the matters; they merely pushed trials and other court applications down the road.

After meeting, the supervising judges decided that all newly filed lawsuits should go immediately into mediation with a judge. To help this along, they generated a short form that required information and brief summaries from counsel and parties. With this form completed, they assumed the parties could move right to an early mediation meeting with a judge.

Before embarking on a new world of full-time JDR, however, they met with the local bar to discuss how an early JDR program might work. After a round of conversations, the judges knew they would need to collect more information during the intake, not only to share with the attorneys but also for the court. Feedback from the local bar suggested that the first area of JDR to focus on should be Family Law (Astor and Chinkin 2002).

With a more complete informational questionnaire used for family law cases, they would find out as quickly as possible what the parties were thinking about: (1) divorce; (2) custody, if children were involved; (3) alimony or spousal support both current and retroactive; (4) child support both current and retroactive; and (5) division of personal and real property. They decided not to ask the lawyers or parties why issues had not been settled and possibly cause them to be defensive. Instead, they asked for new proposals likely to lead to settlement.

They also decided to use the questionnaire to find out: (1) the history of the negotiations (dates being more important than numbers); (2) what court orders were already in place; and (3) objective reasons why the parties had rejected offers proffered by the other side. Lastly, they wanted to know each side's expectations regarding the possible role of independent experts going forward.

The judges knew they had to be creative decision-makers on the bench, but they were less clear about what it would take to be creative problem solvers *during mediation*. They imagined six steps:

1. Objective finding: "What is the goal, wish, or challenge upon which the parties want to work?"
2. Fact finding: "What is the situation or background? What are the facts, questions, data, and feelings involved?"
3. Problem finding: "What is the problem that especially needs focus? What are the concerns that really need to be addressed?"
4. Idea finding: "What are all the possible solutions for how to solving the problem?"
5. Solution finding: "How might the parties and the judge strengthen the solution? How can they anticipate which solution will work best?"
6. Acceptance finding: "What are all the action steps that need to take place in order to implement the solution generated by the parties and the JDR judge?" (King et al. 2009).

Judges want to let clients and attorneys know right up front, during the intake, that they will be openly brainstorming for answers. One of the most useful statements about the value of brainstorming in ADR that we have seen, is as follows from Brown and Marriot:

> One of the ways in which a mediator can help parties to generate options is by brain-storming. This involves the mediator encouraging the parties to put forward as many ideas and options as possible as they come to mind without inhibiting their flow by considering them individually at that stage, or rejecting any, even if at first sight, that may seem unworkable.
>
> The mediator may need to manage the brainstorming session firmly and creatively, helping parties to build on and develop options as they arise and deterring parties from examining them while they are being generated.
>
> It can be helpful when options are being generated to write them all down, on a flip chart if one is being used, and to prioritize them later, rather than eliminating them as they emerge. Even when subsequently considering options, it is not a good idea to eliminate any of them notwithstanding that the parties may agree that particular options are unacceptable. It is not uncommon that options initially considered to be unacceptable later come back into focus as possibilities, perhaps by way of permutation with other ideas (Brown and Marriot 1999).

How did the new JDR intake-based program turn out?

The result of the new program eliminated almost all of the lead times and led to resolutions in almost all of the family and civil cases that came to the court. After the program had run for a year or so, the settlement rate was 90 percent. A senior member of the bar was so enthusiastic about it, he wrote to the chief justice:

> Thank you for allowing [the two judges] to set up a pilot project in [their region] for early case resolution, intake case conferences, mandatory informal case management, and dispute resolution. The informal process on a regular and continuous basis with our clients has led to quicker resolutions of complicated family matters, more efficient court processes, and access to formal dispute resolutions such as vote hearings, judicial dispute resolutions (binding and nonbinding), and quicker access to family law specials, as the case may be.
>
> The mandatory meetings provide useful opportunities for counsel to meet with the justice with their respective clients. In most cases, the meetings narrow down the issues and early case management and resolution are possible.
>
> The pilot project has been going on [in our region] for approximately two years. The presiding justices have taken ownership of the program and are fully prepared: they meet with clients and their respective counsel and have reviewed file materials. In most circumstances, the process has led to quicker access to justice and resolution, and more cost-efficient solutions for what could be time consuming, costly, and complicated matters. The quick resolution has had a tremendous impact on the local bar—fostering mediations, meetings, and working together to solve problems for our respective clients. It has reduced the wait time for family law specials.
>
> Generally, counsel files summaries to outline the position of the respective clients and the justices review file material in anticipation of the meetings. A list of matrimonial properties are exchanged with proposed equalization statements. The lists are not necessarily comprehensive and have fluctuated as to the length depending on the circumstances. In one instance there were four to five pages covering a couple hundred specific items in relation to a business. The parties managed to go through it, allocate a value, and divide up a significant number of matrimonial issues on a rather informal and speedy basis as part and parcel of what was scheduled to be a three-day arbitration process. Parties did reach a consent order on that matter at the end of two days.
>
> When all matters are not resolved at case conferences, usually there has been a significant amount of cooperation, agreement, and at the very least, a narrowing down of issues to the point where more formal judicial processes can be focused on one or two particular issues as opposed to muddying the waters with the dozen or more. Recommendations made from the mandatory intake case conferences include more formal case management, morning chambers, specials, and developing and following the litigation plan or even trials. The matters are determined according to counsel and client wishes along with the specific directions from the justices.
>
> In addition to undertaking the pilot process, taking an active role in management and participation thereof, [the two judges] met with the local bar prior to implementation and on a periodic basis thereafter. There have been informal discussions with various members of the bar as to how the process is going, what can be improved, and whether or not the process should be continued. There is consensus among the local bar that it is reducing wait times, providing an added level of access to justice for our clients, and there is a greater level of satisfaction between most counsel and most of the clients in resorting to and taking advantage of this new process....[1]

---

1. Jeffrey Harcourt, letter to Chief Justice, 5 Dec. 2019.

To conclude, the regional federal district JDR-initiative ended successfully, perhaps predictably so, because of the buy-in and full cooperation of the local bar. The intake format that gathered information for the JDR intake meetings was based on many others used to gather up-front information before initiating ADRs (Stienstra and Yates 2004). Again, the key is not starting a JDR until the parties have completed a thorough intake and the judge has reviewed the information. Much data can be collected in writing by court staff, but some will only be useful if it is the product of face-to-face conversations with the JDR judge, counsel and the parties.

Chapter 16

THE CHIEF JUSTICES AND HOW TO TRIAGE SPECIAL (SPEC) JDR CASES

A little-known way to get litigation into the JDR program is to simply write to the chief (or associate chief) justice and ask to have a case resolved by a senior judge in a special JDR hearing. In Alberta, such JDR case assignments have become known as Special Judicial Dispute Resolution (SJDRs), or SPECs. If the chief justice agrees, the next step is to have the scheduling manager allocate time for a senior justice to conduct the SPEC. In Alberta, this practice is fairly common and saves a great deal of trial time. This chapter explains how and why the chief justice asks a senior judge to do special JDRs ad hoc. Chapter 17 gives examples of real SPEC cases and how they resolved.

In pre-SPEC days, when the chief justice asked a senior JDR judge to take on a challenging case, it was one that would take at least three to four weeks of trial time. SPECs became the label for the most difficult cases, flagged for being in and out of motions court, special hearings and even trials to appeals and back again. They tend to involve numerous counsel and claims in the millions of dollars. It is not uncommon for such cases to actually take a decade to complete. So, *but for* the success of JDR SPEC, the trial time allocated to these difficult cases has been measured in years.

The triaging and docketing of SPEC cases depends on several metrics: heightened animosity between parties, or counsel; the amounts at stake in the controversy; the weeks of trial time likely to be required; the stress on judicial resources at the time; and other unique considerations like the involvement of third parties, counterclaims and multiple jurisdictional complications.

At the outset, the chief justice, or senior judge (on their behalf, with approval of the chief justice) writes a letter to counsel stating that a SPEC justice had been assigned to their case by the chief justice and inviting them to a one-hour court meeting to discuss and develop the SPEC procedures that will be used.

With input from the parties, the SPEC justice tailor-makes the JDR procedure, aiming for something between a normal JDR and a full-fledged trial. While this still involves mediation in a boardroom and not a courtroom, the parties in a SPEC JDR will have additional opportunities to collect and send the justice and each other special pieces of evidence (including appropriate video evidence, transcripts and expert evidence). Following these special procedures, the typical JDR continues almost as a formal "minitrial" in which parties can present positions, evidence and arguments and be questioned (informally, not under oath) by the other side, while the justice facilitates the exchange. The SPEC JDR provides opportunities for experts to attend and provide input, and for the judge's and counsel's examination of their reports.

Through JDR, appropriately selected cases tend to settle consensually. SPEC justices see themselves as lucky to get the biggest and most challenging assignments. They feel privileged to be part of choosing which cases will be pursued in this fashion and having a chance to discuss the case and its scheduling with the chief justice. More, it is rewarding for them to work with their judicial assistants in a new, much more involved way, and to see the litigants' enthusiasm when they realize a settlement process is being designed just for them.

That excitement was clear in a recent SPEC case where the parties needed the SPEC justice for a technical reason *as a precondition* to the actual resolution of any issues. The justice was to handle a preliminary point of law, but they also hoped that same justice would serve as their mediator. They got both with SPEC.

Both sides asked the justice if he would rule on the fine legal point before going further, and they promised to work to resolve it if he did. The justice, of course, agreed but indicated that mediation would follow. All parties filed briefs on the single point of law which the SPEC justice then decided in a very brief, unpublished oral memorandum. Following that, the parties happily proceeded to resolve the case together with the justice.

SPEC JDRs are flexible and can be uniquely fashioned for each case. Judges must do a lot of reading and take part in more meetings than in normal JDRs, but they can literally save those who are drowning in litigation. SPEC JDRs almost always result in settlement. And, it is a thrill for a justice, post-SPEC, to see parties shake hands or even hug following years of acrimony. (Judges never get feedback like that following a trial; seeing instead the sad face of the losing party).

Saving trial time amidst a busy court schedule is especially important. Society also needs healing, however, and SPEC provides that. One-on-one time with fighting parties can calm things down, and meeting with a justice can provide a safe space for problem-solving. There are, of course, the other spinoff benefits: weeks and months of court time saved so that other trials (usually involving significant indictable offenses like murder) can finally be scheduled and heard. To someone sitting in jail, justice delayed really is justice denied, and SPEC can help there, too, such as when a special or tailor-made criminal pre-trial conference is conducted. Finally, settlement and the avoidance of trials offers a positive financial impact by saving much needed resources.

Unique Perspective of the Chief Justice

Chief justices worry about delay in getting cases to trial, particularly for those that have lagged. SPEC focuses on specifically those cases that have been lost in the flow of litigation. Many have dragged on for more than a decade; counsel has done nothing or has not been effective in advancing their case. Chief justices know litigation delays create a widening gap between the parties while communication breaks down and positions harden waiting for trial. Without resolution, tension builds between the parties, creating blinders to the possibility of settlement, because winning the fight becomes more important than ending it. What is lost in all this is the search for fairness, not to mention fractures in evidence; a witness's memory fades, they move away, or sometimes even pass away, before trial.

Chief justices get involved in SPEC invitations, but there is related procedural correspondence that someone else has to handle; the chief justice usually does not send out personal letters and neither are they supposed to intervene in trials. As busy as they are, chiefs do not constantly review the hundreds or thousands of pending cases and motions. They do respond, however, to the letters they receive. For parties in need of a mediation, there is something special about getting a phone call out of the blue from a justice's assistant, announcing a SPEC opportunity. The little-known JDR process has a unique appeal—sometimes merely because it adds excitement and moves things along.

There is a hope among jurists that SPEC can build trust in the judicial system. Coupled with the use of modern technologies to communicate (as with OJDR, discussed in Chapter 19), chief justices know that SPEC will be seen as a life raft for drowning parties heading over a waterfall.

Chief justices bring people together and with their invitation provide a new push to settle. When the opportunity is explained to parties, it seems to enhance their readiness and willingness to work things out voluntarily through the SPEC process. It also helps parties put their matter in perspective: when fighting parties realize there are hundreds of other cases waiting to be litigated and they can mediate theirs right away while freeing up room for others, they may not help each other (and litigation between them proves that point), but will help third parties they do not even know by moving to mediate and free up trial time.

The entire court benefits from the resolution of disputes. SPEC successes attract attention. It feels like a shared success, even for a trial justice, to receive an email from the chief justice congratulating everybody on the consensual resolution of a long-scheduled case.

The chief justice has a direct hand in these successes by offering SPECs to senior judges, thereby opening up their schedules. As discussed, it is part of the administrative role of a chief justice to worry about all of the long trials and challenging cases that are pending. SPEC saves months or even a full year of trial time and millions of dollars in resources inside the court and between parties. It allows the chief justice to free up multiple judges to do other trials, especially criminal trials in which a defendant's liberty is at stake.

Why not Assign SPEC JDR Exclusively to One or More Senior Judges?

With all of these benefits, it is clear that senior justices with ADR or JDR training should be slotted into SPEC JDR assignments on a regular (even full time) basis. These tend to be justices who have accumulated considerable JDR experience on the bench and may have had substantial ADR experience before their appointment to the bench. Specialization happens in other professions, so it is not surprising that specialized JDR judges are emerging in the judiciary. These judges are held to a high standard by the chief justices who appoint them. This underscores the most important point we are trying to make in this book: JDR is a specialized skill, and only appropriately-trained judges should take on these assignments. Based on their success, some of those will become full-time SPEC justices. It may take a few years to ensure the necessary range of trial experiences. From these challenging trials comes an understanding of evidence and written decisions across the spectrum of all legal disputes—and an understanding of lawyers and how to deal with them in highly adversarial situations. These disputes include criminal trials, constitutional cases, and ruling on the validity of legislation.

This range of experience builds a JDR judge's disposition to help parties settle. They know there is long-term harm in declaring winners and losers when most lawsuits are fact based, not law based, and really are private fights. By the time a JDR judge is senior enough to mediate full time, they likely know the court staff, the reputation of most counsel, most law firms, and have received advice from ADR-trained judicial staff and court counsel, not to mention having worked with the chief justice enough to gain his or her confidence. We don't know for certain whether all Canadian chief justices will move in the direction of appointing SPEC JDR judges or whether individual judges will accept such appointments. Those who have, clearly make the case for the value of the SPEC system, and the advantages of pointing SPEC JDR judges.

The ad hoc special JDR program saved so much time, it became a permanent fixture in the Court of Queen's Bench. Our next chapter completes the picture with the advantages of SPEC from the perspective of the judge who did them full time and explains how and why they were successful.

Chapter 17

SPECIALIZED JDRs (SPECs)

A Look at Three Cases and the Impact
of the COVID-19 Pandemic

This chapter continues our discussion of JDR SPECs (Specialized JDRs) as described in Chapter 16 from the perspective of trial judges who do SPECs. We are interested in why judges might want to take on SPECs, which are unusually difficult JDR assignments.

SPEC JDRs started in Alberta around 2015 when the then-chief justice asked one of his experienced JDR judges to tackle some of the court's most difficult and time-consuming cases slated for several months' court time. In preparation for the SPEC JDR, the judge called the parties into open court to propose this special JDR and to help him create tailor-made procedures, such as identifying the most critical pieces of evidence and considering if the parties wanted a "minitrial" within the JDR. This collaborative approach, particular to each case, meant each SPEC had slightly different procedures. They took longer than typical JDR cases—running about three days—but like typical JDRs, the settlement rates were very high, exceeding 80 percent.

As discussed in the previous chapter, SPECs are directed at resolving complicated litigation involving parties who have been in a serious disagreement. Given the amount of work involved, why would a judge want to be assigned to such a case, or be added to a SPEC roster? The answer is not immediately apparent. First, such cases have probably been in litigation for many years, often including appeals and returns to trial court; the record can be voluminous. Some SPEC cases include upwards of 100,000 pages of discovery and written and oral depositions; a judge's workload can be quite onerous. Second, the preparation time required is extensive especially when complicated by the fact that jurisdictional lines have been crossed.

JDR has evolved to handle challenges like these, but the work depends on the abilities of the SPEC JDR judge. A SPEC process might involve both a hearing and a mediation, or both. SPECs are almost like conducting a mediation, negotiation and trial all at the same time. There are opening and closing statements as well as witness statements that can happen all at once, with none being available at the beginning of the trial. SPECs are time consuming and the energy required of the judge is substantial. The clients in these cases often hold entrenched positions; for some, at least at the outset, the shift to a SPEC JDR may be seen as nothing more than a postponement along their pathway to trial, something they have pursued for decades and spent millions of dollars on legal fees to achieve. All of this makes the SPEC JDR judge's job harder.

Nevertheless, SPECs appeal to some judges because helping parties reach a resolution—after a decade of delay—offers the judge and the parties great satisfaction. Parties find the experiences memorable by reaching a conclusion on their own; often times, they are mystified that a negotiated settlement is possible when for years there was no solution available. And, of course, they appreciate not having to continue paying counsel for extended trial work.

One of the huge procedural advantages of JDR SPEC as opposed to a normal JDR is that the judge has more control over his or her own schedule. That's appealing to many judges; time management is something judges lose control over the first day they are appointed. Because SPEC JDRs are totally unpredictable, judges need to maintain more flexible calendars; SPEC JDRs usually last two to three days, although sometimes they can go twice that long. The judge's time must be coordinated with multiple counsel and the parties' schedules, as well. A judge's assistant sets up intake and pre-SPEC meetings, assists online, assembles the documents needed to complete the mediation process, and ensures that resolution and Settlement Orders get filed at the end of the SPEC. Thus, the judge and assistant must have unprecedented scheduling flexibility to make SPEC JDR work. They face long hours; SPEC hearings start early and go late, often with the judge and staff getting little or no time off for lunch as they shuttle between caucuses, joint sessions and taking time to read additional documents. SPEC cases may also require time set aside for site visits or to hear expert evidence.

A new judge assigned exclusively to SPEC may lose some of the benefits of hearing a wide range of cases. Exposure over time to multiple legal areas and listening to parties arguing very different points of law are learning opportunities that build a judge's body of experience.

The SPEC roster allows JDR judges to specialize in the kinds of cases they take, unlike sitting judges who, once appointed, have very little control over the content of their schedule. SPEC judges may be criticized by their colleagues for being JDR "experts" in what is a general jurisdiction court—where all judges are expected to sit as equals in all areas. In fact, a SPEC JDR judge is no different from other judges who come to the bench having been career prosecutors or defense counsel to handle mostly criminal trials. The same is true for career civil trial lawyers who wind up judging long civil trials, or administrative law judges who go on to hear administrative decisions. On the bench, those judges can end up doing judicial reviews of tribunals. Put another way, specialized counsels who become judges often sit as specialized judges in the same areas in which they had worked. There is nothing unusual about this. Senior judges, for example, tend to sit in areas of their greatest strength, especially in their senior years.

One cannot underestimate the value of SPEC for judges. The majority of SPEC JDR judges, complicated as their cases are, usually see the parties reach a settlement. The satisfaction of seeing adversaries reach mutual agreements, gain control of their lives and shake hands—is something trial judges never see. These more than counteract the challenges of SPEC JDR.

Three SPEC Cases

The three cases described in the next few pages are based on actual court filings and were all resolved through SPEC JDR. The names and some facts were changed to ensure privacy and protect confidentiality.

Car crash

This case involved a man who had been involved in a car accident that resulted in paraplegia (loss of movement in his lower extremities and torso). Following the accident, he moved on with his life, working hard to develop new talents. He pursued a sport that he loved, curling, in a wheelchair, becoming so proficient that he won national matches. In time, he qualified for the Olympics where his team did very well, and he later became a coach and mentor for athletes across Canada.

Over the years he continued non-competitive curling, coaching and even had a small rink built in his backyard. To visit friends, he drove his specially equipped truck which allowed him to steer and brake with his hands. Life was as good as he could make it.

One day, while sitting at a red light in his truck, another vehicle hit him from behind causing neck and upper body injuries. He joined friends on a long trip that weekend, but subsequently experienced nerve and shoulder pain throughout his upper body. After seeing several specialists and a lawyer, he filed suit against the owner of the vehicle that rear-ended him.

The driver of the vehicle had moved out of the country, but never denied his responsibility for the collision and agreed it was more than just a fender bender. The defendant gave a statement indicating that he hit the back of the plaintiff's vehicle at about thirty kilometers per hour. The insurance company defended on behalf of the driver, mainly arguing that anyone hurt that badly would never have taken on a long trip.

The litigation began and the attorneys established the battle lines and tried to get to trial. During the pre-trial period, a variety of depositions were taken but few offers were exchanged. The pending litigation became increasingly costly and emotionally and mentally challenging for the plaintiff. On the defendant's side, frustration grew as privately gathered evidence (post-accident) did not, in their mind, support the complex injury claims alleged in the lawsuits. The trial docket was full, and more time passed. The plaintiff became so depressed that he quit curling. He did join a group that enjoyed bowling, but he quit the sport he loved.

The judge assigned to this SPEC case recognized that, like most long trials, the parties had been in a holding pattern for quite some time—almost a decade. Because of the extended delay, the case became a candidate for special resolution.

At the pre-SPEC intake meetings, the judge asked counsel for JDR briefs and any critical evidence he should read to understand the interests of the parties. On request, the plaintiff produced medical records documenting his injuries that were corroborated by statements from his family and close friends. They all said that once he quit curling, his life changed for the worse.

On the other hand, the defendant's insurance company stressed the plaintiff's pre-existing injuries and produced surveillance videos of him driving to and from bowling, meeting friends and grocery shopping. The defendant asserted that the footage discredited the plaintiff's upper body complaints and claims of complications following the rear-end accident.

During the first day of the SPEC, the plaintiff and his counsel were surprised and quite upset with the extensive, professional—and likely costly—surveillance evidence. They were doubtful the insurance company would pay any damages, let alone those that might help him rekindle his interest in leaving his house for bowling or curling. As the SPEC process began, however, with the judge requiring the insurance company to release the entirety of the footage, the videos took a back seat to determining what parties actually wanted. The judge allowed more time so all they could all view the videos in their entirety, and he urged the parties to think about what would work to get them to a settlement.

The parties realized that the litigation had already cost them much more than they had imagined it would, and a trial would dramatically increase those costs. They asked the SPEC judge if he would make the result of the JDR binding: if the mediation was not successful, the judge would make a final decision. He agreed, but in doing so, revealed his personal approach—to continue to mediate as if nothing had changed. The judge also noted that he had never made a final binding decision in a JDR in eleven years; every case he had mediated had settled consensually.

This case settled too, and while each side got about half of what they were seeking, the plaintiff received one hundred thousand dollars (paid to him within days of the SPEC) that allowed him to upgrade his curling rink—something he had wanted to do for some years—and to make needed repairs to his truck. The insurance company was satisfied with the file closed and a settlement consistent with the limit they had set initially. Both sides avoided the cost of trial—which covered most of the insurance company's settlement costs. The defendants seemed happy not only for the insurance company, but for the plaintiff as well.

Ski accident

This SPEC JDR case involved a professional skier who perished after a collision on the slopes. Prior to the accident he had—for reasons not previously understood by his doctors—begun taking medication prescribed by his psychiatrist for hallucinations. The medicine had side effects that included occasional thoughts of suicide.

On the day in question, according to witnesses, he was skiing normally and then started swerving for no reason, turning off the path and colliding with a tree. He was pronounced dead at the scene. The ski patrol that investigated concluded that he had run into the tree on purpose.

The skier left behind a mourning wife and two children. They sued the ski resort for its failure to properly identify and maintain the terrain, and others for professional negligence.

The ski resort, claiming the plaintiff contributed to his own negligence, felt confident they would win at trial. During the discovery process and document production, they realized they were protected by contractual interpretation in the plaintiff's ski coverage. Exceptions to coverage were exclusions for "going out of bounds" as well as "participating in any sport while taking prescription medications." Hearing this, the family was disheartened, assuming there would be no recovery at all, when they really needed the money.

This lawsuit became part of a SPEC JDR somewhat inadvertently. A senior judge would have to hear the trial and decide the matter because of the many different claims that were going to be raised at trial (e.g., contractual interpretations and several unique circumstances of negligence). As is typical with SPEC, the trial itself was calendared as lengthy because of the number of witnesses and legal issues facing the judge.

On the day of the SPEC, several counsel and clients attended including some from out of province. The defendants' attorneys strongly opposed any settlement—at least while they were in the same room—but, as is his usual practice, the judge separated the clients. During these agreed-upon caucusing sessions in private rooms, it became clear to the judge that speaking to counsel and clients separately yielded very different findings. (One wanted to protect a client's reputation; another did not want a bad precedent and at the same time really did not want to pay trial costs given the uncertainty about the result.)

The case resolved successfully, litigation costs came to an end, and the defense was thankful to avoid setting a precedent. The judge thanked the parties for reaching a settlement and noticed that the family was in tears. He imposed a moment of silence so the family could regain its composure and then waited a bit longer, not knowing what to say. The plaintiffs broke the silence and thanked the judge and insurance company for a result they never believed possible at trial. They finally had the funds they needed, and while it was just under half of what they had hoped for—about $100,000—they were grateful and had the money in their hands in a matter of days.

Plastic surgery

The final case involved plastic surgery that went terribly wrong. The plaintiff, a woman in her mid-thirties, had wanted surgery since birth for congenital impairments as well as cosmetic concerns. Over the years, she and her family took considerable time selecting a plastic surgeon, wanting the best in Canada.

On the day of the surgery, everything seemed to go well except for some post-surgical bleeding that the doctor felt was of no major consequence. He re-opened the surgical site to cauterize and stop the bleeding. However, he did so rather quickly, without talking to the woman's family and getting further consent for the additional surgery. The doctor said he wanted to stop what appeared to be normal surgical bleeding.

Post-surgery, the plaintiff still had issues with her appearance and functioning, neither of which had been improved. Acutely self-conscious, she quit work, moved in with her family, and avoided all social interactions, believing she would never marry or have normal relationships.

Eventually, the plaintiff and her family deemed the surgery a total failure and sued the doctor. They alleged not only professional negligence during the operation, but also failure to get her consent for the second surgery.

The doctor defended on the grounds that the surgery was appropriate given the congenital obstacles; the post-surgical intervention was necessary to stop the bleeding; and that he followed professional standards for that type of sensitive surgery. Confronted with the allegation of negligence (because he made semicircular incisions that were far larger than ever contemplated), he claimed these were absolutely necessary because of the unusual physiology of the plaintiff. He further argued that he was a fully competent surgeon, that no other specialists were needed to undertake the procedure, and he did not agree with the plaintiff's allegation that her physical appearance represented improper surgical procedures.

During the SPEC mediation, the judge immediately recognized the plaintiff's deep emotional pain and trauma created by the surgical scars. Relatively quickly, he realized that she sought an apology as part of the process. She believed the doctor's position would always be upheld and that no settlement could ever obviate the awful and costly process of litigation (especially depositions) that had felt degrading and caused her further emotional distress.

After working though intense sessions with each side, the case settled. The amount (half of the plaintiff's best possible outcome at trial, but still a seven-figure settlement) restored the plaintiff's belief that people can be compassionate, and that litigation can have a positive conclusion, painful though it may be. In addition, the plaintiff avoided spending hundreds of thousands of dollars to prosecute a claim of professional negligence.

Why would a Judge Prefer to do SPEC JDRs over Her Normal Caseload?

As we have discussed, SPECs can be rewarding for the JDR judge, but they are challenging—emotionally and otherwise—and the differences with trial are notable. A trial judge gets nothing at the beginning of a trial except Pleadings, Agreed Statements of Fact, or Admissions (hopefully), and Exhibit books to be entered in due course. There is nothing to read, but as evidence is provided along the way, there are rulings on evidence and a lot of findings to which the judge must apply the law. Mostly, trial work is relatively straightforward because a judge can sit back and let the attorneys do the heavy lifting. For long trials, this means the judge gets to do nothing but listen and decide.

A JDR SPEC judge cannot just listen from the dais, but rather interacts constantly with all the parties. So, given an already busy court schedule, why would a judge prefer to do a SPEC assignment, especially full time? She has to prepare extensively, continually engage all parties, take notes, generate settlement options and put herself between people who do not like each other.

Judges who do SPECs are those with a considerable ADR background either in private practice or elsewhere like agency, board, or commission work. They know how to solve litigation problems by involving the parties early, before the case gets to trial.

Thus, a SPEC judge sees her new assignment as a return to resolving problems instead of deciding who was right and who was wrong. She has a normal predisposition to settle cases as opposed to making rulings, "calling balls and strikes" or creating precedents.

SPEC judges care very little about *stare decisis*; they measure their success in terms of helping parties settle cases and move on with their lives. These judges consider themselves fortunate to be doing SPECS full time.

How did the COVID-19 Pandemic Present SPEC Opportunities?

Though SPEC assignments began years before the pandemic, they grew even more important as trial time became even more precious than before. As court hearings were temporarily suspended, SPECs became quite popular. Litigating parties were told to stay home. Trials and motions adjourned. Parties and attorneys (for health reasons and later for legal prohibitions) could not meet in courtrooms. These restrictions applied to judges and their staff, sheriffs, clerks, assistants and many others. COVID closed the courthouse, but SPECs continued into the new isolated world of online Judicial Dispute Resolution (OJDR). As described in Chapter 19, mediation blossomed.

At first, remote hearings, motions and even remote SPEC JDRs moved slowly. Counsel, parties and others were afraid of doing something wrong. A few months after COVID started, SPEC hearings gained significant traction. For the SPEC judge and his assistant, after a brief pandemic pause, there was burgeoning enthusiasm for JDR. Their bookings became overwhelming as word got out in the legal community. In fact, during the summer of 2020, the SPEC judge's assistant booked seventy-two SPEC or pre-SPEC JDR hearings for a single SPEC judge, from June through September. Even though some were continuations, the settlement rate at the end of the summer was very high. With non-settling matters being adjourned for further dates, with "homework" still to do, the SPEC judge pressed parties to solve problems based on new out-of-the-box thinking about how they might work together, with or without him. As the months rolled on, SPEC JDR settlement rates ended up around 90 percent.

Conclusion

During the SPEC process, before and after COVID, judges and their assistants collected feedback using surveys and keeping personal notes. Their experience and the survey results suggest that SPECs are successful because they are (1) fast; (2) flexible; (3) provide a form of social justice; and (4) deepen the court's commitment to resolution. We are left with these conclusions:

(1) In Alberta, the court can get parties into a pre-SPEC meeting with a judge in just a couple of weeks. The exchanges of complex mediation briefs can be accomplished in one or two months.
(2) Once the pre-SPEC meeting happens, parties may need some time to get organized. By having total booking freedom (for the SPEC JDR judge), the pressure of litigation decreases and deadlines and hearings can follow a realistic timeline, based not so much on court pressures but on what works best for all the parties.

(3) All lawsuits can participate (not just civil), and all people are potential candidates for SPEC. During COVID, even smaller cases (one- to two-week trials) qualified for SPECs, rather than the usual three- to four-week trials. Parties are begging to be heard and being contacted by the judge—as opposed to hearing everything through their lawyer. This gives them a sense that their interests are being taken seriously. Further, travel is not an issue, so resolution is possible wherever the internet is available.

OJDR offers a new reality and many possibilities. Platforms such as OJDR create a more level playing field; parties may participate without representation even if they have limited financial resources. While most SPEC parties are represented by counsel, it is not a precondition of an ordinary JDR, SPEC JDR, or OJDR.

Participating in OJDR involves substantially less pressure than being in an actual courtroom. Almost everyone has access to video technology, and most have had some experience using it and can participate from their own home. Even for documentary and video evidence, SPEC's remote hearings resonate with an increasingly technologically sophisticated society that has learned how to use cloud computing, picture storage and wireless devices.

(4) Parties are impressed with the court's commitment to the JDR process. It is common for a SPEC judge to tell parties he will sit on Saturdays or evenings, an otherwise unusual commitment that pleases parties and counsel. Sitting late is a trade-off for the increased flexibility—offered by the SPEC judges' cleared schedules—to arrange the dates as they see fit.

In summary, SPEC JDR offers a major payoff for the court and for society. In Alberta, within the first few months of COVID, the time saved by resolved litigation added up to over one whole *year* of trial time! Further, there were substantial financial benefits due to reduced operating costs—no court clerks, sheriffs, court reporters and so on—especially during a time of economic turmoil. More importantly, the public's sense of social justice was strengthened by the parties' increased control over the timing, management and outcome of litigation. The attorneys still have a role, but JDR gives the parties much more control.

Chapter 18

HOW TO PREPARE FOR AND WHAT TO DO DURING A JDR

The Power Pole Case

Signing up for JDR is easy; preparing for the mediation itself takes real work. Counsel and their clients need to be ready. All sides need to know what kind of briefs are required. Will the lawyers be expected to make traditional legal arguments? How will the judge start the JDR? Will the judge expect the parties to base their arguments on legal precedent? Should counsel reveal their best offer to the judge at the outset? If not, when?

The Power Pole Case provides a provisional set of answers to these questions. We describe the ways in which the judge and the parties interacted during the JDR. From there, we shift to a series of eighteen tips that can help lawyers and their clients prepare properly for JDR, drawn from our study of *The Well Fire Case*, *The Negligent Land Transfer Case*, and *The Medical Malpractice Case*—all three of which are also presented in the book's Appendix.

The Power Pole Case

On a spring day in the late 1990s, three individuals drove a grain feed truck on or near the Happy Valley Farm Ltd. in central Alberta. The truck was mounted with an unloading auger which, when extended, moved feed out of the truck bed through its spiral shaft. While driving underneath power lines, the still-extended auger—usually retracted during transport—collided with the lines, damaging them. Happy Valley hired a journeyman electrician to repair the damage. To access the lines, he climbed a nearby power pole that suddenly broke and fell on top of him.

As a result of the fall, he fractured his left pelvis and right elbow, and suffered major contusions and additional minor injuries requiring several surgeries and extensive physical therapy. On top of the expenses and lost income related to medical care and rehabilitation, as well as the damages associated with his pain and suffering, he alleged that his injuries inhibited his ability to perform basic household tasks, leaving him dependant on the assistance of others. Further, he claimed that the lasting effects of his injuries would make it impossible for him to fully compete with his healthy coworkers, disadvantaging him professionally and limiting his opportunities for future advancement. Because his injuries were sustained on the job, he received some disability benefits from the Workplace Compensation Board (WCB), a provincial agency responsible for administering disability insurance. These benefits were limited, however, and terminated several months after the accident.

Seeking to recover damages, the electrician sued Happy Valley, claiming that the farm, as owner of the property on which the power pole stood, had been negligent in ensuring the premises were reasonably safe for visitors. In particular, their failure to inspect the pole, take necessary steps to ensure its safety, and to warn or advise the electrician of the risk, led to his injuries. In total, he claimed nearly $7 million in damages.

With this background in mind, how did the judge begin the JDR, and how did each side present its arguments?

Prior to the non-binding JDR session, the parties (which included the electrician, his lawyer, Happy Valley's lawyers, as well as a WCB adjuster), filed JDR briefs with the JDR judge. These briefs articulated fairly rigid positions similar to those an attorney would present in court. Based on these briefs, the judge prepared a Scott Schedule. The reference is to George Scott, a Referee of the UK High Court of Justice who developed a helpful format for summarizing all of the issues that need to be decided in a case and the position of each of the parties on each issue.[1]

On the day of the case, the judge invited the parties to present fifteen- to twenty-minute opening statements. He explained that beyond arguing their legal theory of the case, this was an opportunity to explain why the case was important to them in personal terms. Following the opening statements, the judge said that he would allow clarifying questions, but not arguments. One of the lawyers indicated afterwards that a broader range of responses was actually permitted. The injured plaintiff was allowed to "get things off his chest" and ensure that the other side heard what he had to say.

This particular judge did not like emphasizing legal arguments in JDR. He put the parties in separate groups and shuttled between them. Like most JDR judges, he did not tell the parties his view of the case; he kept asking questions in an effort to help them discover grounds for a possible settlement. He avoided a discussion of possible precedents. Our research team pieced together the following story:

After an initial opportunity for the parties to talk among themselves, the judge began a private discussion with the plaintiff. At this stage, he avoided providing his own assessment of the case, and instead went back and forth between the parties, a stage characterized as "shuttle diplomacy." One of the lawyers explained: "A good mediation justice will let them go through the process," and organically adjust their expectations. The judge said the Scott Schedule allowed him to identify where disagreements persisted. Though the judge initially refrained from providing his own assessment of the case, he stated that—as is usual in his mediation experience—the initial discussion did not move them far beyond their initial positions. He then began to "reality test" their assumptions by offering opinions as to whether their requests seemed realistic or fair. None of the individuals involved mentioned invocation of specific precedents during this phase. In fact, there seemed to be a general reluctance to invoke them for fear of falling back into positional bargaining.

---

1. See *Cornelius Grey Construction v. Folz*, 2018 ONSC 647 (Canlii), para 18, footnote 4.

As with most JDRs, this one was a success. The judge stayed neutral, asked questions, tested how strongly committed the parties were to their opening positions, and knew how to use precedents without making them the focus. Our research team, reported the following:

When testing the assumptions of the parties during the session, the judge was an impartial authority. For example, when he began to question the size of some of the plaintiff's damage claims, his experience with similar disputes and the general aura of respect that surrounds the judiciary provided credibility that would not necessarily have been accorded to a non-judge mediator.

The parties' initial briefs and opening arguments appeared to be the part of the JDR most laden with precedent. Past cases can reinforce initial positions and inform what is considered fair, but prior results can also block the emergence of a tailored resolution. It seemed that much of the judge's work was aimed at disentangling the parties from their initial positions (based on the precedents cited by their lawyers) and getting them to focus on the facts and needs of each side. When one side's demands seemed particularly high, he spoke to the lawyers separately and quietly invoked relevant precedents, urging counsel to bring their demands into more realistic territory.

We also learn the importance of preparing for opening statements from this case:

"Articulating what happened and how he was injured in his opening statements not only proved cathartic for the plaintiff, it increased the WCB adjuster's sympathy for him and led to a resumption of his benefits. His lawyer suggested this short-term decision may have been more valuable to his client than his share of the final settlement."

The following nineteen tips will help attorneys and parties through the JDR process.

1. Be clear that you are booking a JDR to *resolve* the case, and not to "kick the litigation tires." A judge will not be impressed if the parties or counsel are merely using a JDR to get a preview of the evidence the other side intends to present or to gauge the weaknesses of their arguments. If the JDR unfolds in that direction, the judge is likely to quickly end it and send the matter to trial. Judges may or may not even want to see the formal pleadings (Complaint/Answer). They prefer the details of the lawsuit, as important as they are, to be part of the introductory narrative. Most attorneys wrongly start a JDR by stating their client's high end or legal position. The JDR judge will not welcome this approach because it inevitably leads into a "zero-sum" trap, also called "distributive negotiation"—a win/lose game where each side's gain is the other's loss.

2. Make sure to ask questions of the JDR judge (through his or her assistant); the sooner the better! The judge will want you to think about the steps and some of the fundamental elements in the JDR process: (a) preparing for the first meeting; (b) understanding the roles the judge will play; (c) knowing whether the judge will offer opinions (yes, if BJDR); (d) knowing whether the mediation will be recorded (it is usually not); (e) being aware that the judge will expect to hear from the client, not just the lawyer, during the opening; (f) asking the judge how much time he or she wants for their opening comments; (g) asking the judge how he or she expects to probe the interests of the two sides and whether there will be caucusing; and (h)

asking the judge how he or she expects to sort out facts that are in disagreement to establish common ground.

3. Confirm that the client will be at the pre-JDR meeting ready to talk about their view of the case. If that is not possible, be sure the client has written answers to all of the questions the judge is likely to ask. If there are new client questions arising from conversation with the judge, promise to send written answers before the JDR starts. Both the attorney and client must be prepared when the JDR opens; the judge surely will be. In *The Medical Malpractice Case*, both lawyers noted that their justice understood the importance of "getting into the weeds" of the case. She made this clear in her detailed and probing questions about the facts, strength of the evidence, and legal arguments. Knowing in advance that the justice operated in a highly efficient and evidence-based manner encouraged the parties to come into the JDR well aware of their bottom-line numbers and the principled reasons supporting them. The parties' lawyers appreciated and complied with the justice's emphasis on principled rather than positional negotiation.

4. Parties always want to know what JDR materials they are required to send to the court. The judge's pre-JDR letter and/or meeting will make this clear; follow the judge's advice. (See Appendix 1 at the end of this chapter for a pre-JDR judge's letter.) Your attorney's submissions per the judge's normal direction should set out the factual background of the case and include relevant case references. The main focus, however, should be on the fact that this is a judicial settlement meeting, not a meeting to make a point of law—though the law may certainly be relevant to certain interests. The judge will want to know your side's real interests and want to hear options for resolving the issues in your lawsuit.

5. If the judge wants to know anything confidential, like settlement positions or your sense of your BATNA (or even previous informal or formal offers) you can send these privately to the judge or the judge's assistant. All your *other* submissions will always be copied to opposing counsel. It is important *not* to file anything with the court clerk; JDR meetings are private, while anything filed with the clerk is public (unless a judge seals the materials).

When filing submissions, make sure you let the judge know if expert reports will also be included (again, not to be filed with the clerk, but with the judge's assistant). These additional reports must meet the court and judge's rules related to filing deadlines.

Let the judge know if you would like expert(s) to attend the JDR. JDR meetings accommodate expert opinions but treat them less formally than in court. If experts attend a JDR, there is less rigorous cross-examination, but there is certainly the opportunity for questioning if the parties and judge set up the JDR that way.

The Well Fire Case did not rely heavily on expert testimony and other technical expertise that, at trial, might have played a key role. At trial, the plaintiff and the defense would have presented their own expert testimony about oil well safety, proper equipment and vapor storage, firefighting preparedness, and other matters relevant to determining each party's responsibility for the damage. The experts would then have been subject to cross-examination. Ultimately, the judge would weigh the expert testimony, assess the credibility of the witnesses, and issue a decision and appropriate damages.

In contrast, the JDR process allows each party to submit a written expert report highlighting key sections that support their positions. Typically, there is neither in-person expert testimony through which the JDR judge might assess credibility, nor a formal mechanism used for asking clarifying questions. Primarily, it is the written document and each party's brief that shapes the judge's assessment of the relative merits of each side's claims. The judge uses these documents to develop a Scott Schedule, designed to "try and hit the high points" of a case to ensure that each judge understands the core issues in a case without getting bogged down in the technical minutiae.

On the point of disclosing offers, some judges want this information while others do not. *The Medical Malpractice Case* revealed one judge's practice with regard to offers:

> Before the JDR session, the justice meets briefly with the plaintiff and defense counsels to review the facts of the case. She asked if the parties had any prior settlement discussions, and if not, she tells them to return to the JDR once they have. If the parties have already engaged in settlement discussions, she asks them to disclose their last offers. Sometimes during this conversation, a lawyer will disclose that his client knows that their last settlement offer is not realistic. This helps the justice determine where she needs to put her energy in working toward settlement during the JDR.

And the same judge, with a lot of bench experience, did not want or need any precedents to be filed (see Chapter 14 for a full discussion of the limitations of precedents). For example, the plaintiff's attorney noted that because the justice had experience litigating and adjudicating cases involving medical malpractice and insurance payouts, the justice had a general sense of the ballpark of damages for the specific injury that Smith had suffered. The justice therefore did not pressure the plaintiff to settle for an exceptionally low number—something that had happened to the plaintiff's attorney in other JDR sessions.

6. The question almost always arises about the appropriate length of JDR submissions. Most judges expect around ten to twenty pages; any more than that would necessitate asking the judge or the judge's assistant ahead of time. You will not be filing submissions with the clerk of the court; again, that would make everything public. "Filing submissions" means sending them electronically or in hard copy to the JDR judge and opposing counsel. Some counsel adhere closely to the page limit to avoid being at a disadvantage. Prior to *The Negligent Land Transfer Case* JDR, each party filed a mediation brief with the judge laying out their legal positions. One counsel noted that the briefs were not required, but "if you don't do it, you're at a severe disadvantage." The plaintiff's counsel stated that the judge walked into the room fully briefed and prepared for the complexities of the conflict.

7. Talk with your client about developing possible settlement options. Let them know this is what the JDR judge will be doing as she searches for mutually acceptable trades. Explain that the judge will expect the parties to help with this.

8. Just how informal is the JDR? Whether the venue is a board room or courtroom office, business attire is expected—and so is your comfort. JDR's informality allows parties to have a beverage, unlike in a court room, but do ask the judge's assistant if you can bring a snack or sandwich because you will probably be working through lunch. Without the judge's permission, the sheriff may not let you bring food into the court's boardroom. Cell phones should be off, but unlike in courtrooms, you can bring cell phones to the JDR and use them if necessary. To be sure, however, check with the judge's assistant. Lastly, it is not mandatory to call the judge "your honor," or rise when the judge enters the boardroom. The judge will not be wearing robes at the JDR.

9. You will need to know if the JDR is binding or non-binding. This question will be discussed with the opposing side. If binding, let the judge know so he or she can send you their BJDR agreement.

10. Feel free to ask the judge during the pre-JDR meeting whether there will be caucusing, and, if so, how the judge will conduct the sessions. You especially want to find out whether the judge favors an evaluative or a facilitative approach to mediation. Here is a bit more detail on the judge's approach to caucusing in *The Medical Malpractice Case*:

   The JDR officially began with the justice addressing the parties together for a brief introduction to the process. For the remaining time together, she almost exclusively caucused with each party and their lawyers. These conversations were confidential, but at times she encouraged parties to share information with each other, especially if there was information asymmetry; she feels that balancing it out brings the parties closer to settlement. This justice also stated that it can be more effective for a party to hear the "bad news" about the case directly from the other side rather than through their lawyer, which could make them feel that their lawyer is not fully on their side. Thus, she was not only highly conscious of the need to reality-check the parties, but also on focusing on the multiple relationships in play, and which source of information each party might find most credible.

   At her initial meetings with each side, the justice asked the parties to recount their experiences, requesting from the plaintiff, ".... a snapshot of yourself before the accident, versus now." She also drilled down on specifics: How did the plaintiff know "x"? How did "y" feel? Her goal was to get to know the parties, build rapport, and get a sense of how they would fare as a witness at trial and how sharp their recall is. If a party seemed to be a poor historian, the justice may say: "I have a sense from the ten minutes that we talked that you find it difficult to go through dates and times and places." She cautions that remembering dates while testifying is a necessary part of trial, and a trial might be especially stressful if a party has trouble calling up details. She did ask the lawyer to tell their client as candidly as possible how they thought he will fare at trial.

   The justice also worked with each party to make a list of issues that would be important if the case went to trial, such as negligence, standard of care, different types of damages, etc. She asked the lawyer for a summary of what they would say at trial about standard of care and what they thought the best and worst parts of the case would be at trial. Lawyers are often reluctant to discuss the weaker parts of the case in front of their client, which makes this exercise even more useful as a reality test.

If the justice noticed that an issue was particularly weak for one side after holding caucuses, she shared her reaction with that party. The purpose of caucusing is to provide parties with a structured way to analyze the strengths and weaknesses of their case; to correct information asymmetries that are barriers to settlement; and to weigh the costs and benefits of going to trial over settling.

11. Should you contact witnesses, and will they appear at a JDR? The answer for either fact or expert witnesses depends on the JDR judge and how time is allocated. But if both sides use the *same* witness (as has happened) be sure to coordinate with the other side as well as the judge to ensure the neutrality of the witness's opinion. If there are many witnesses—in BJDRs, specifically—ask the judge how to handle the flow and timing. A popular option is to have "will say" statements or even affidavits or statutory declarations. In complex JDRs (SPECs) it is common to have dozens of witnesses that may need to have their statements incorporated into the JDR.

12. Who should speak to the judge, and where will counsel seat their client? Most judges prefer to speak directly to clients, not counsel, and thus it is better to seat the clients closest to the judge. The judge will probe issues in a forthright manner, including the client's emotional state, which reflects upon their ability to be candid. Don't be surprised to see the judge try and balance hearing from each side equally.

13. Should you make an opening statement at the beginning of the JDR to summarize your side's view of the case? There are pros and cons: in a divorce case where custody is an issue, for example, an opening statement focused on the best interests of the children, as opposed to denigrating the other parent, may be a good thing. Further, hearing from each side in front of the other unmasks perspectives that may not be known—and not covered in the court filings. *The Well Fire Case* describes one perspective on opening statements:

At the start of the JDR session, the judge asked the lawyers for opening statements that laid out their positions. One attorney noted to us that such statements may bring up feelings, but he tries to keep his emotions in check. "Sometimes it just pisses you off … but you never want to look angry because the whole point of the meeting is to settle, and you don't settle by being obnoxious." Each party also had a chance to speak, and though some of them said they had nothing to add, others shared how the case had affected them emotionally, professionally, or financially. The attorneys noted that such moments can be cathartic for the parties and add a human element to negotiations.

14. Be careful not to move to agreement too soon. Talk out all of the issues and explore settlement options until you and the judge are satisfied there is no more value that can be added to the agreement.

15. This may seem obvious, but always make sure the client who attends has full authority to settle.

16. The judge will expect the clients to give instructions to settle; it is their decision and their choice. The judge will expect counsel's help in analyzing and reviewing the settlement for legal issues.

17. It is okay to ask the JDR judge for a time out if emotions are getting out of hand or a party needs time to ask counsel for advice.

18. Do you need the final settlement to be in a court order? Depending on the history of the parties (and other matters), sometimes you do. Here are observations from *The Negligent Land Transfer Case* where emotions ran quite high:

   Though the JDR was non-binding, the agreement did result in a court order. All the parties concurred that the agreement should be memorialized in this way and kept in the judge's file so that the parties could not, as the judge said, "go behind it." Given the low level of trust between the parties—particularly after the Walker defendants allegedly reneged on the 2007 land transfer agreement—all felt that filing the decision as a court order was prudent. This is a situation in which an agreement made with a judge in the room, rather than one negotiated in a private mediation, may have been more beneficial for the parties. After the fallout from betrayals stemming from a private contract, the parties were only confident in their settlement because it had the official backing of the judiciary.

19. What will the judge do with all the materials collected the once the JDR is over? The court will shred them. You may want to keep copies on file for your own purposes.

These nineteen points may be summarized as follows: The judge will attend the JDR and will want to meet and get to know the clients. He will speak to them directly and work diligently with lawyers and clients to tailor-make the JDR procedures to reach an agreeable settlement. JDR judges work extremely hard to ensure they are familiar with the facts and materials and ask attorneys and their clients to do the same. They do not want to argue at the JDR about who is right and wrong as a matter of law; their goal is to work jointly with all parties to create a reasonable solution for everyone involved. This confidential JDR meeting will be your only opportunity to work with a judge who, in this creative role, will be looking for mutually acceptable trades in settling this case. A judge will be settling the case so your file can be closed and the litigating parties can move on with their lives. With help from the parties, the judge will be making any court orders necessary to give effect to the settlement reached.

We are envisioning a new paradigm in the legal profession, one which will force lawyers to become dialogical beings responsive to the context, not inferential beings responsive to the inferences of rules, principles, and standards. The most general advice for JDR may be: conduct yourself as if you are having a dialogue with somebody who is collaborating with you to solve a problem satisfactorily and efficiently—and as if you are being watched by a judge.

Chapter 18 Appendix 1: Judge's pre-JDR Letter to Parties

<date>
Addresses and emails of Attorneys
Dear Counsel:
Re: (specify binding or non-binding) Judicial Dispute Resolution
[Set out date, time and place]
Reference: [set out name of case A *versus* B]
Action Number: [set out the formal action number]

In preparation for our JUDICIAL DISPUTE RESOLUTION Conference on the above-noted date, kindly ensure that you each provide me with the following:

1. A brief synopsis of the facts, not to exceed 10 pages.
2. A list of the issues in this action - and any that have been agreed upon.
3. The relief that is sought by the parties, under separate headings where appropriate. (See paragraph seven below.)
4. If relevant, the expert's reports or opinions that you are relying upon to substantiate your client's perspective of this matter. Please highlight the most persuasive portions of these reports if you are submitting them to me and mark the highlighted pages with tabs.
5. *If* it affects your proposed settlement, please provide copies of the significant case law upon which you will be relying and why the cases include procedural or substantive matters that may affect the settlement. Ensure the relevant portions are highlighted and tabbed.
6. Costs are not normally negotiated as both sides pay their own. If Costs are relevant, a Bill of Costs must be included in your materials.
7. Please bring to the JDR your *options* for settlement. It helps me if you provide your best/least favorable options for each issue in the lawsuit. Feel free to summarize this in a table format. For each issue in the lawsuit, be prepared to discuss the other side's position with me. Additionally, I will not discuss your alternatives to settlement with the other side because that is confidential. If you are already aware of the other side's settlement proposal(s), I will ask you to explain why you do *not* prefer the other side's options but more importantly, be prepared to give me your corresponding proposal that would be better within the context of the issues raised in the lawsuit. As the JDR progresses, I will work with all sides to improve these alternatives. Finally, the information in this paragraph should be provided *confidentially* to me.
8. Any other material deemed critical to settlement of the case.

The information requested is not intended to be presented in any formal fashion nor is it intended to require the kind of extensive briefs that are normally associated with a trial, mini-trial, or special application.

I would request these materials to be delivered to my office [give address] *unfiled*, no later than [give date]

If parties have any questions, we can address them at the pre-JDR meeting. Meantime, I have enclosed some draft guidelines to better acquaint you and your clients with the process. Keep in mind these guidelines are intended to be flexible to accommodate each individual case and can be varied as counsel or their clients' desire. Please ensure that your clients attend this JDR and have full monetary authority to settle for different amounts from those set out in your JDR briefs.

Thank you for your attention to these matters.

Yours very truly,

[Judge's name]

Encl.

Chapter 18 Appendix 2: JDR Guidelines

1. The purpose of judicial dispute resolution is to reach a settlement on all issues, or to resolve as many issues as possible with the assistance of a judge of this court.

2. Generally, all counsel and parties must agree in advance to the JDR.

3. If you have any questions about the JDR, contact the judge's assistant who will work with the trial coordinator to give you an exact date. When finished, the results of the JDR and/or court order will be provided to the trial coordinator (unless the order is sealed by the judge).

4. Your JDR judge will arrange through his assistant to have a pre—JDR meeting. At that meeting, you will discuss with the judge materials and procedures required for the JDR. Counsel and parties may request that a judge provide an opinion or decide, but that is not done without consent and usually never done at the beginning of a JDR.

5. Counsel must have parties or representatives at the JDR with full authority to make any settlement decisions.

6. All parties to the JDR must participate in good faith in reaching a resolution of the lawsuit.

7. The JDR will normally be conducted in a board or conference room setting. Gowning is not required.

8. The JDR process is confidential. Statements made by counsel or parties are confidential and without prejudice and cannot be used for any purpose or referred to at trial, should the matter proceed to trial. After the JDR, all briefs, submissions, notes and papers in the judge's possession will be destroyed.

9. Unless the parties consent, and in the unlikely event the JDR is unsuccessful, the judge will not hear any applications or here the trial of this matter.

10. During the JDR, parties and their counsel may meet privately, with or without the judge. If the judge meets privately with them, anything said by a party or counsel to the judge and confidence will remain confidential and will not be disclosed to the other party unless the confidentiality of the communication has clearly been waived.

11. The only document which will survive a successful JDR will be a court order or memorandum of settlement. Various terms of the settlement agreement may require consent orders, discontinuances, releases or other documents that will be prepared and filed by counsel in consultation with the JDR judge.

12. The JDR judge is non-compellable as a witness in any proceedings related to this lawsuit.

Chapter 19

THE NEW WORLD OF ONLINE DISPUTE RESOLUTION (OJDR)

Introduction to the Technology

Decades ago, the internet "started the fire" of online dispute resolution (ODR) and the COVID-19 crisis poured gas on it (American Arbitration Association 2003). The expansion of communication provided by the internet has created more disputes, while offering unexplored ways of resolving them. Though ODR has been criticized as a distortion of traditional face-to-face encounters, it has become widely popular in the last thirty years not as an alternative to in-person dispute resolution, but as the default setting.

Online judicial dispute resolution (OJDR) offers a blend of dispute resolution and digital justice. ODR consists of the application of information and communications technology to prevention, management and resolution of disputes. Digital justice requires an understanding of the role of law, legal processes and institutional design. New arrangements in each of these areas have enabled individuals to resolve and prevent disputes using digital technology. ODR and digital justice have a lot in common, but one difference is that ODR is commonly extended to private providers, while digital justice is offered only by judicial authorities or public officials entrusted by the law.

The growth of technology over just the last few decades is remarkable. In the words of Richard Susskind:

> [s]ince [the 1980s] there have been breathtaking advances in video and related technologies. While the most sophisticated systems, such as immersive telepresence, create a remarkable sense of being gathered together (…) even more modest systems, running as basic apps on laptops and handhelds (for example, Skype and FaceTime) enable a very high level of interaction. Systems that, technologically speaking, sit between telepresence and mobile phone video–telephony, are widely installed in courts across the world (Susskind 2019).

Susskind felt the newer technology plus never-ending human desire to resolve legal battles via ADR would lead us to a point where parties will design their own dispute resolution systems. At least this was the aim of the ODR pioneers (Susskind 2019). But are we there yet? And, if so, how did we get to the point where ODR has become one of the main options for disputing parties?

An International History and Comparisons of Models

The first example of ODR was in 1982 at Carnegie Mellon University when faculty were informed through a digital message board that an oil spill had occurred (Katsh and Rabinovich-Einy 2017). When a faculty member, Scott E. Fahlman, realized the message was intended as joke, he wrote: "I propose the following character sequence for joke markers: :-)." This was the first instance of ODR and perhaps the first emoticon ever used; digital technology to prevent future conflicts in the virtual environment (Katsh and Rabinovich-Einy 2017).

As innovative and influential as Fahlman's emoji was, the inauguration of ODR is often marked by the design of the eBay ODR System in 1998. This was not only one of the first game-changing dispute resolution systems, but also a prototype to be used in subsequent designs. eBay contracted the University of Massachusetts' Online Ombuds Office (directed by Ethan Katsh) and the National Center for Technology and Dispute Resolution to conduct a pilot project to explore whether disputes between buyers and sellers could be negotiated, mediated, or adjudicated online (Katsh and Rabinovich-Einy 2017).

By 2012, eBay was handling around 60 million disputes annually through a software-assisted program that first, identified a problem; second, softened the communications between the seller and buyer; third, allowed space for negotiation; fourth, assigned a mediator to facilitate the resolution of the problem; and finally, if still unresolved, shifted the case to a decision-making body to adjudicate resolution.

The eBay ODR program continued as a project of SquareTrade.com and emerged as a comprehensive system developed by Colin Rule. The system was based on the "staircase" model of dispute resolution: intractable conflicts were left to human mediators or adjudicators, while the largest share of disputes were addressed and resolved primarily through software applications. The first stage replaced a human facilitator with a software-assisted questioning process that "identif(ied) dispute types; exposing parties' interests; ask(ed) questions about positions; reframe(ed) demands; suggest(ed) options for solutions; allow(ed) some venting; establish(ed) a time frame; ke(pt) parties informed; disaggregate(ed) issues; match(ed) solutions to problems, and draft(ed) agreements" (Katsh and Rabinovich-Einy 2017). If these steps didn't produce a result, an assisted online mediation would kick in, and if this didn't help, then a body of human decisionmakers would handle the dispute. In Colin Rule's words:

> We decided to take a staircase approach, beginning with problem diagnosis (where we worked with the complainant to identify the root of the problem and likely solutions), then escalating to direct negotiation assisted by technology, and finally moving to an evaluation phase where eBay and its payment system provider, PayPal, would decide the case if the transaction partners could not do so. Each party could decide unilaterally when it wanted the process to move on to the next phase. The goal of the system was to prevent as many disputes as possible, amicably resolve as many as possible, and then decide the remainder as quickly and fairly as possible (Rule 2017).

It is important to stress that the eBay approach was not merely e-ADR or an online tool for dispute resolution. It was a complex system that gathered data from the users, revealed information about disputes and disputing, and offered better ways to prevent, manage and resolve disagreements. An ODR system uses information technology to prevent future disputes. Or as Katsh and Rabinovich-Einy say in their book, *Digital Justice*, "[i]n an ODR system, data is generated that reveals patterns of disputes and provides opportunities to both facilitate and monitor consensual agreements, thus making disputes in the future less likely" (Katsh and Rabinovich-Einy 2017).

Why do we focus on eBay's model in a chapter about OJDR? There have been other ODR initiatives, such as ICANN's ODR mechanism for resolving domain name disputes (Lindsay 2007) or Wikipedia's ODR mechanism for building agreement around what edits should remain or be erased in a published piece (Jemielniak 2014). eBay's robust and populated system, however, showed us specifically how to apply the stairway model to resolve legal disputes—how to start with algorithmic initial phases and open the space for a mediator or eventually an adjudicator to jump in if necessary.

In Canada, the stairway model is not new. In 2012, the British Columbia Civil Resolution Tribunal (CRT) was established and became the first online tribunal in the world. It deals with disputes under $5,000, strata-property issues (e.g., legal problems derived from shared ownership of common property) of any amount (except land title disputes), and motor-vehicle accident and injury claims of up to $50,000. The first step at the CRT is handled by the "Solution Explorer," a problem-diagnosis mechanism that helps the parties identify and narrow the scope of their disagreement. It suggests resolution options like templates and other legal aid mechanisms. If this fails, parties can move to the second step—the dispute resolution phase—which starts with an online negotiation and moves ahead to mediation or adjudication. Only 6 percent of the claims filed reach the adjudication phase (Allsop 2019). This suggests that digital justice enhanced with artificial intelligence (AI) tools can make a difference in the judicial system and ultimately streamline court procedures and promote justice.

The Pandemic and Finding Virtual Resolutions

Like so many others during the COVID-19 crisis, judges needed to shift their workplaces to their homes and conduct virtual hearings through Zoom, Webex, GoToMeeting and other online communication platforms. JDR experienced what we might call the "virtual turn." Indeed, the first OJDR was conducted during the first weeks of the initial quarantine and it picked up speed. With COVID in full swing, some provinces started online projects to resolve matters of family justice. Nova Scotia, for example, set up "eCourt," a pilot for family legal matters. At the outset, OJDR was more a form of eJDR; an electronic and virtual version of person-to-person JDR.

The difference between eJDR and OJDR is important. eJDR simply translated the physical setting into a virtual one without taking advantage of the benefits of technology: the parties join a meeting and the judge can do joint-sessions or caucus in breakout rooms. At this point, most JDR judges are reluctant to use technology in a way that would change the traditional format. For example, a judge would probably be unwilling to record the session due to confidentiality, even though it could be useful and recording on Zoom is easy. A recording could generate an instant transcript of all the dialogue and possibly help everyone understand the interests, options and alternatives available to them. Confidentiality concerns may also make a judge disinclined to use an online pre- or post-OJDR survey, though it could help in understanding the reservation values of the parties, their priorities and what they hope to accomplish during the OJDR.

Parties' feedback from post-OJDR surveys helped gauge satisfaction with the process. (We provide the first results of Alberta's post-OJDR surveys later in this chapter.) In general, most participants felt that OJDR "worked well or mostly worked well." Among the benefits they noted were reduced travel costs and availability during the pandemic. All issues were resolved in more than half of the OJDRs, and some or all of the issues in most OJDRs. The overwhelming majority of participants were either very satisfied, satisfied, or somewhat satisfied. As far as the advantages of the OJDR process, participants reported that it saved time, was easier to prepare for, kept emotional tensions at bay, and that it allowed parties to comply with social distancing guidelines.

Although online hearings became pervasive post-COVID, they actually had beginnings long before in North America. In 1972, real-time, two-way video conferencing was used by the Illinois Court to conduct bail hearings. In fact, by 2002, "eighty-five percent of federal district courts had access to video-conferencing equipment in at least one of their courtrooms, but the extent of video-conferencing in both civil and criminal federal court proceedings was still fairly limited" (Sela 2016). Despite the slow uptake of online hearings, some initiatives were quite successful. For instance, in Michigan in 2001, there was an move to create the first virtual online court to hold virtual hearings, generate an automated court report, and let parties and lawyers participate remotely from anywhere. The Michigan Cyber Court never received funding, however, so it never went ahead (Toering 2013).

Also in 2001, the UK's Money Claim Online (MCOL) was conceived and successfully launched. The MCOL can be used to resolve disputes of claims for sums up to £100.000: the court receives a claim through a web-form limited to 1080 characters. The claimant explains their concerns and what is owed. The defendant responds to the claim through an online form or by mail. If the defendant fails to respond or admits they owe the money, a judgment is entered online and the payment is made to the claimant. If the defendant doesn't pay, the claimant can file a warrant of execution to force the defendant to pay. If the defendant receives the claim and wants to argue against it, the case is then referred to a mediator or to the court's Money Claim Online Portal. Ayelet Sela reports: "MCOL offers many benefits to litigants: it is accessible year-round, twenty-four hours a day; it takes about thirty minutes to file or defend a claim, and it is subject to lower court fees (...) Today, MCOL issues more claims than any other local county court in the United Kingdom" (Sela 2016).

In the Netherlands, "the Burenrechter" has also been a successful source of digital justice in neighborhood disputes. It involves a tiered process that facilitates discussion through an online platform:

> The two parties begin the process by completing an online intake process reporting their position, continue in direct dialogue via a web interface, and progress to an online mediation

by a judiciary staff member. If resolution is not achieved, a judge intervenes, either facilitating a settlement or issuing a binding decision. The process includes an online follow-up mechanism to enable the court to monitor whether the neighborly situation improved after the case was concluded (Sela 2016).

It is noteworthy that many digital justice initiatives have followed eBay's stairway model. By structuring the process in stages, the designers recognized that ODR and digital justice is not merely about managing or solving disputes; it is also about preventing future disputes and educating parties about their rights and ways to access negotiation or mediation. The idea is to move justice closer to the people without relying on lawyers or court officials as intermediaries.

In 2017, a pilot was established in the U.K. creating the first court without lawyers. According to Lord Briggs, the online court functions as a three-step process: (i) first stage will be an automated triage where participants describe and articulate their view of the case, (ii) the second step is an ADR phase (a conciliation) where parties are directed to the most appropriate dispute resolution mechanisms available for their dispute (i.e., ODR, assisted negotiation, telephone or face-to-face mediation and judicial early neutral evaluation, etc.), and (iii) the third step involves a judge who will resolve the case, if it comes to that (Astin 2016).

In Alberta during the pandemic, the senior federal judge assigned to OJDRs exclusively, conducted over one hundred OJDR meetings. While some of them involved second or third hearing days, he nevertheless conducted OJDRs for the SPEC cases (the most difficult ones, see Chapter 17) almost every day of the week including—as a rule— two cases per week. Within those cases, there were usually three to six attorneys and sometimes three different parties involved in a lawsuit. He did this for over six months with inspiring success: the judge settled over 80 percent of the cases with only the usual IT difficulties like bandwidth and so on. At the beginning of the OJDRs, the senior judge had staff handle initial steps such as opening the room, preparing parties for caucus rooms and dealing with sharing documents. As the year progressed the assistant was there simply to open the room and transfer hosting to the judge who finished the day online with the parties. At the end of his full-time OJDR SPEC pandemic assignment, the judge reported the same level of success (still over 80 percent) whether he conducted OJDR or in-person JDRs.

In most digital dispute resolution initiatives, a large amount of data are being collected. In some instances, machine learning patterns are being documented. Particularly, in China, AI is being incorporated in an effort to develop algorithms that will improve the digital responses of online systems. This has been possible there because "[a]s of February 2020, there were over 81.5 million judgments and other judicial documents on the SPC's China Judgments Online, representing the world's largest digital repository of judicial information" (Zou 2020).

OJDR in Canada has not yet incorporated machine learning tools, nor is ODR very widespread. As noted, Alberta is in full swing mostly because the pandemic caused a shift. Other provinces like Nova Scotia moved quickly.

OJDR's Potential

In 1876, a Western Union electrician said to the president of the company, with regard to the telephone: "[t]his 'telephone' has too many shortcomings to be seriously considered as a means of communication. The device is inherently of no value to us" (Allsop 2019). Similarly, today many judges believe that virtual hearings and online settings have too many shortcomings to be seriously considered as a means of dispute resolution. We disagree.

In 2015 in British Columbia, the possibility of OJDR was clearly anticipated in Chapter 25 of the Civil Code regarding the dispute resolution services that may be used by the Court. Under rule 25(2): "[f]acilitated settlement may be conducted in person, in writing, by telephone, videoconferencing or email, or through use of other electronic communication tools, or by any combination of those means" (British Columbia 2010). Nevertheless, the Canadian Department of Justice acknowledges that "in Canada, most courts and tribunals have not yet adopted ODR technology as part of their case management system either as part of the negotiation, mediation, or adjudicative process" (Canada 2012).

Ayelet Sela distinguishes "instrumental" from "principal" ODR systems (Sela 2018). An instrumental ODR system is "a virtual space for convening the dispute resolution process: a specialized communication platform that enables conducting the process online" (Sela 2018). This is how OJDR is currently being implemented—enabling remote communication among the parties and the judge. Principal ODR systems, on the other hand:

> go beyond enabling communication and access to information; they take a proactive role facilitating the resolution of the dispute. Typically powered by artificial intelligence, principal ODR systems automate classic third-party capacities such as identifying interests and goals, educating parties about available options, refining preferences and defining strategies, diagnosing applicable rules and applying them, classifying and routing cases to relevant resolution paths, calculating tradeoffs and enabling maximization of mutual gains, generating resolution options, and determining final outcomes (Sela 2018).

As Colin Rule and Ethan Katsh argued, "we may learn from offline approaches in designing ODR systems, but the larger challenge is to take advantage of what we can do with technology that we could not do before. As a result, as the full potential of ODR is realized over time, future applications are likely to diverge more and more from how disputes were handled in the past" (Katsh and Rule 2016).

We have to learn how to use machine learning and AI to take full advantage of OJDR procedures. Perhaps the best starting point is to collect a lot of data from users so their perspectives drive the benchmarks used to calibrate the quality and the effectiveness of OJDR systems. Ayelet Sela has suggested some variables that can be used to capture the *ex post* perceptions of participants. Below is the table she designed for generating potential surveys that can help us understand the impact of technology on dispute resolution (Sela 2018).

Concept	Dimension	Indication
Procedural Justice	Process Fairness	Agree/Disagree: Process was objective? To what degree: Process was neutral? To what degree: Process was fair?
	Voice/ Participation	Agree/Disagree: Able to present your views? Agree/Disagree: Parties could present their side?
	Process Control	Agree/Disagree: My views were considered in the process. To what degree: I controlled the process.
	Decision Control	Agree/Disagree: My needs were considered in the outcome. My influence over the outcome: none—a lot
	Bias Suppression	Agree/Disagree: Treatment was influenced by my race, sex, age, nationality, or other characteristics
	Accuracy	Information collected was: Accurate—Inaccurate
International Justice	Neutral Attentiveness	Neutral was: Attentive—Inattentive Agree/Disagree: Mediator listened when I expressed my views.
	Neutral Respectfulness	Neutral was: Respectful—Disrespectful Agree/Disagree: Neutral treated me with respect.
	Neutral Trust-worthiness	Agree/Disagree: Neutral was trustworthy
Informational Justice	Explanation of the Process	Neutral explained the process: not at all—fully
	Neutral Clarity	Neutral was: Clear—Confusing
Neutral Performance	Neutral Fairness	Neutral was: Fair—Unfair Neutral was: Effective—Ineffective
	Neutral Effectiveness	Neutral was: Helpful—Unhelpful
Disputant Personal Experience	Affect (negative emotions)	Agree/Disagree: Process upset me. Agree/Disagree: Process was stressful. I felt in process: Hopeless—Hopeful
	Empowerment (self-efficacy)	Process effect on self-image: Positive—Negative Process effect on competency resolving disputes: Positive—Negative
	Certainty	During process I experienced: Certainty—Uncertainty
	Satisfaction	Process: Satisfied—Unsatisfied Process overall impression: Positive—Negative

Once this information is available, JDR (re)designers will have enough information to determine what is working well and what is not. OJDR can then be improved on an ongoing basis.

We are not sure whether, as Ayelet Sela suggests, ODR is "the first viable means for realizing Sander's vision of the multi-door courthouse" (Sela 2018). It is too soon to tell. We do agree, however, that it does open new doors. Machine learning and AI can revolutionize JDR, but only if the concerns of litigants, disputants and judges are fully taken into account.

OJDR, like any new program, is evolving—and has had some hiccups. The Alberta senior judge who offered OJDRs full time during the pandemic reported that some parties initially started OJDRs by standing up in their homes like they would in the courtroom. The judge, of course, told them that was not necessary, but more than that, he had to remind them that he could see them; during one of the virtual meetings, a participant's spouse walked around in their bedroom half clothed without even knowing it (although everyone else did). The lesson? All parties in OJDR hearings from home must add a virtual background! Alberta's SPEC judge's virtual courtroom appeared so real that parties asked the judge repeatedly if he was physically in court. When interviewing children, that same judge uses a friendlier background from a popular children's film to make it more fun and less stressful for them.

Audio can be a challenge to get right. During the initial OJDR SPEC hearings, the same Alberta judge tried different sound configurations. The computer microphone was easiest but allowed background noise. He eventually settled on wireless headphones because the mute function was superior, the sound was clearer and wireless allowed him to get documents, or refer to law books without removing them. There were certainly challenges reading and downloading evidence and judges experimented with different electronic formats, including Cloudsharing, Dropbox, USB sticks and old-fashioned paper copies as a last resort.

Even when the technology went smoothly, some participants expressed a strong desire to meet face-to-face with the judge. They relented when he explained health concerns due to COVID, and OJDR's advantages, such as his close-up view their facial expressions and how it allowed counsel to quickly share and edit the proposed settlement consent order right on the screen (viewed by everybody) in real time. These factors are all consistent with JDR's collaborative approach. OJDR also provided unexpected convenience and cost savings: the judge could meet with parties earlier or later in the day and even on the weekends because unlike in-person court, he did not need to rely on clerks or sheriffs to open conference rooms and standby for assistance. Lastly, judges have found it less stressful to work remotely and have been grateful to avoid travel and courtroom formalities.

CHAPTER 19 APPENDIX 1: OJDR SURVEY RESULTS N=28

When questioned about the **Parties' Reactions to OJDR**, 54% said it worked well and 32% said mostly well; 7% wanted breakout rooms which were not then-available.

When questioned about the **Perceived Benefits of OJDR**, 75% said it was the reduced cost of traveling to a central location; 21% said there was no need to be in the room with an adverse party; 82% referred to the ability to conduct OJDR during the pandemic; and 14% commented on other benefits like efficient caucusing; faster, more relaxed atmosphere for the client, and the ability to share screens.

When asked to state the **Possible Disadvantages of OJDR (over regular JDR)**, 14% said the lawyers were unfamiliar with the use of OJDR tools; 11% said the judge was unfamiliar with OJDR tools; 21% said the parties were unfamiliar with the use of OJDR tools; 18% said the OJDR tools got in the way of effective face-to-face problem-solving; and 18% said OJDR did not work as well as normal JDR.

When questioned about the **Success of OJDR in Resolving Some or All** issues in the lawsuit, 50% said *all* issues were resolved; 18% said *some* issues were resolved; and 18% said no issues were resolved. Some of the respondents to the survey did not check a box.

When asked about their **Personal Level of Satisfaction in the OJDR**, 57% were very satisfied with the outcome; 21% were somewhat satisfied; 7% was very dissatisfied, and some participants did not check a box.

When asked if **OJDR Changed their Opinion about JDR in general**, 46% said they had neither a pro or con opinion about normal JDR before this case; 4% had a positive opinion before but was slightly less positive now; 32% had a positive opinion before, and was even more positive now, and some participants did not check a box.

When asked about the **Advantages of OJDR over Normal JDR**, 64% mention saving time by not going to court; 43% mention the ease of preparation; 43% mentioned the decrease in intensity of emotional tension; 18% said the feelings can be controlled better online (than in-person); and 86% mentioned they could do it while social distancing measures were in place.

Notes: For each question, the participants were asked to check *one* box except questions 4 and 8, where they could check *any* box that applied. The percentages do not always equal 100% because some parties did not answer all the questions.

COURT OF QUEEN'S BENCH OF ALBERTA

Virtual JDR Survey

Role in JDR:
☐ Plaintiff
☐ Defendant
☐ Third Party

Type of Case [CHECK ALL THAT APPLY]:
☐ Breach of Contract
☐ Family
☐ Personal Injury
☐ Commercial
☐ Other:

1. Your Experience with JDR
☐ A. First time involved with JDR (either binding or non-binding)
☐ B. Involved once or twice before in non-binding JDR
☐ C. Involved once or twice before in binding JDR
☐ D. Involved in many non-binding JDRs
☐ E. Involved in many binding JDRs

2. Reactions to Virtual JDR ("VJDR") [CHECK ONE]
☐ A. Worked well
☐ B. Mostly worked well, but online interaction posed some difficulties
☐ C. Mostly did not work well, online interactions posed serious difficulties
☐ D. Did not work well. Would not recommend virtual JDR to anyone else
☐ E. Other:

3. Perceived Benefits of VJDR
☐ A. Reduced cost of travel to a central location.
☐ B. No need to be in the room with an adverse party
☐ C. Ability to conduct VJDR during Pandemic
☐ D. Other:

4. **Possible disadvantages of VJDR (over regular JDR) [CHECK ALL THAT APPLY]**

☐ A.   VJDR took too long to calendar

☐ B.   Lawyers unfamiliar with use of VJDR tools

☐ C.   Judge unfamiliar with use of VJDR tools

☐ D.   Parties unfamiliar with use of VJDR tools

☐ E.   VJDR tools got in the way of effective face-to-face problem-solving

☐ F.   VJDR just didn't work as well as normal JDR

5. **Was the VJDR successful at resolving some or all of the issues?**

☐ A.   Yes, all issues were resolved

☐ B.   Yes, some issues were resolved

☐ C.   No, no issues were resolved

6. **Personal Level of Satisfaction [CHECK ONE]**

☐ A.   I was very satisfied with the outcome of the VJDR

☐ B.   I was somewhat satisfied with the outcome of the VJDR

☐ C.   I was somewhat dissatisfied with the outcome of the VJDR

☐ D.   I was very dissatisfied with the outcome of the VJDR

7. **Did this VJDR change your opinion about JDR in general? [CHECK ONE]**

☐ A.   I didn't have either a pro or con opinion about normal JDR before my involvement in this case

☐ B.   I had a positive opinion before, but I am slightly less positive now

☐ C.   I had a positive opinion before, and I am even more positive now

☐ D.   I had a negative opinion before, but I have a more positive opinion now

☐ E.   I had a negative opinion before, and I still do

8. **What advantage does VJDR have over normal JDR? (check as many as you like)**

☐ A.   You save time by not going to court.

☐ B.   It is easier to prepare and go through a virtual session.

☐ C.   The emotional tension in the room is not as intense.

☐ D.   Feelings can be controlled better online.

☐ E.   It can be done while social distancing measures are in place.

9. **How can VJDRs be improved?**

Please note that all responses will be stored anonymously.

EPILOGUE

The Future of JDR

We have reported on the outstanding success of JDR in Canada. Our findings should encourage those in positions of power and responsibility to expand the availability of JDR both in terms of SPEC for complex cases caught for years in the vortex of the legal system, as well as JDR more generally because it enhances the quality of justice, reduces the cost of funding the judiciary, and speeds the disposition of legal claims.

JDR enhances the quality of justice in seven ways: (1) it gives plaintiffs and defendants more control over the outcome of the disputes; (2) it allows cases to be treated as the unique matters that they are, rather than pinning results to precedents set in other places and times when the circumstances may have been only somewhat similar; (3) it takes full advantage of the knowledge, skill, and stature of judges, but still leaves matters in the hands of clients and their lawyers; (4) it seeks to maximize the value to both sides in every legal dispute, rather than just picking a winner and a loser; (5) it improves relationships between the parties; (6) it gives certainty of result to the parties who might be experiencing unmanageable ambivalence about a conflict and (7) it preserves and sustains the public's faith in legal institutions as sites where peacemaking is fostered and conflicts are resolved.

In the long run, JDR builds citizens' capacity to deal with their very personal and emotional differences in peaceful and collaborative ways rather than increasing the litigious nature of society. JDR certainly makes sense in a wide variety of family law and other civil suits and it could help in some criminal matters as well, especially in terms of sentencing (building on the restorative justice and Aboriginal justice systems) or diversionary programs.

Decisions to expand Canada's JDR system are completely in the hands of the chief justices of the various provincial and national courts. Under the banner of improving case management, they can build on JDR's advantages; no further legislation is needed from Parliament. As JDR grows, some lawyers might have to make adjustments in how they practice and bill for time, and they might have to acquire continuing legal education to bring them up to speed. The public, as well, will need to educate itself a bit more on how to take advantage of JDR so they can reduce the amount they pay their lawyers and the amount of time they spend in and out of court. Many judges will have to acquire additional JDR training, but it will be worth it to them to gain considerable control of their schedules, not to mention stress relief as they end their cases under reserve and advisement. Law schools will want to educate future lawyers in the theory and practice of JDR so they know how to help their clients prepare for court. The media will have to begin reporting on something they usually ignore. And legal scholarship will probably shift to help us understand more about this form of dispute resolution. Because Canada has come so far with JDR, it will be relatively easy to spread JDR operations across the country, building on existing initiatives.

The most important point to continue to emphasize is that decisions to switch to JDR are always voluntarily. Anyone who prefers the win/lose battle of traditional litigation will always have that option. With JDR, though, they can have their cake and eat it, too.

Will JDR Expand to the U.S.?

Some might say JDR is already happening in the U.S. through settlement conferences. We have described their similarities and differences and consider it will be a much bigger challenge to expand JDR throughout the U.S. state and federal courts system as practiced in Canada, even though it was almost forty years ago when the late Chief Justice Burger asserted that litigation had failed society partly because it increased stress and did not heal human conflicts. He went on to say that even when a result was achieved, litigation drained much of its value due to its demands of time and expense. Similarly, former U.S. Supreme Court Justice Sandra Day O'Connor felt parties should not go to court until they had first tried alternative methods to resolve their disputes.

Private mediation has a strong foothold in the U.S., much of it offered by former judges who retire early to make more money providing services through for-profit companies. Court-annexed private mediation, however, doesn't offer JDR's advantages of an active judge's intervention at the parties' request. Frankly, aside from some magistrate judges, litigants in the U.S. have never had a chance to seek voluntary resolution from a judge, and sitting judges do not expect to provide dispute resolution assistance.

It is possible that ODR options may take root in the U.S., even after the pandemic allows everyone to return to public buildings. But these are not likely to take the more consequential form of OJDR, as in Canada. The U.S. does not have a history of appointing, training, and supporting judges with an inclination to mediate. Whether online or in person, U.S. judges are too accustomed to deciding cases from the dais to easily shift into JDR mode.

We recognize the legal community would very likely oppose any growth of JDR into the U.S. Lawyers haven't been trained to advocate for their client's interests in a mediation context, and they are likely to worry about the short-term loss of billable time as cases resolve more quickly. There might have to be state and federal legislative efforts to clarify the terms under which the use of JDR could expand. The powers that be would likely lobby hard to make such legislation difficult to pass, even if it would enhance the quality of justice provided by the U.S. legal system.

Will JDR Expand in Other Parts of the World?

In countries around the world that already have some form of JDR, it may be OJDR that provides the impetus for expansion; if JDR were going to spread, it probably would have already. It is not clear whether JDR's growth is likely in Israel, Indonesia, and the Philippines. In many of these counties, private mediation—especially court-annexed mediation—has not blossomed, so there is no mediation tradition to build on. Once again, we would expect the legal profession to push hard to maintain its status and central role in the current win/lose system of litigation. Law schools in these countries should train lawyers and future judges how to mediate and explain how JDR could enhance the quality of their justice system. Although some form of JDR exists internationally, it is not nearly as prevalent as Canada and there is relatively small number of judges involved. It's possible that a progressive and influential senior (supreme court?) justice could lead the way to expand JDR in some of these countries, but absent some surprising leadership, it is unlikely to happen.

In countries that have nothing like JDR at present, it is possible that the advent of ODR—especially if provided by private international marketing companies or law firms—could allow JDR to make its way into national court systems. If international law firms find local judges and courts to partner with they could offer OJDR on a large scale very quickly, especially if they enlist local jurists to serve as the key JDR providers. They would need to invest in local marketing and offer current lawyers financial incentives to promote JDR with their clients. Absent the arrival of OJDR, though, we doubt that JDR more generally will make much headway in countries that have seen very little of judges or court systems operating collaboratively. Judges in these countries do not see themselves providing a mediation option through the courts, lawyers are not pushing for it, and clients don't realize that such a thing is possible. So, again, even though we believe that a version of JDR could be implemented quickly, especially on an experimental basis in any cultural context where the rule of law applies, we don't expect much to happen in countries that don't already have a strong mediation tradition.

We are convinced that JDR enhances the quality of justice provided by the Canadian court system and have provided evidence to support this claim. Because confidentiality has been key to the administration of JDR in the Canadian court system, however, very few people understand how it works. We hope this book will open more eyes in the legal profession to this powerful instrument for justice and that it provides the instruction, evidence, and arguments needed to push for the expansion of JDR and OJDR in Canada and elsewhere.

If any readers are moved to advocate for the broader use of JDR and OJDR, we urge them to remember that only properly trained judges with the right temperament should be given JDR responsibilities; merely being appointed or elected to the judiciary does not mean that someone can mediate effectively. The same is true for lawyers; a law degree does not mean that they are equipped to help their clients participate in JDR. We hope that others who study the law will find a way to access additional information on the practice of JDR, monitor on-going practice, and share their findings.

BIBLIOGRAPHY

Agrios, John. 2004. *A Handbook on Judicial Dispute Resolution for Canadian Lawyers*. Unpublished Manuscript. https://cfcj-fcjc.org/sites/default/files/docs/hosted/18586-jdr_handbook.pdf.

Alberta. 2018 [2000]. *Judicature Act*.

Alberta Court of Appeal. 2002. *Heller v. Martens*. ABCA 122.

Alberta Court of Appeal. 2005. *J.W. Abernethy Management & Consulting Ltd. v. 705589 Alberta Ltd. and Trillium Homes Ltd*. ABCA 103 (CanLII).

Alberta Court of Appeal. 2007. *L.N. v. S.M.* ABCA 258 (CanLII).

Alberta Court of Appeal. 2010. *Adeshina v Litwiniuk and Company*. ABQB 80 (CanLII).

Alberta Court of Appeal. 2014. *Imperial Oil Limited v Alberta (Information and Privacy Commissioner)*. ABCA 231 (CanLII).

Alberta Court of Appeal. 2017. *Luft v Taylor, Zinkhofer & Conway*. 2017 ABCA 228 (CanLII).

Alberta Law Reform Institute. 1990. *Dispute Resolution: A Directory of Methods, Projects and Resources (Research Paper No. 19)*. Edmonton: Alberta Law Reform Institute.

Allsop, James. 2019. "Technology and the Future of the Courts." *University of Queensland Law Journal* 38(1): 1–12.

American Arbitration Association. 2003. *ADR & the Law: Developments in the Law. Dispute Resolution Services Worldwide*. Huntington, NY: Juris Publishing Inc.

Amsler, Lisa, Martinez, Janet, and Smith, Stephanie. 2020. *Dispute System Design: Preventing, Managing, and Resolving Conflict*. Stanford, CA: Stanford University Press.

Aristotle. 1962. *The Politics*. Translated by Thomas Sinclair. Harmondsworth: Penguin.

Aristotle. 2000. *Nicomachean Ethics*. Translated by Roger Crisp. Cambridge: Cambridge University Press.

Astin, Diane. 2016. ""Navigation Without Lawyers": Access to Justice and the Online Court." *Legal Action Group*, October 2016. https://www.lag.org.uk/article/202069/-lsquo-navigation -without-lawyers-rsquo---access-to-justice-and-the-online-court.

Astor, Hilary, and Chinkin, Christine. 2002. *Dispute Resolution in Australia*. Australia: Lexis-Nexis Butterworths.

Auerbach, Jerome. 1983. *Justice Without Law?* New York: Oxford University Press.

Boulle, Laurence, and Kelly, Kathleen. 1998. *Mediation: Principles, Process, Practice*. Toronto: Butterworths.

Bowal, Peter. 1995. "The New Ontario Judicial Alternative Dispute Resolution Model." *Alberta Law Review* 34(1): 206.

Bowling, Daniel, and Hoffman, David. 2000. "Bringing Peace into the Room: The Personal Qualities of the Mediator and Their Impact on the Mediation." *Negotiation Journal* 16(1): 5–28.

Braithwaite, John. 1999. "Restorative Justice: Assessing Optimistic and Pessimistic Accounts." *Crime and Justice* 25: 1–127.

Brenner, Donald, and Baird, Carol. 2003. *Whose Court Is It Anyway? A Symposium for Judges: Summary Report*. Canada: Royal Roads University.

Brill-Case, Israela A. 2015. "The Importance of Intake Mediation." In: Nancy Wiegers Greenwald, Kristen Blankley, and Kim Taylor (eds), *Mediation Convening and Intake Best Practices: Presented at the ABA Section on Dispute Resolution 2015 Conference*. Boston: Law Collaborative in Conna Weiner. http://connaweineradr.com/wp-content/uploads/2015/04/Mediation -Convening-and-Intake-Best-Practices-1_opt.pdf.

British Columbia. 2010. "Civil Resolution Act, Chapter 25, SBC 2010." http://www.bclaws.ca/
civix/document/id/complete/statreg/12025_01#section25.

British Columbia Supreme Court Rules.

Brown, Henry, and Marriot, Arthur. 1999. *ADR Principles and Practice*. London: Sweet & Maxwell.

Burger, W., Levin, A., and Wheeler, R. (eds). 1980. *The Pound Conference: Perspectives on Justice in the
Future*. St Paul, MN: West Publishing Co., p. 111.

Bush, Robert. 1988. "Defining Quality in Dispute Resolution: Taxonomies and Anti-Taxonomies
of Quality Arguments." *Denver University Law Review* 66(3): 335–380.

Canada. 2012. Dispute Resolution Reference Guide. Department of Justice, Canada. Dispute
Prevention and Resolution Division. https://www.justice.gc.ca/eng/rp-pr/csj-sjc/dprs-sprd/
res/drrg-mrrc/10.html#note3.

Canada's Truth and Reconciliation Commission. 2015. *Summary of the Final Report of the Truth and
Reconciliation Commission of Canada*. Toronto: Lorimer.

Canadian Bar Association. 1996. *Task Force on Systems of Civil Justice*. Ottawa: The Association.

Canadian Code of Civil Procedure.

Canadian Criminal Code reference: Criminal Code (R.S.C., 1985, c. C-46), at https://laws-lois
.justice.gc.ca/eng/acts/C-46/ accessed.

Canadian Court of Appeal. 2016. *JP v JP SKCA168*.

Canadian Criminal Code.

Canadian Forum on Civil Justice. 2010. "What Does It Cost to Access Justice in Canada? How
Much Is 'Too Much'? And How Do We Know?" (Literature Review). Edmonton.

Canadian Forum on Civil Justice. 2012. "The Cost of Justice: Weighting the Costs of Fair &
Effective Resolution to Legal Problems." http://www.cfcjfcjc.org/sites/default/files/docs
/2012/CURA_background_doc.pdf.

Canadian Judicial Council, Sub-Committee on Access to Justice (Trial Courts) of the
Administration of Justice Committee. 2008. "Access to Justice: Report on Selected Reform
Initiatives in Canada." *CJC*. http://www.cjc-ccm.gc.ca/cmslib/general/2008_SelectedRef
ormInitia tives_Report_final_EN.pdf.

Carrie, Menkel-Meadow. 1985. "For and Against Settlement: Uses and Abuses of the Mandatory
Settlement Conference." *UCLA Law Review* 33 (2) (December 1985): 485–516.

Chatterjee, Charles, and Lefcovitch, Anna. 2008. *Alternative Dispute Resolution: A Practical Guide*.
New York: Routledge.

Clarke, Gay, and Davies, Iyla. 1991. "ADR – Argument for and Against Use of the Mediation
Process Particularly in Family and Neighborhood Disputes." *Queensland University of Technology
Law Journal* 7: 81–96.

Court of Queen's Bench of Alberta. "Judicial Dispute Resolution. What is Judicial Dispute
Resolution?" https://www.albertacourts.ca/qb/areas-of-law/jdr.

Court of Queen's Bench of Alberta. 2008. *Stewart v. Stewart*. ABQB 348.

Darley, John M., and Thane S. Pittman. 2003. "The Psychology of Compensatory and
Retributive Justice." *Personality and Social Psychology Review* 7 (4): 324–36.

Delgado, Richard et. al. 1985. "Fairness and Formality: Minimizing the Risk of Prejudice in
Alternative Dispute Resolution." *Wisconsin Law Review* 1985, no. 6: 1359–1404.

Denlow, Morton. 2010. "Breaking Impasses in Judicial Settlement Conferences: Seven (More)
Techniques for Resolution." *Court Review: The Journal of the American Judges Association* 337.
https://digitalcommons.unl.edu/ajacourtreview/337.

Druckman, Daniel and Lynn, Wagner. 2016. "Justice and Negotiation." *Annual. Review of
Psychology* 67: 387–413.

Farrow, Trevor. 2014. *Civil Justice, Privatization and Democracy*. Toronto: University of Toronto
Press.

Farrow, Trevor. 2017. "The Cost of Civil Justice in Canada: What Do We Know What Don't We
Know What Should We Know." Edmonton: Canadian Forum for Civil Justice.

*Federal Rules of Civil Procedure. 3. Rule 1.

Fiss, Owen. 1984. "Against Settlement." *The Yale Law Journal* 93(6): 1073–1090.

Fogel, Michael. 2002. "ADR: What is the Real Alternative?" *Canadian Arbitration and Mediation Journal*, Winter: 10–13. http://adric.ca/journals/CAMJournalwinter2002.pdf.

Folger, Robert, Rosenfield, David, Grove, Janet, and Corkran, Louise. 1979. "Effects of "Voice" and Peer Opinions on Responses to Inequity." *Journal of Personality and Social Psychology* 37(12): 2253–2261.

Fuller, Lon. 1971. "Mediation–Its Forms and Functions." *University of Southern California Law Review* 44(2): 305–339.

Galanter, Marc. 1985. ""… A Settlement Judge, Not a Trial Judge:" Judicial Mediation in the United States." *Journal of Law and Society* 12(1): 1–18.

Galanter, Marc. 1988. "Compared to What—Assessing the Quality of Dispute Processing Introduction." *Denver University Law Review* 66: xi–xiv.

Glaholt, Duncan, and Rotterdam, Markus. 2018. *The Law of ADR in Canada: An Introductory Guide.* Canada: Lexis Nexis.

Goldberg, Stephen B., Sander, F. E., and Rogers, N. H. 2020. *Dispute Resolution: Negotiation, Mediation, Arbitration, and Other Processes* (7th ed.). Wolters Kluwer.

Green, Ross. 1997. "Aboriginal Community Sentencing and Mediation: Within and Without the Circle." *Manitoba Law Journal* 25: 77–125.

Green, Ross Gordon. 1997. *Justice in Aboriginal Communities: Sentencing Alternatives.* Saskatoon, Canada: Purich Publishing.

Grillo, Trina. 1991. "The Mediation Alternative: Process Dangers for Women." *The Yale Law Journal* 100, no. 6: 1545–1610.

Hang Ng, Kwai, and He, Xin. 2014. "Internal Contradictions of Judicial Mediation in China." *Law & Social Inquiry* 39(2): 285–312.

He, X. 2022. "The Judge as a Negotiator: Claims Negotiating and Inequalities in China's Judicial Mediation." *Law & Social Inquiry* 47(4): 1172–1200.

Hollander-Blumoff, Rebecca, and Tyler, Tom. 2011. "Procedural Justice and the Rule of Law: Fostering Legitimacy in Alternative Dispute Resolution." *Journal of Dispute Resolution* 1: 1–20.

James, William. 2018 [1907]. *Pragmatism.* New York: Dover Edition.

Jemielniak, Dariusz. 2014. *Common Knowledge?* Palo Alto: Stanford University Press.

Julie, Macfarlane. 2012. "ADR and the Courts: Renewing our Commitment to Innovation." *Marquette. Law Review* 95(3): 927 (2012).

Julie, Macfarlane. 2017. *The New Lawyer: How Settlement Is Transforming The Practice of Law* Vancouver: UBC Press.

Katsh, Ethan, and Rabinovich-Einy, Orna. 2017. *Digital Justice: Technology and the Internet of Disputes.* New York: Oxford University Press.

Katsh, Ethan, and Rule, Colin. 2016. "What We Know and Need to Know About Online Dispute Resolution." *South Carolina Law Review* 67(2): 329.

King, Michae, Frieberg, Arie, Batagol, Beck, and Hyams, Ross. 2009. *Non-Adversarial Justice.* Annandale: The Federation Press.

Kovach, Kimberly. 2005. "Mediation." In: Michal Moffitt and Robert Bordone (eds), *The Handbook of Dispute Resolution.* San Francisco: Jossey Bass.

Kun, Fan, 2023. "Beyond law and politics: an empirical study of judicial mediation in China." *Journal of International Dispute Settlement* 2023, 14(1): 47–75.

LaGratta, Emily (ed.). 2017. *To Be Fair: Conversations About Procedural Justice.* New York: Center for Court Innovation.

Lande, John. 2006. "Introduction to the Vanishing Trial Symposium." *Journal of Dispute Resolution* 1.

Landerkin, Hugh. 1997. "Custody Disputes in the Provincial Court of Alberta: A New Judicial Dispute Resolution Model." *Alberta Law Review* 35: 627–686.

Landerkin, Hugh, and Pirie, Andrew. 2003. "Judges as Mediators: What's the Problem With Judicial Dispute Resolution in Canada." *Canadian Bar Review* 82(2): 268–298.

Landerkin, Hugh, and Pirie, Andrew. 2004. "What's the Issue: Judicial Dispute Resolution in Canada." *Law in Context: Socio-Legal Journal* 22(1): 25–63.

Leacock, Jill. 2004. "British Columbia Court of Appeal Judicial Settlement Conference Pilot Project." *Advocate, Vancouver Bar Association* 62(6): 879–880.

Lee, Jeffrey. 2014. "Mediation in Mainland China and Hong Kong: Can They Learn From Each Other?" *Asian-Pacific Law & Policy Journal* 16(1): 101–121.

Lind, Allan, and Tom Tyler. 1988. *The Social Psychology of Procedural Justice*. New York: Springer.

Lindsay, David. 2007. *International Domain Name Law: ICANN and the UDRP*. Oxford: Hart Publishing.

Luban, David. 1995. "Settlements and the Erosion of the Public Realm." *The Georgetown Law Journal* 83(7): 2619–2662.

Malhotra, Deepak. 2016. *Negotiating the Impossible: How to Break Deadlock and Resolve Ugly Conflicts*. Oakland: Berrett-Koehler Publishers.

Manitoba Queen's Bench Rules.

Margalit, Avishai. 2010. *On Compromise and Rotten Compromises*. New Jersey: Princeton University Press.

Maurice, Rosenberg. 1964. *The Pretrial Conference and Effective Justice*. New York: Columbia University Press.

Mayer, Bernard. 2000. *The Dynamics of Conflict Resolution: A Practitioner's Guide*. San Francisco: Jossey-Bass.

McEwan, Joan. 1999. "JDR: Judicial Dispute Resolution." *National* 8(7): 36.2.

Menkel-Meadow, Carrie. 1993. "Lawyer Negotiations: Theories and Realities - What We Learn from Mediation." *Modern Law Review* 56(3): 361–379.

Menkel-Meadow, Carrie. 2020. "Hybrid and Mixed Dispute Resolution Processes: Integrities of Process Pluralism." In: Maria F. Moscati, Michael Palmer, and Marian Roberts (eds), *Comparative Dispute Resolution*. Cheltenham, UK: Edward Elgar Publishing.

Miller, David. 2017. "Justice." In: Edward N. Zalta (ed.), *The Stanford Encyclopedia of Philosophy*. https://plato.stanford.edu/archives/fall2017/entries/justice/.

Mintz, Steven. 1992. "Children, Families and the State: American Family Law in Historical Perspective." *Denver University Law Review* 69: 635–662.

Mnookin, Robert, Peppet, Scott, and Tulumello, Andrew. 2004. *Beyond Winning: Negotiating to Create Value in Deals and Disputes*. Cambridge: Belknap Press.

Model Standards of Practice for Family and Divorce Mediation. 2001.

Money Claim Online Portal. https://www.moneyclaim.gov.uk/web/mcol/welcome.

Moore, W. K. 1995. "Mini-Trials in Alberta." *Alberta Law Review* 34(1): 194–205.

Murphy, Colleen. 2017. *The Conceptual Foundations of Transitional Justice*. Cambridge: Cambridge University Press.

Murphy, Renalda, and Molinari, Patrick. 2009. *Doing Justice: Dispute Resolution in the Courts and Beyond*. Montreal: The Canadian Institute for the Administration of Justice Conference.

National Symposium on Court-Connected Dispute Resolution Research. 1994. https://ncsc .contentdm.oclc.org/digital/api/collection/adr/id/56/download.

New-Brunswick. Rules of Court of New-Brunswick.

Nova Scotia. Service Nova Scotia and Internal Services. "Online Dispute Resolution for Family Legal Matters a First in Canada." October 23, 2000. https://novascotia.ca/news/release/?id =20201023002.

Nova Scotia Rules of Civil Procedure.

Online Etymology Dictionary. https://www.etymonline.com.

Ontario Bar Association. 2013. "A Different 'Day in Court'. The Role of the Judiciary in Facilitating Settlements." Report of the Ontario Bar Association Judicial Mediation Taskforce. https://www.oba.org/getattachment/News-Media/News/2013/July-2013/A-Different-%E2 %80%98Day-in-Court-The-Role-of-the-Judiciar/ADifferentDayInCourt7122013.pdf.

Ontario Rules of Civil Procedure, Rule 50.

Ontario Superior Court of Justice. 2006. *Rudd et al v. Trossacs Investments Inc., et al. 79 OR (3d) 687. OJ No. 922.*

Otis, A. 2006. *Judicial Dispute Resolution In Commonwealth Jurisdictions. Comparing the Evolving Judicial Role in Canada, Singapore and Australia.* LL.M. Thesis. National University of Singapore. https://scholarbank.nus.edu.sg/bitstream/10635/15179/1/Final%20Version%20LLM%20Thesis%2016%20May%202006.pdf.

Otis, Louise. 2000. "The Conciliation Service Program of the Court of Appeal of Québec." *World Arbitration & Mediation Review* 11(3): 80.

Philippine Justice Administration. "Consolidated and Revised Guidelines to Implement the Expanded Coverage of Court-Annexed Mediation and Judicial Dispute Resolution (JDR)." https://sites.google.com/view/e-codal/remedial/criminal-procedure/special-rules/a-m-no-11-1-6-sc-philja-cam-and-jdr.

Pirie, Andrew. 2000. *Alternative Dispute Resolution: Skills, Science, and the Law.* Toronto: Irwin Law.

Provine, Marie. 2000. *Settlement Strategies for Federal District Judges.* Washington: Federal Judicial Center.

Quebec Court of Appeal. 2011. *Bloom Films 1998 Inc. c. Christal Films Productions Inc.* QCCA 1171 (CanLII).

Rawls, John. 1971. *A Theory of Justice.* Cambridge, MA: Harvard University Press.

Rawls, John. 1999. *A Theory of Justice* (Revised Edition). Cambridge, MA: Harvard University Press.

Resnik, Judith. 1982. "Managerial Judges." *Harvard Law Review* 96(2): 374–448.

Resnik, Judith. 1995. "Many Doors? Closing Doors? Alternative Dispute Resolution and Adjudication." *Ohio State Journal of Dispute Resolution* 10(2): 211–265.

Richler, Joel. 2011. "Court-Based Mediation in Canada." *The Judges Journal* 50(3): 14–17.

Rogers, Carl. 2003. *Client-Centered Therapy: Its Current Practice, Implications and Theory.* London: Constable.

Rooke, John. 2010. *The Multi-Door Courthouse is Open in Alberta: Judicial Dispute Resolution is Institutionalized in the Court of Queen's Bench.* LL.M. Thesis. Edmonton: University of Alberta Faculty of Law. https://era.library.ualberta.ca/items/8f8a29e5-c9ec-4067-b57f-1162eb6055f6.

Rosen, Michael. 2012. *Dignity: Its History and Meaning.* Cambridge, MA: Harvard University Press.

Royal Commission on Aboriginal People. 1996. *Report of the Royal Commission on Aboriginal Peoples: Perspectives and Realities,* Vol. 4. Ottawa: Indian and Northern Affairs Canada.

Royce, Terry. 2005. "The Negotiator and the Bomber: Analyzing the Critical Role of Active Listening in Crisis Negotiations." *Negotiation Journal* 21(1): 5–27.

Rule, Colin. 2017. "Designing Global Online Dispute Resolution System: Lessons Learned From eBay." *University of St. Thomas Law Journal* 13(2): 354.

Salter, Shannon. 2017. "Online Dispute Resolution and Justice System Integration: British Columbia's Civil Resolution Tribunal." *Windsor Yearbook of Access to Justice* 34(1): 112–129, at 114.

Sanchez, Valerie. 1996. "Towards History of ADR: The Dispute Processing Continuum in Anglo-Saxon England and Today." *Ohio State Journal on Dispute Resolution* 11(1): 1–40.

Sander, Frank. 1979. "Varieties of Dispute Processing." In: A. Levin and R. Wheeler (eds), *The Pound Conference: Perspectives on Justice in the Future.* St Paul, MN, West Publishing Co., p. 111.

Sander, Frank. 1983. "Family Mediation: Problems and Prospects." *Mediation Quarterly* 2: 3.

Sander, Frank, and Goldberg, Stephen. 1994. "Fitting the Forum to the Fuss: A User-Friendly Guide to Selecting an ADR Procedure." *Negotiation Journal* 10(1): 49–68.

Saskatchewan Court. 1993. *Condessa Z Holdings Ltd. v. Rusnak.* CanLII 5526.

Saskatchewan Rules of the Court of Queen's Bench, Rule 191.

Schwarz, Roger M. 2017. *The Skilled Facilitator : A Comprehensive Resource for Consultants, Facilitators, Coaches, and Trainers.* Third edition. Hoboken, New Jersey: John Wiley & Sons, Inc.

Sela, Ayelet. 2016. "Streamlining Justice: How Online Courts Can Resolve the Challenges of *pro se* Litigation." *Cornell Journal of Law and Public Policy* 26: 331.

Sela, Ayelet. 2018. "Can Computers Be Fair: How Automated and Human-Powered Online Dispute Resolution Affect Procedural Justice in Mediation and Arbitration." *Ohio State Journal on Dispute Resolution* 33(1): 91.

Sela, Ayelet, and Gabay-Egozi, Limor. 2020. "Judicial Procedural Involvement (JPI): A Metric for Judges' Role in Civil Litigation, Settlement, and Access to Justice." *Journal of Law and Society* 47(3): 468–498.

Shiravi, Abdolhossein, and Javad Abdollahi, Mohammad. 2017. "Privacy and Confidentiality in Alternative Dispute Resolution Methods." *Journal of Economic & Management Perspectives* 11(3): 835–844.

Singapore State Courts. "Overview of State Courts Centre for Dispute Resolution." https://www.statecourts.gov.sg/cws/Mediation_ADR/Pages/Overview-of-State-Courts-Centre-for-Dispute-Resolution.aspx.

Sourdin, Tania, and Archie, Zariski. 2013. *The Multi-Tasking Judge: Comparative Judicial Dispute Resolution*. Pyrmont: Thompson Reuters.

Spencer, David. 2006. "Judicial Mediators: Is the Time Right? Part I." *Australian Dispute Resolution Journal* 17(3): 130–139.

Stanford Legal Design Lab. "Online Dispute Resolution in British Columbia." https://justiceinnovation.law.stanford.edu/online-dispute-resolution-in-british-columbia/.

Stienstra, Donna, and Yates, Susan. 2004. *ADR Handbook for Judges*. Washington, DC: American Bar Association Section of Dispute Resolution.

Stitt, Allan. 2003. *Mediating Commercial Disputes*. Aurora: Canada Law Book.

Stone, Douglas, Heen, Sheila, and Patton, Bruce. 2010. *Difficult Conversations: How to Discuss What Matters Most*. New York: Penguin Books.

Supreme Court of Canada. 1988. *B.C.G.E.U. v. British Columbia*. (Attorney General), 2 S.C.R. 214 [25].

Supreme Court of Canada. 2017. *Clyde River (Hamlet) v. Petroleum GeoServices Inc.* 2017 SCC 40, 1 S.C.R. 1069 [24].

Susan, Prince. 2009. "ADR after the CPR: Have ADR Initiatives Now Assured Mediation an Integral Role in the Civil Justice System in England and Wales?." In: Déirdre Dwyer (ed), *The Civil Procedure Rules Ten Years On*. Oxford: Oxford University Press.

Susskind, Lawrence. 2004. "Expanding the Ethical Obligations of the Mediator: Mediator Accountability to Parties Not at the Table." In: Carrie Menkel-Meadow and Michael Wheeler (eds), *What's Fair, Ethics for Negotiators*. San Francisco: John Wiley and Sons.

Susskind, Lawrence. 2006. *Breaking Robert's Rules: The New Way to Run your Meeting, Build Consensus, and Get Results*. Oxford: Oxford University Press.

Susskind, Lawrence. 2014. *Good for You, Great for Me*. New York: Public Affairs.

Susskind, Lawrence, Babbitt, Eileen, and Segal, Phyllis. 1993. "When ADR Becomes the Law: A Review of Federal Practice." *Negotiation Journal* 9(1): 59–75.

Susskind, Lawrence, and Cruikshank, Jeffrey. 1995. *Breaking the Impasse: Consensual Approaches to Resolving Public Disputes*. New York: Basic Books.

Susskind, Lawrence, and Madigan, Denise. 1984. "New Approaches to Resolving Disputes in the Public Sector." *The Justice System Journal* 9(2): 179–203.

Susskind, Lawrence, and McMahon, Gerard. 1985. "The Theory and Practice of Negotiated Rulemaking." *Yale Journal on Regulation* 133(3): 133–165.

Susskind, Richard. 2019. *Online Courts and the Future of Justice*. Oxford, UK: Oxford University Press.

The Supreme Court of Canada. 2001. *Of Re Therrien*. 2 SCR 3.

The Supreme Court of Canada. 2014. *Union Carbide Canada Inc. v. Bombardier Inc.* 2014 SCC 35.

Thibaut, John, Walker, Laurens, LaTour, Stephen, and Houlden, Pauline. 1974. "Procedural Justice as Fairness." *Stanford Law Review* 26(6): 1271–1289.

Toering, Dougal. 2013. "The New Michigan Business Court Legislation: Twelve Years in the Making." American Bar Association, January 31. https://www.americanbar.org/groups/business_law/publications/blt/2013/01/03_toering/.

Tomporowski, Barbara, Manon, Buck, Bergen, Catherine, and Binder, Valarie. 2011. "Reflections of the Past, Present, and Future of Restorative Justice in Canada." *Alberta Law Review* 48(4): 815–830.

Tyler, Tom, and Bies, Robert. 1990. "Beyond Formal Procedures: The Interpersonal Context of Procedural Justice." In John Carroll (ed.), *Applied Social Psychology and Organizational Settings*. New York: Routledge.

Tyler, Tom, and Blader, Steven L. 2003. "What Constitutes Fairness in Work Settings? A Four-Component Model of Procedural Justice." *Human Resource Management Review* 13(1): 107–126.

UK Civil Procedure Rules 1998.

United States Congress (U.S.C.). 1976. 1 28 § 2071.

United States Congress (U.S.C.) §§ 620-629. 1976. Act of Dec. 20, 1967, Pub. L. No. 90–219, 81 Stat. 664.

Ury, William, Goldberg, Stephen, and Jeanne, Brett. 1988. *Getting Disputes Resolved: Designing Systems to Cut the Costs of Conflict*. San Francisco: Jossey-Bass.

Winslade, John, and Monk, Gerald. 2000. *Narrative Mediation: A New Approach to Conflict Resolution*. San Francisco: Jossey-Bass.

Youngzhu, Chen. 2015. "The Judge as Mediator in China and Its Reform: A Problem in Chinese Civil Justice." *Journal of Comparative Law* 10(2): 106–125.

Zariski, Archie. 2018. "Judicial Dispute Resolution in Canada: Towards Accessible Dispute Resolution." *Windsor Yearbook of Access to Justice* 35(1): 433–462.

Zou, Mimi. 2020. "Virtual Justice in the Time of Covid-19." *Oxford Business Law Blog* 16. https://www.law.ox.ac.uk/business-law-blog/blog/2020/03/virtual-justice-time-covid-19.

APPENDIX

TEACHING GUIDE

Table of Contents

Teaching Guide

The nine case studies that follow were prepared by students of our Harvard Law School research seminar in the Spring of 2019. Based on interviews with the key litigants, lawyers, and presiding JDR judges, they detail actual JDRs in Alberta, Canada and are are published with the permission of the parties. Names are fictional and some facts have been changed to preserve the confidentiality of the parties involved.

In a law school course on mediation or ADR, all nine cases can be used to raise important questions about the practice of mediation, particularly the role of lawyers; styles of mediation (i.e., facilitative vs. evaluative vs. transformative); the ethical obligations of the mediator; the rights of the parties; and the difficulties of evaluating outcomes. Although numerous published case studies recreate the details of mediation processes, we have found none that provide a detailed review—after the fact and from the perspectives of all the parties—of mediation as it is practiced by sitting judges. As we discussed in the book, JDR in Canada is similar in some respects to U.S. mini-trials, judicial conferences, and court-annexed private mediation, all of which were shaped by the "multi-door courthouse" idea derived from the contributions of our Harvard Law School colleague Professor Frank Sander.

The cases cover a range of civil disputes and can be used as a focal point for discussion in law school classes on torts, property, family law, environmental law, negotiation,

Table 1 Fitting the cases to the applicable courses.

Cases	Page #	Applicable courses
The Contaminated Land Case	35	Torts Property Environmental Law Negotiation Mediation ADR
The Divorce Case	41	Family Law Negotiation Mediation ADR
The Motor Vehicle Accident with Pedestrian Case	61	Torts Negotiation Mediation ADR
Temperament in an Estate Dispute Case	73	Family Law Jurisprudence Law & Psychology Negotiation Mediation ADR
The Negligent Land Transfer Case	77	Property Negotiation Mediation ADR
The Falling Rocks Case	101	Torts Negotiation Mediation ADR
The Medical Malpractice Case	115	Torts Procedural Law Negotiation Mediation ADR
The Well Fire Case	119	Environmental Law Torts Insurance Law Negotiation Mediation ADR
The Power Pole Case	141	Labor Law Negotiation Mediation ADR

labor law, procedural law, law and psychology, and insurance law. Table 1 indicates which cases are most relevant to various law school classes along with corresponding page numbers where the case is referenced in the book to highlight a key feature of JDR as it is practiced in Canada. It is followed by a summary of each case and the key teaching points that deserve special attention.

Case Summaries and Key Teaching Points

The Contaminated Land Case

This case involves a plaintiff who took out a mortgage to purchase a land parcel for development. Despite the obstacle of the land being contaminated, the plaintiff went to great lengths to pay off his debts to the mortgage lender, including handing over his family's country home. Nonetheless, these efforts over many years did not meet the lender's expectation regarding interest and principal repayment and resulted in several lawsuits. The case was ultimately settled using JDR with both sides walking away from all their claims.

Key teaching points

- *Role of lawyers in JDR*

Lawyers have special responsibilities to their clients during JDR. The unrestrained advocacy by counsel expected during litigation is not appropriate during JDR. JDR participants need very different kinds of advice and assistance. For one thing, they need help clarifying their interests (i.e., the kinds of things important to them in rank order). They also need help figuring out the interests of the other side (so they can offer "trades" that are likely to be accepted). JDR participants need help telling their story in their own words so the judge can understand their emotional needs. And, it helps if they can clarify their BATNA—whether through the JDR judge's forecast of what is likely to happen if they proceed to litigation or through some other kind of analysis. What they don't need is an exaggerated estimate of the likely outcome of litigation or a review of the strengths of their case in terms of past precedent—exactly what lawyers are expected to provide in litigation. Key question for discussion: How are ADR/JDR counsels' roles and responsibilities different from what they are in litigation?

- *JDR judges and mediation expertise*

JDR judges need in-depth mediation training. They must know how to interact with the parties (together and in caucus), as well as when and how to offer forecasts or opinions (privately) to the parties regarding the likely outcome of litigation, if mediation fails. To the extent a JDR judge has substantive legal background (e.g., has previously studied, litigated, or participated in environmental lawsuits), they must consider when, whether, and how to offer substantive suggestions to one or both of the parties regarding the conflict. Simultaneously maintaining a neutral or non-partisan stance is a challenge for all mediators. Given the weight of a judge's words, offering the parties new options or solutions can backfire. Key question for discussion: What special training in mediation should the court require of JDR judges? Is this any different from the training that all mediators need?

- *JDR vs. private (out-of-court) mediation*

One alternative to JDR is private mediation. The same parties headed to JDR might instead, choose to work with a private mediator who is not connected to the court (although that mediator might be a former judge of some kind). The parties have to pay for the services of a private mediator while there is no charge for JDR. The parties might not be as convinced of the (non-judge) private mediator's forecast of the likely outcome if the case goes to litigation. The mediator has no power to bind the parties to whatever agreement they reach, unlike JDR where the parties can ask the judge for binding decision, ensuring that the case is closed and the likelihood of compliance is high. Key question for discussion: What are the pros and cons of JDR vs. private (out-of-court) mediation?

- *Missing parties at JDR*

The environmental regulator was not at the table in this case. We are not aware of guidelines around missing parties at a JDR, and we did not encounter any established process in our research. According to Justice Tilleman, however, it is permissible—with the concurrence of the parties and their lawyers—for a judge to notify a missing party of a pending agreement that has been reached during the JDR. Presumably, this could occur prior to the final resolution of the case, with reactions relayed to the parties who could then decide whether to modify the agreement. Key question for discussion: What should a JDR judge do when a party, whose concerns are important to the resolution of the case, is not at the table? Can counsel act for a party who is not there? Should s/he act without their client present in a JDR?

- *Building a relationship with the parties in a JDR case*

In this case, the JDR judge spent a lot of time in private caucus with each party and their lawyer. Once the parties reached a point of trusting the judge to be fair and feeling that he had listened to their versions of the story, they seemed open to the judge's suggestions. The judge, drawing on his prior experience as an environmental attorney, convinced the defendant that he would still face substantial clean-up costs even if he secured control of the parcel in question because the regulators would not relent. That appeared to help the defendant make a more accurate appraisal of his interests. Key question for discussion: What are the ways in which a JDR judge can build a bond of trust and credibility with the parties? Is this different from what a private mediator can do?

The Divorce Case

Howard first filed for divorce from Patricia in February 2017, and the JDR occurred in October 2018. The case was settled amicably in a two-day, non-binding, informal case management (ICM) meeting with a judge serving as the mediator. ICM is a type of JDR that began as a pilot program in northern Alberta, in June 2018, only four months before this case was settled. If the case had not settled in the ICM, the parties would have gone to trial with a different judge presiding over the case. In addition to the divorce, the case involved child support, parenting time, and the division of property.

Key teaching points

- *Satisfaction and compliance*

In family law matters, future relationships between disputants is important. Co-parenting means a relationship of some kind between the parties will continue after a divorce. If no children are involved, there may be ongoing financial matters that require attention and conversation over time. JDR promises higher levels of satisfaction and compliance with the results of settlement negotiations because the parties get to choose the result rather than it being imposed. JDR can also generate an enforceable contractual agreement by the time it concludes. Key question for discussion: What are the ways in which JDR might enhance levels of participant satisfaction and compliance with the terms of negotiated agreements?

- *When mediation/JDR should not be used in a family law context*

In the family law and dispute resolution fields, it is assumed that ADR/JDR should not be used when there is a past history or a threat of violence, especially if children are involved. There may be other considerations besides the threat of violence, but this should be at the top of the list. Key question for discussion: When should mediation/JDR not be used to resolve family law disputes?

- *Mediation benefits that can't be matched in litigation*

Mediation, especially in the context of JDR, offers benefits that litigation does not: the parties control the outcome; it often takes much less time to reach a settlement; it costs less; the emotional and interpersonal dimensions of the dispute remain entirely relevant; the parties and the mediator are not bound by legal precedent; the entire process and outcome remain confidential; there is no "loser"; and the parties get to tell a judge their side of the story in their own words without cross-examination by an adversarial lawyer.

Litigation offers its distinct merits, as well: setting legal precedent (taking the public interest into account); cross-examination in the search for the "truth"; decisions based solely on the strength of legal arguments and argumentation; a definitive result; and no requirement that either party speak before the court. Key question for discussion: What are the benefits of JDR in family law cases that litigation is not likely to provide?

The Motor Vehicle Accident with a Pedestrian Case

The plaintiff in this case was seriously injured when he was was hit by a truck while crossing a highway. Statements filed with the court may have given the impression that this case could not be settled: on one side was the plaintiff's claim of heart-breaking losses and allegations of personal liability, and on the other, the defendant had an equally compelling argument of his regrettable involvement in an accident over which he had no control due to the plaintiff's fault and negligence.

In the JDR session with a sitting justice on the Alberta Court of Queen's Bench, all parties agreed to settle. The plaintiff received a payment of approximately $150,000 and all claims were dismissed.

The justice's process was key to the resolution. She was clear with the plaintiff that the case had to focus on compensation. Her risk analysis with both parties— weighing a trial's likely outcome and expenses—helped frame the discussion, as did her emphasis on finding a global settlement number rather than particular damages. Including a deadline gave the JDR a sense of urgency when it might have otherwise gone unattended until trial. Lastly, but possibly most importantly, the plaintiff felt heard.

Key teaching points

- *How to discuss and determine damages in JDR/ADR*

In this case, there was very little discussion during the JDR about the expert medical reports provided by the parties. They began by discussing each element of the claimant's list of damages and the suffering caused by the accident, but moved quickly—at the judge's suggestion—to a single number, or a possible "global settlement." The judge set a very clear deadline and met multiple times in separate caucuses with both sides, sharing that it would be very difficult to forecast what would happen if the case went to litigation, and that most claims of this type tend to settle. Even though the pre-JDR materials submitted by both sides indicated that a settlement was highly unlikely, the case did, in fact, settle within the time frame set by the JDR judge. Key question for discussion: How should damages be valued in a JDR/ADR context?

- *Fairness and justice in JDR/ADR*

Mediation in JDR and in a private context outside of court both aim to provide a process for collaborative decision-making that feels fair to both sides. ADR and JDR are less concerned about ensuring a substantive outcome that matches past court decisions in similar situations. While the JDR judge can offer an opinion, if asked, about what a likely court outcome would be, unless the parties ask for a binding decision (BJDR) from the judge, the judge need not be satisfied that the outcome agreed to by the parties is substantively just. In a sense, JDR presumes that a fair process (with the parties controlling the outcome and with the advice of counsel) will yield a just outcome. Key question for discussion: What constitutes a fair or just outcome in ADR/JDR?

- *How to cope with suffering and losses in ADR/JDR*

The judge in this case made very clear from the outset that the mediation process could not possibly repair the damage caused by the accident; the only issue was determining fair compensation. She listened patiently and empathetically to the difficulties the plaintiff reportedly suffered and how his life had been changed, and this, in particular, set the stage for an agreement. It seems unlikely that a private mediator doing the same thing would have had the same effect. The fact that there was no cross-examination by the defendant's insurance company made the whole process more bearable for the plaintiff. Key question for discussion: How can ADR and JDR address suffering and losses in ways that litigation cannot, and how do these features of mediation make it more likely that the parties will reach a voluntary settlement?

Temperament in an Estate Dispute Case

In this case, two siblings discussed how to distribute their deceased parents' estate that included a residence where the sister lived, personal investments, and a cabin. The dispute, however, was not limited to distributional details. The bigger issue was that both siblings were grieving in their own ways. The judge knew he had to turn their attention to their shared loss instead of focusing first on their divergent views on how to distribute assets.

All matters that were partially agreed upon and decisions made regarding further actions were included in interim and consent orders.

Key teaching points

- *The power of storytelling in ADR/JDR setting*

It is clear in this case that the JDR judge was able to use storytelling and the tools of narrative to help the parties and their lawyers see how JDR could help them. The judge shared details of a case that had dragged on in litigation for a long time to illustrate that JDR or BJDR made agreement possible. Key question for discussion: How can mediators or JDR judges use storytelling techniques to bring the parties to the table?

- *How to manage the distributive and value-creation tension in ADR?*

In all ADR and JDR contexts, the parties and the mediator face a variety of distributive tasks. Every agreement includes implicit and explicit determinations of who gets what (relative to their interests, goals, and values). Even though it is less obvious and often overlooked, every dispute resolution effort also offers value-creating opportunities. By reframing the dispute, linking certain agreed upon commitments to other promises, or including contingent elements of various kinds (i.e., "If this happens our deal is this, but if that happens, we will switch to an alternative arrangement spelled out as an appendix to our agreement"), the parties can almost always create value (and not in a zero-sum fashion). Value creation and value distribution can be encouraged and managed by a JDR judge. Usually, value creation comes first. Key question for discussion: What are the ways in which the JDR judge helped the parties create value?

- *How to move beyond the facilitative/evaluative dichotomy*

In most writing about JDR or ADR mediation, there is usually reference made to the style or strategy of the mediator. Are they facilitative (i.e., focused exclusively on helping the parties reach agreement and offering no judgements or forecasts of their own) or are they evaluative (i.e., quick to offer their personal prediction of how the case is likely to be decided if it goes to court)? The distinction is both interesting and important. While some private mediators draw on both approaches in the same case, they are usually selected because they are one or the other. JDR judges, however, must be eclectic. The primary assumption in JDR is that the parties will control the outcome, so the JDR judge must be working mainly in a facilitative mode. But, the if the parties ask for the ADR judge's best guess about what will happen if they go to court (often in the hope that the answer will cause the other side to be more realistic about their BATNA), most JDR judges will provide a response. This case illustrates the nuanced way a JDR judge can weave an evaluative move into what is basically a facilitative approach. Key question for discussion: In what ways must a JDR judge incorporate both evaluative and facilitative elements into their mediation style?

- *Training for JDR mediation*

In law school, judges do not learn in the necessary skills to be able to provide JDR services. On the other hand, all JDR judges cannot be expected to have prior professional mediation experience when they join the bench. This means, newly appointed judges must go to "judge school" (or training organized by the bar) to learn how JDR works. JDR training is typically led by a sitting or former judge and the focus is on logistics and the judge's responsibilities (i.e., what information needs to be collected in pre-trial interviews; when and how caucuses should be organized; and when and how expert information should be incorporated, etc.). A few days at judge school, however, is not sufficient to prepare a new judge with no prior mediation experience to develop the frame of mind required to be an effective facilitative mediator. More, since judges do not talk with others on the bench about their JDR experience, new judges must learn from their own judicial experience. If law schools included mandatory ADR training as part of their curricula, all lawyers (and, presumably most future judges) would know how facilitative mediation works. Key question for discussion: Which JDR/ADR skills are teachable, and which are mostly a byproduct of the JDR judge or private mediator's own character?

The Negligent Land Transfer Case

This emotional and complex case involves a dispute between Betty and Tom Walker and their three children, Lila, Will, and Ellis. The parents had made their son Will the registered owner of three parcels of farmland where they lived. Lila was made an owner of only one parcel, the "family home parcel," where their home was located. In 2006, Ellis spoke with his family about being added to the title of the three parcels of land. Despite a verbal agreement that he would become a co-owner of the land, his brother Will refused to execute the documents. Tom hired a lawyer to represent him in adding his son to the title for each of the three parcels. Betty, Will, and Lila retained their own lawyer, and a settlement was negotiated in early 2007, which Tom signed, but Ellis did not. Soon after, revised documents modified Ellis's share, but Ellis was not informed. Nearly a year after the modified settlement had been executed, one lawyer contacted the other to obtain additional affidavits to support the transfer. While waiting on the documents, Tom Walker died.

The case settled in a four-hour JDR process. The judge suggested giving a wholly separate, family-owned property to Ellis, to which the family agreed. Negotiation between the family members was paramount in this process.

Key teaching points

- *How caucusing or shuttle diplomacy can help to resolve disputes*

Many mediators insist on limiting their interactions with parties to face-to-face meetings with all the parties present rather than separate caucuses. In *The Negligent Land Transfer case*, the JDR judge relied entirely on what is known as "shuttle diplomacy," moving from one private caucus to another. The case had been in limbo for so long that the relationships among the parties (who were family members) had been irretrievably fractured. In the opinion of the JDR judge and the lawyers, there was too much animosity to mediate with all of them in the same room. In a court room, of course, private caucusing would not be an option. Key question for discussion: When and how should caucusing or shuttle diplomacy be used in JDR?

- *Judge's role in shaping the ZOPA in court*

The Zone of Possible Agreement (ZOPA) in a dispute is bounded by the BATNAs (or, the "reservation values" as economists call them) of the parties. A deal or an agreement is possible if the least one party will accept is less than the most the other party is willing to offer. Once a JDR judge—in private caucuses with each side—understands there is a ZOPA (no matter how small), they can proceed to mediate and tell the two sides that the chances of reaching agreement look good. If, however, the JDR judge determines at the outset that no ZOPA exists given the parties' positions, the he or she can suggest to one or both sides that they reconsider their BATNA. One way the judge can do this is to offer a prediction of the case's likely outcome if it goes to trial. Another way is by helping the parties create value by reframing the dispute, adding new issues, or negotiating trades that the parties have not considered before. In this case, the judge found a way to generate a new solution to the dispute; rather than focusing on money, he addressed how Ellis had felt wronged by their deceased father. Key question for discussion: What role can a JDR judge play in reshaping the ZOPA at the outset of a dispute resolution effort?

- *What satisfaction means in assessing the outcome of a mediation effort*

The goal of mediation, whether ADR or JDR, is to meet the interests of the parties in a way that seems fair, efficient, and wise to them. In JDR, it's helpful to think about the judge as a party, unlike how we tend to think of an independent mediator in a private mediation. The ADR judge represents the public interest and has to go along with the terms of settlement. In *The Negligent Land Transfer Case*, we focus on the extent to which the parties are satisfied with the agreement they reached. (There was no BJDR requested.) Ellis, who initiated the lawsuit was satisfied because he received a land bequest, even though it was not the land he originally requested. Indeed, the arrangement was only possible because the JDR judge urged the other family members to offer a parcel that was never in dispute (and not part of the litigation). The monetary value of the parcel was not relevant; satisfaction can mean something entirely different to each party in a JDR/ADR. A judge has to probe to discover what it is really going on to generate a satisfactory agreement. This is not possible in litigation where the parameters of the lawsuit are set at the outset and cannot be changed. While private mediation could have produced the same result, the JDR judge was able to go a step further when the parties asked him to issue an order embodying the details of the terms of their agreement, something a private mediator could not do. This gave everyone confidence that compliance would be forthcoming. Key question for discussion: What can JDR offer, by way of satisfying the interests of the parties, that litigation or ADR more generally cannot?

- *What to do when JDR/ADR comes too late to repair relationships*

JDR only happens after parties have hired a lawyer, filed a case, had the case accepted by the court, and the court assigns a JDR judge. Throughout that pre-case filing period, private mediation could be utilized, while JDR cannot. This case points out this weakness of JDR; by the time the case reached a JDR, it was too late to repair relationships within the family that were at the heart of the case. Key question for discussion: Under what circumstances might it be too late for JDR to repair interpersonal relationships?

The Falling Rocks Case

This was a ten-year litigation between a Canadian municipality and the owners of a private building near the city hall. A storm passed through the city and allegedly blew loose rocks from the private building's roof onto city hall, breaking its glass pyramids. The city advised the building owners to take immediate action to avoid similar incidents in the future. Three more storms allegedly caused more damage, and the city hired an expert to investigate and then file a lawsuit against the building owners. The city accused the building owners of nuisance in the design, inspection, and replacement of the roof, as well as nuisance for allowing the rocks to accumulate. The city sought an injunction requiring the building owners to remove the blowing rocks or make repairs to avoid any damage to the city hall again.

The case settled in a single day with the court issuing a consent dismissal order requiring that the city and its insurance company receive almost half of the amount they requested, along with a small portion of their litigation costs. They received around $500,000 compensation two months later, marking the close of the case.

Key teaching points

- *The Role of Scientific Experts in JDR/ADR*

The litigation that preceded the JDR had gone on for a long time. Each side had lined up numerous scientific and technical experts to support their arguments and cost estimates. There is usually no involvement of experts in JDR, but it is allowable (if both sides agree) for the JDR judge to meet with and cross examine an expert (without the direct involvement of counsel for either or both sides.) In this case, the parties did not seek to involve the experts in the JDR. When we think about the goal of mediation, it doesn't seem very important to involve experts to impeach the arguments of the other side; the focus is exclusively on the terms of settlement. Key question for discussion: What role is there for scientific experts in JDR/ADR?

- *How insurance coverage might affect the outcome of a mediation effort*

This case is basically an effort to mediate liability litigation, and it included five counsels. The counsel for an insurance company had to call their office in the middle of the settlement negotiations to get permission to offer more money than they had originally intended. There is no question that the available insurance coverage played a part in shaping the outcome of the mediation. The lawyer for the insurance company was clearly influenced by the evaluative statements of the JDR judge, even though this was not an instance of BJDR. Key question for discussion: What role does insurance coverage play in shaping the outcome of an ADR/JDR mediation?

- *Reality testing in JDR/ADR*

The JDR judge plays a "reality testing" role in the mediation process, often via private caucuses with each side and their counsel. A private mediator (especially if they are a former judge) can do the same, but our research suggests that a sitting judge's estimate of what might happen if the case goes to litigation has more of an impact. Key question for discussion: How can a JDR judge who is trying to help the parties reach a voluntary settlement serve as a reality tester for both sides?

- *Confidentiality in disputes in which there is a public interest*

Various authors point to the confidentiality promised in JDR as a strength, while others suggest it is a drawback, especially when a case involves issues that can have a bearing on the public interest. In *The Falling Rocks Case*, one of the parties is a city government. A confidential outcome of a longstanding and expensive litigation process means that the public (and the media) will not have a transparent view of the basis for settlement. For the parties, confidentiality makes it easier to reach agreement (i.e., no one has to explain to anyone else why the terms of settlement were reached), as does the absence of a court decree announcing winner and loser. Key question for discussion: Is the confidentiality requirement in this case a plus or a minus from the standpoint of ensuring that the public interest is well served?

The Medical Malpractice Case

The medical procedure giving rise to this action and successful JDR was a vitrectomy. Smith, the eventual plaintiff, underwent a vitrectomy surgery to improve vision in his right eye. After multiple rounds of topical anesthesia and pain, Smith still claimed that his eye was not numb, but the ophthalmologist went ahead and began the surgery. Smith again experienced extreme pain and moved suddenly, causing the ophthalmologist's needle to perforate the globe of his eye, resulting in vitreous and preretinal hemorrhage. Further anesthetic was added, and the ophthalmologist completed the vitrectomy successfully. However, Smith had to undergo several more surgeries over the coming years to attempt to correct the damage resulting from the perforated globe.

Ultimately, the plaintiff was convinced that he should accept a much lower settlement because his initial claim had been undermined and rendered unjustified by the defense's evidence. The confidential settlement consisted solely of monetary damages and costs. There was no admission of liability by the defendants and the settlement did not become a court order.

Key teaching points

● *Power imbalances in JDR/ADR*

Although this case does not focus specifically on the ways that power imbalances emerge in JDR or ADR—or how the JDR judge or mediator can stop them from emerging—it does highlight some of the ways a JDR judge can help even out each party's "airtime"; the extent to which each party is taken seriously; and the extent of each side's contribution to the agenda for settlement negotiation. In JDR or mediation, unequal representation by high-priced or inexperienced attorneys can be counteracted by a JDR judge who is providing varying levels of coaching to each side, depending on the help they need. Key question for discussion: Are the power imbalances that can arise in litigation also likely to emerge in ADR/JDR? If they do, what are the ways the JDR judge or the mediator can and should respond?

● *Calculating monetary damages and costs*

The confidential settlement in this case consisted solely of monetary damages and costs. Whatever calculations were made by each side, they kept to themselves. The plaintiff's lawyer said the settlement amount was fair, but not huge and a lot less than the plaintiff's initial demand in litigation. The funds were delivered without any issues from the defendant's insurance company to the plaintiff's attorney within fifteen days, and without the need for the judge to assist with compliance. There was no admission of liability by the defendants, and the settlement was not incorporated into a court order. The judge did require the parties to sign a settlement sheet, which she kept for two years following the JDR. Key question for discussion: Do the parties in ADR/JDR need to agree on how and why monetary damages should be set at a certain amount, or is it sufficient that they just agree on an overall amount?

- *The pros and cons of facilitative JDR*

For the most part, the JDR judge in this case took a facilitative approach to the mediation. In private caucus, however, she helped each side see the weaknesses that might undermine parts of their legal argument if they went to court. Through repeated caucusing, she moved the parties closer to settlement, using what many ADR analysts would consider an evaluative style. She played a "reality testing" role for both sides (separately), but she did not define her style or strategy as evaluative. She avoided offering her opinions on the strength of each side's overall case and instead focused on what appeared to be weaknesses in specific elements of each side's presentation. She offered her opinions, privately, to each side if she felt they were rejecting reasonable offers. That's different from helping the parties clarify their BATNAs. Key question for discussion: What are the pros and cons of facilitative JDR?

- *Confidentiality and non-liability in a settlement*

Neither side wanted the case to go to litigation and have their reputations adversely affected. The doctor didn't want his alleged malpractice debate to be made public, and the plaintiff's lawyer was concerned about her reputation if her client did not come off as fully credible in court. Key question for discussion: What are the various reasons that parties in JDR attach importance to confidentiality, and how can confidentiality add to the prospects for voluntary agreement?

The Power Pole Case

A truck's extended auger damaged the power lines on a farm property. When the electrician climbed a power pole to repair the damage, it broke and fell on him leaving him with injuries that required several surgeries and extensive physical therapy. On top of the expenses and lost income related to medical care and rehabilitation, as well as the damages associated with his pain and suffering resulting from the fall, he alleged that his injuries inhibited his ability to perform basic household tasks, leaving him dependent on the assistance of others. Further, he claimed that the lasting effects of his injuries would render him unable to fully compete with his healthy co-workers, disadvantaging him professionally and limiting his opportunities for future advancement.

The plaintiff had received some disability benefits from the Workplace Compensation Board (WCB) but these benefits were limited and terminated several months after the accident. Claiming nearly $7 million in damages, he sued the farm for negligence. The case settled at the JDR for a monetary payment to the electrician of under $100,000 (delivered shortly after the session), in exchange for which the electrician signed a standard release and discontinued the suit.

Key teaching points

- *Storytelling and narrative in JDR/ADR*

The JDR judge in this case invited each side to tell their story in very personal terms at the outset. This was cathartic for the plaintiff and it increased the sympathy of the defendant's insurance representative. Personal storytelling or narratives—not an option during litigation—allows emotional and physical injuries to be acknowledged, independent of monetary claims. Not every JDR judge or mediator will proceed in this fashion, but it certainly made a difference in this case. Key question for discussion: What are the ways in which inviting the parties to "tell their story" in very personal terms (without the intervention of their lawyers) can make it easier to reach a voluntary settlement?

- *The role of precedent in JDR/ADR*

When a sitting judge offers a forecast of what is likely to happen if a case goes to litigation, it can be as powerful as a legal precedent drawn from prior case law. Parties tend to listen and recalibrate their thinking. The opening briefs in this case were laden with all kinds of references to legal precedents that convinced each side of the strength of their own positions. The JDR judge, though, worked to get the parties to let go of these positions. The case is somewhat confusing: it is a story of how a timely supreme court decision had a significant impact on a JDR. At the same time, the JDR judge appeared to argue that the likely result if the case went on to litigation was more important to generating agreement acceptable to both sides than any legal precedents. This issue is a key topic for discussion.

- *Measuring satisfaction in JDR/ADR*

While both sides in any dispute resolution effort are sure to be concerned about the justice or fairness of the outcome in their case, their satisfaction, as we see in this case, might be mostly a function of how speedily and inexpensively the dispute resolution process is run. Key question for discussion: What are the key determinants of parties' satisfaction with the outcome of JDR or ADR?

The Well Fire Case

A fire broke out at a fracking site when gases escaped from a tank and alit on a nearby diesel engine. Allegedly, the tank was unvented and inappropriate for flammable gas storage, the engine was too close to the tank, and the site's crowded layout made it difficult to access and extinguish the blaze. The fire caused more than $3.3 million in damages to equipment, as well as a loss of profit due to the shut-down and clean-up operations.

The JDR closed on the second day without a finalized agreement and a date for trial in two years. It did eventually settle before trial, however, when the plaintiff's lawyer accepted a lower number. The site supervisor and operator assumed the majority of the liability and the rest of the defendants were assigned "descending levels of contribution" based in large part on guidance from a supreme court case that had come down the previous year, a precedent which made the deal feel fair overall. The site supervisor ended up with a settlement that was too good to pass up: under his insurance policy limit and protection from any personal liability. A different—even better—settlement may have been achieved at trial, but would have cost more.

Key teaching points

- *Using expert reports in JDR/ADR*

Resolution of this case did not depend on expert testimony and technical expertise that would surely have been important if it had gone to trial. Although expert testimony and cross-examination is permitted in JDR, the judge did not invite any experts to present and the lawyers did not cross-examine their opponents' evidence. The judge developed a "Scott Schedule" that is often used in JDR: based on pre-conference submittals and preliminary conversations with the parties, the judge lists the various types of damages that will need to be addressed, as well as the monetary value of these damages claimed by each side. According to the judge, all of this preliminary information was sufficient to generate an effective Scott Schedule. Note that the Scott Schedule is based on the claims of the parties and not an independent assessment of the scientific or technical basis for each side's position. Key question for discussion: How should disagreements over scientific or technical aspects of a dispute be addressed in JDR/ADR?

- *The dilemmas and dangers of a JDR judge trying to forecast the likely results of litigation*

In this case, it turned out that comparing settlement offers to the likely results of a trial did not have much influence on what the parties viewed as fair or realistic. There were complicating concerns on both sides, which if introduced in court—and it was not obvious that they would or could be—might have determined the likely outcome. This meant that there was a lot of uncertainty surrounding any effort to predict the results of a trial. In such a setting, working out a mutually acceptable agreement is the smartest way forward. Key question for discussion: How should the JDR judge proceed when it's difficult to predict a litigation result?

- *The role of precedent in JDR/ADR*

In this case, a supreme court decision right before the JDR set a precedent that had a substantial impact on this case. The way liability should be assigned (in varying amounts) discussed in the supreme court decision increased all the parties' sense of what would be fair in the JDR. In theory, liability is supposed to be based on fault, not capacity to pay. But in practice, including this case, insurance policy limits can set a boundary that both sides accept. Key question for discussion: What role should judicial precedents play settling ADR/JDR disputes?

CASE STUDIES

THE CONTAMINATED LAND CASE

Jessica Ljustina

Facts

This case involves a plaintiff who took out a mortgage to purchase a land parcel for development. Despite the obstacle of the land being contaminated, the plaintiff went to great lengths to pay off his debts to the mortgage lender, including handing over his family's country home. Nonetheless, these efforts over many years did not meet the lender's expectation for interest and principal repayment and resulted in several lawsuits. The case was ultimately settled at JDR with both sides walking away from all their claims.

Lead-up

In January 2005, two friends, Edward and David, purchased a piece of industrial land that they perceived to have development potential. They made the purchase through a newly incorporated company, 270 Incorporated (270 Inc.), in which they were equal shareholders. Each agreed to finance half of the $750,000 purchase price. Edward financed his half with a vendor-takeback loan from the seller, who was his sister. David obtained and personally guaranteed a mortgage loan from a third party, Forte Banking Corporation (Forte Banking), which had previously provided David and his wife a mortgage for their country home.

A month later, David's counsel (who incorporated 270 Inc. for David and Edward) told David that the land had a caveat on behalf of Coal Creek Oil and Gas due to contaminated waste beneath the soil. David and Edward had a difficult time making mortgage payments and otherwise advancing their development project. Within several months of purchasing the land, Edward sold his 50 percent share in 270 Inc. to the sole shareholder of Forte Banking, and his sister transferred the mortgage to Forte Banking. It would eventually come to light that Edward and his sister engaged in a series of related party transactions for increasingly greater amounts that inflated the land's value and looked like a classic straw buyer mortgage fraud.[1]

---

1. A straw buyer "is someone who agrees to put their name on a mortgage application on behalf of another person, typically for a cash payment." Real Estate Council Alberta. (2019, March). *Straw Buyer Mortgage Fraud.* Retrieved July 31, 2020, from https://www.reca.ca/wp-content/uploads/2019/03/Straw-Buyer-Mortgage-Fraud.pdf.

Even though Edward left the deal, David still felt there was development potential in the land and made further agreements with Forte Banking to help with the payments over several years. In early 2006, Forte Banking lent David additional funds securitized by a mortgage on David's private home in the city, and also received David's 50 percent shares in 270 Inc. as security for his debt.

Nothing improved for David. The industrial land was not suitable for development in large part due to the contaminated subsurface and surface. With no cash flow and further financial difficulties, David and his wife turned over their entire country home to Forte Banking in 2012. David was told that this would cover the overdue interest and some of the principal on his outstanding Forte Banking debt. David, however, felt that giving the bank his country home covered his entire debt. Accordingly, he demanded that his 50 percent shares in 270 Inc. be returned to him so he could develop the land.

Forte Banking, its individual shareholder and the shareholder's family (who became involved in the lawsuit) did not want to return the 50 percent shares. Their refusal was in part because they paid the utilities and tax bills, and because David allegedly ran a rent-free business on the property. Several lawsuits were filed between 2016 and 2017, including Forte Banking moving to foreclose the property on David. David claimed damages against Forte Banking totaling around $1 million for breach of contract, breach of good faith, fraud and unjust enrichment.

Forte Banking not only defended on the basis of paying the taxes and utilities, it also claimed for re-zoning costs, appraisals, environmental studies and negotiating remediating costs with Coal Creek Oil and Gas. Forte Banking counterclaimed for the remaining unpaid mortgage and the bills it had paid for David, totaling around $300,000. The provincial environmental regulator was also involved and required cleanup of the hazardous waste. (David had offered to use his own time and efforts to do the cleanup, but Forte Banking refused on the basis of his lack of skill and underestimation of the size of the problem.)

Outcome

The case was settled at JDR in September 2019, with both sides walking away from their claims and counterclaims on a "without costs" basis, which meant that each side paid their own costs and fees.[2] Upon joint application by the plaintiff (counterclaim defendant) and defendants (counterclaim plaintiffs), the JDR judge granted and signed a court order dismissing the action in its entirety. The dismissal was to have the same force and effect as if it had been pronounced as the court's decision after a full and complete trial of the action on its merits. Moreover, it was on a "with prejudice" basis, meaning neither side could subsequently sue the other for the same facts and claims or counterclaims.

---

2. In Canada, unlike in the U.S., the losing party pays the winning party's court-assessed costs and fees in almost every action.

Attorneys' and Judge's Attitudes toward the Case

For many years, the defendants had told the plaintiff that his case had no merit, though neither the plaintiff nor his lawyer were ready to give up on the lawsuit. The plaintiff had taken on a $400,000 high-interest-rate mortgage and the payments became significant. He was disappointed when, after paying $800,000 (a notable amount of interest and most of the principal) he still did not end up owning the property. The plaintiff ran a small business on the land which did not generate significant cashflow, and he effectively paid $800,000 in rent over seven years when he could have leased another property for significantly less. In this context, it was helpful to have a respected judge review the case, get the defendants' perspective toward the plaintiff, and convey that information to the plaintiff; since the plaintiff did not pay back the principal and interest according to the loan terms, it was unclear how the lender had committed fraud.

This was a difficult and emotional case because both sides felt betrayed. The debtor felt he was cheated and left with nothing, having lost both his residential property and his 50 percent share of the industrial land. The lender alleged that the borrower ran a rent-free business on the site. The environmental regulator's requirement that the land to be cleaned posed a further complication as well as significant costs for the owner of the land. At the outset, given the overlap in contractual and environmental problems, the JDR judge did not know how the case would settle.

JDR Process

Prior to the JDR, each side wrote and exchanged briefs of their arguments. In addition, the judge invited both sides to submit confidential settlement proposals that only he would see. These proposals included each side's view of its best and worst day in court. The defendants' best day scenario was the plaintiff's claim being dismissed and the outstanding interest paid, and on their worst day all claims would be dismissed. On the plaintiff's best day, he would be awarded $1 million, and on his worst day he would receive $500,000.

The defendants' attorney viewed the submission of these confidential settlement proposals to the judge as key in framing the conversation to effect a resolution. In particular, he felt the defendants' worst-day proposal provided the judge with credible evidence of their willingness to compromise with the plaintiff. (This was the first JDR in which the defendants' attorney encountered this procedural step, and he later used it in another JDR.)

This judge typically conducts JDR sessions in boardrooms on a different floor from the courtroom. He starts with everyone together for introductions and sets up the JDR as a mediation where court rules apply unless he says otherwise. In contrast with a trial, no opening statements were made by the lawyers or parties in this JDR. The defendants' attorney saw this as setting a tone of compromise rather than the two sides digging into their respective positions.

The JDR session proceeded through individual, confidential caucusing between parties in separate rooms and shuttle diplomacy. The defendants' attorney saw this approach as a key factor that contributed to the case settling in spite of feelings of hurt and betrayal; what is said in a breakout room typically stays in that room. The judge encouraged each side to identify the five to ten issues in litigation and chart three options: their best option, walkaway option, and a third option where the judge can seek to create value. As the judge moved between the rooms, he talked with the parties about their respective interests, identified overlaps, and offered suggestions regarding possible agreements. This is in contrast to another JDR approach of bringing everyone into the same room to try and hash things out.

The defendants approached JDR as though it were a trial: they made their best pitch to the judge, answered any and all questions and provided comprehensive materials. The judge noted that the defendants' attorney's preparation, calm demeanor and ability to guide his client through JDR contributed to the success of the process and enabled the judge to focus his mediation efforts on the plaintiff's side. While in the plaintiff's room, the judge offered an empathetic ear, relayed the other side's story and provided objective views—particularly on the environmental issues and costs required to clean up the land.

Halfway through the day, the judge had built up enough rapport with both sides that they changed the JDR from non-binding to binding. The defendants' attorney had anticipated this possibility, though clients on both sides were not completely convinced of the logic of this procedural change. They were, however, confident in the judge's opinion and trusted in the decision. Ultimately, the parties consensually reached a settlement through binding JDR (BJDR) and a court order was entered.

Themes

JDR judge's expertise and capacity to mediate

The judge's mediation skills were critical to the case's outcome. He identified and implemented appropriate process choices, including requesting confidential settlement proposals at the outset, caucusing and making the JDR binding.

His mediation style was primarily facilitative, with some evaluative characteristics. The parties felt his genuine empathy as he listened to their stories. The defendants' attorney thought that the judge had told the plaintiff that his case was relatively weak and noted this was an example of a more evaluative approach, which the attorney believes contributed to the case resolving in a fair and efficient manner.

The judge's environmental expertise also proved helpful for addressing the contamination issues related to the case. The judge recalled being sympathetic to the plaintiff's case and believes there was a shift to resolution when he pointed out that the owner of the land would be finally realizing the significant clean-up costs imposed by the environmental regulator. This move by the judge seems neither purely facilitative nor evaluative and stands out as something unique to JDR that would not have been possible in a litigation setting.

In addition to the confidential settlement proposals and individual caucusing, the defendants' attorney noted that the ability to change the JDR from non-binding to binding facilitated parties reaching a settlement. He characterized BJDR as binding arbitration, where the judge is empowered to settle the file for the parties if they cannot reach a settlement. This contrasts with non-binding mediation under non-binding JDR, and in the defendants' attorney's opinion, had the effect of incentivizing the side with a relatively weak case to agree on a settlement. The judge explained that his BJDR mediation approach is the same as in non-binding JDRs, and that he has never had to make a decision for the parties. Thus, even if the option of the judge deciding the case is seldom chosen, having this alternative on the table may incentivize parties to reach a mutual agreement rather than have their case settled for them.

Satisfaction and fairness

The defendants' attorney and the judge saw the resolution as fair and satisfactory for both sides. The attorney expressed a general view that judges often want to try to give something to both sides. In this case, the defendants' reservation value allowed the judge to tell the plaintiff that the defendants were willing to walk away from the outstanding interest the plaintiff owed, and further, to persuade the plaintiff to walk away from his claims. The judge felt it was a just outcome even though the plaintiff did not end up with the land that he thought he was entitled to; the plaintiff accepted that owning the land came with additional obligations, and development prospects appeared bleak to an objective observer.

An important contributor to party satisfaction may have been the process itself. For all involved, JDR was less costly, less time-consuming and less acrimonious compared to other options (see below). The judge's efforts to be understanding and share his expertise on the law and substantive issues seemed to enable parties on both sides to accept the outcome as one that they could live with.

JDR vs trial or private ADR

In contrast to litigation, JDR gives parties an opportunity to step back from their adversarial positions and consider their underlying interests and alternatives. JDR's track record of success, condensed time frame and relatively low cost to litigants and the courts often makes it a more favorable option than trial or private ADR.[3]

The judge in this case referred to the Special Resolution Project (SPECS), where three- to four-week trials on the judicial calendar are allotted focused time and may be resolved through JDR in a few days. Under current Alberta court rules as of the writing of this case (March 2020), parties could not book trial time unless they had completed ADR (including JDR or private mediation) or received a court order exempting this

---

3. While JDRs entail an added single-day cost for cases that do not resolve, the judge in this case estimated that 80 percent of JDRs succeed and noted that the judge's time is free. Moreover, cases that do not fully resolve and proceed beyond the JDR benefit from the experience both in terms of clarification of facts and how the law may apply.

requirement under limited circumstances (e.g., class action, small dollar value claims, some family matters). The defendants' attorney described mandatory ADR as "smart," noting that in the past when ADR was not required, there was a negative impact on trial time.

The defendants' attorney favored JDR over ADR for two reasons. First, JDR is free, compared to private mediation which can be extremely expensive: a one-day mediation including preparation time with one of the most sought-after private mediators—a former judge of the Ontario Supreme Court—could cost $30,000 to $40,000. Second, JDR takes parties and litigants "behind the curtain," sharing how judges might feel about their case. An experienced JDR judge may also offer insights regarding how other judges on the bench might view the case and could even be their presiding trial judge. The judge pointed out JDR's advantage of enforceability over private ADR. Whereas private ADR results in a private agreement, JDRs can result in a court order which is enforceable through normal processes, including contempt of court. Compliance is not an issue in all cases, however, especially when principled attorneys help ensure that an agreement is followed. Thus, the judge may not sign a court order in some JDRs, or may issue a court order containing a general clause that parties agree to file discontinuances and legal documents, transfer funds, and so on, to give effect to the agreement as soon as possible.

2

THE DIVORCE CASE

Tessa Tompkins Byer

This case involves a divorce between Patricia and Howard. Interviews were conducted with the judge overseeing the Judicial Dispute Resolution (JDR), Patricia and her attorney and Howard's attorney.

About JDR

Parties may choose to participate in non-binding JDR or binding JDR (BJDR). In BJDR, the judge makes final decisions about the case if the parties do not come to an agreement, much like a mediation-arbitration process: the judge as mediator becomes an arbitrator and rules on the case. In non-binding JDR, the case goes to another judge for a trial if the parties do not come to an agreement, much like a traditional mediation process. One procedural downside to BJDR is that it cannot be appealed; an issue less important in divorce than in other types of cases. The judge in this case reported that he sees more parties choose BJDR than JDR because they want the case to be done after the process. In contrast, the two attorneys in this case both prefer non-binding JDR noting that the process may be more relaxed and less like a trial.

The judge in this case reported that about eight out of ten cases that engage in JDR are resolved. In his experience, one of the main reasons has to do with efficiency: every aspect of the case is resolved within two days of meetings, or the judge and parties agree to another date for resolution. He also attributes some of JDR's success to elements of the process that do not exist in litigation, such as encouraging both parties to step back, take a breath and truly listen to each other. When he prevents parties from interrupting each other, he noted, they may realize what they are hearing from the other side actually works for them. He also asks parties if an apology will help to move things forward. Another strategy he recently developed in divorce cases is to allow couples to get divorced immediately and then hammer out the remaining issues in JDR. The relief of the divorce can create a more conciliatory tone for the rest of the JDR. These components are not available in traditional litigation settings but can be instrumental in contributing to a cooperative resolution of a case.

Another advantage in JDR is enforcement: when parties reach an agreement, the court stands behind the resolution and allows them to return to court if one party is not following the agreement. Trust is not necessary for compliance as it is in a private Alternative Dispute Resolution (ADR) process. That said, the very nature of the JDR process tends to build trust among parties as they hear each other's perspectives and work together toward a resolution.

Facts

Howard first filed for divorce from Patricia in February 2017, and the JDR occurred in October 2018. The case was settled in a two-day, non-binding, informal case management (ICM) meeting with a judge serving as the mediator. ICM is a type of JDR that began as a pilot program in southern Alberta, in June 2018, only four months before this case was settled. If the case had not settled in the ICM, the parties would have gone to trial with a different judge presiding over the case. In addition to the divorce, the case revolved around child support, parenting time and the division of property.

In February 2018, a parenting time order was issued. It outlined that Patricia and Howard were to share joint custody of their son, Sam: Howard would have Sam in his care from Thursday through Sunday every other week and from Thursday to Tuesday every other week in summers. Their other child, Emily, who was not Howard's biological daughter, was not mentioned in the order. The order accommodated Howard's schedule of working alternating weeks. After the order went into effect, however, Howard's schedule changed to two weeks on and two weeks off, which would have made him unavailable for half of the time he had Sam. Patricia and Howard agreed to alter the parenting arrangement without officially amending the order through court; Howard was then able to have Sam for two weekends in a row rather than every other weekend.

After successfully working within the new arrangement for the spring, Patricia informed Howard that for the summer months she wanted to return to the order where Howard had Sam every other weekend. In response, Howard filed a Family Application to officially amend the order so he could continue to have Sam in his care for two full weeks in a row throughout the summer. Additionally, Patricia had to work every other Saturday, leaving Sam with a babysitter and Howard objected to contributing to childcare costs when Sam could instead be with him.

Patricia's objections to Howard's proposed parenting arrangement were multifold: first, she was uncomfortable with Sam being away from her for two weeks at a time. Because she took the lead on the children's health and education, she was concerned about these areas of their lives that might suffer. Second, Patricia attested that she wanted to honor Sam's request that he spend no more than a week with his father. Third, Patricia's work schedule allowed her to have Friday and Saturday off every other week; therefore, she wanted to have Sam in her care on the long weekends that she did not have to work. She mentioned buying kayaks specifically for summer recreational time. The original order accommodated this schedule, but the informal interim arrangement allowed her to see Sam on only one of these long weekends a month. Finally, Patricia contended that Howard was asking for more parenting time so as to avoid paying child support.

In Patricia's response to Howard's application, she asked for back child-support for Sam as well as for Emily, because she said that Howard was the only father Emily had known. To cover her living expenses, Patricia also requested spousal support. In addition, Patricia asserted that Howard was hiding assets and income because he owned an oilfield operation company but his income showed considerably less than the industry average. With these points of contention, the parties opted to participate in an ICM meeting and attempt to resolve the case outside of litigation.

Outcome

Before the ICM took place, Howard's attorney sent Patricia's attorney a settlement proposal. The proposal was not discussed directly between the parties before the ICM, but it provided a place to start the discussion. As a result of the JDR, Patricia and Howard agreed to a set parenting schedule for Sam, but they left it open in regard to Emily. Howard was able to see Sam for two weeks in a row during the summer. Patricia reported that Emily decided to accompany Sam to Howard's home for all but one night during these two-week periods. Patricia and Howard followed the child support guidelines (that involved Sam, only), and Howard paid some spousal support and some back child-support in monthly installments.

Howard got an exemption for their matrimonial home since he owned it prior to the marriage, and Patricia kept the house that they bought after the marriage. They divided the rest of their belongings, such as cars and clothing, based on who purchased it or who used it the most. Howard agreed to retain liability for $150,000 in shared debt. Howard's attorney recalled that Howard's acceptance of the debt was the only difference between their proposed settlement and the final settlement agreement.

Neither the two attorneys nor Patricia had a copy of the court order in this case, and none of them mentioned needing it after the JDR concluded. Though a return to court to enforce the agreement has not been necessary since the successful conclusion of the JDR, it is conceivable that lack of easy access to the order itself may have played a part.

JDR Process and Timing

The JDR occurred in October 2018 over two days. The first day was devoted to child and spousal support and parenting time; the second day revolved around division of property. The parties were able to get a divorce at the end of the JDR, finalized in December 2018.

To start the JDR, the judge descended the dais, placed his robes aside and brought the parties into a boardroom. He began in a joint caucus allowing both parties to detail their priorities, which he recorded on a white board and referenced throughout the process. He also made it clear that he would speak with both parties separately and confidentially. They held separate caucuses, but they also spent a lot of time in joint caucuses, allowing Patricia and Howard to hear from each other directly. Both attorneys described the ICM as a constructive conversation.

Attitudes

The judge who conducted this ICM believes that almost every family law case can be resolved in JDR, especially when there are children involved. The one exception is if there is violence or allegations of violence between the parties. Barring that, he approaches every family law case as a resolvable conflict that takes time, patience and face-to-face interaction.

Patricia's attorney only endorses JDR when it is non-binding informal case management, such as this case. To her, BJDR, which requires the parties to exchange briefs and write arguments, is too similar to trial and prepares people to become entrenched in their positions and to fight one another. When they do not have to exchange materials, she feels they can speak broadly and consider creative resolutions. As part of the JDR process, she appreciates when a judge acknowledges feelings and offers an evaluation of the facts and the legal aspects of the case. On the other hand, she does not like when a judge tries to push an agreement by threatening parties with the cost of litigation if a deal is not reached. She wants her clients to hear facts and be able to make their own decisions about how to move forward without undue pressure from the judge. Prior to this case, she had participated in only about five ICM meetings. If JDR had been available for more of her fifteen years of family law practice, however, she would not necessarily have chosen it; she likes being able to fight for her clients, and JDR removed the need for confrontation. Despite this stance, she thought JDR was the right decision for this case.

Howard's attorney reported that, if available, she always chooses JDR because her clients are more relieved after JDR than they are after a trial. She believes the satisfaction comes from being heard by both the judge and the other side. She noted a colleague who does not like JDR because he feels like he is no longer an attorney when not making legal arguments. Conversely, Howard's attorney said she still prepares for a JDR the way she would prepare for a trial; the difference is that, unlike trial, her clients are going to have opportunities to address the issues in the relationship. In her twenty to thirty JDRs, all but one was non-binding, and about 75 percent of those cases were resolved.

Patricia remembers her attorney first describing a JDR to her as an experimental way to resolve cases. Patricia was enthusiastic about the prospect because the case had gone on for almost two years with accompanying legal fees, and she relished the possibility of finally resolving the case. She also appreciated that a JDR process would give her some control in the outcome of the case. After the experience, she said she would choose JDR over litigation if she ever had to go to court again.

As these attitudes suggest, JDR elevates the parties' involvement and self-determination in the outcome of the case; attorneys who favor JDR often do so inasmuch as the process benefits their clients, not themselves.

Evaluation

All parties agreed that the case could have been resolved in litigation but that JDR secured long-term benefits not offered in litigation. They each offered their thoughts as to why the JDR process and the outcome were successful.

Patricia's attorney felt that the parties came to an agreement first and foremost because they wanted the process to be done, and they were willing to make compromises to prevent ongoing litigation. She also thought the judge was effective in listening to both parties, and she believes there is power in having an authority's undivided attention. In addition, she thought the informality of the ICM process relaxed the parties and enabled them to cooperatively come to an agreement. Finally, she mentioned how helpful it was for the parties to hear the judge's opinion as they decided how to proceed.

Howard's attorney agreed that this case settled in JDR because the parties were eager for closure. She found Howard willing to work with Patricia and accommodate her needs. She also liked having their proposed settlement agreement as a starting point; they landed in a place very close to it. To her, the judge's evaluative nature was crucial to the success of the process: the parties listened when the judge offered his opinion about what was reasonable and encouraged productive conversation that moved the case forward. In particular, she feels it is invaluable when a judge says, "If I were hearing this at trial, this is what I would do."

Patricia agreed that the process was an unmitigated success. Like the others, she noted timing as a main draw: the case resolved in two days, after almost two years of waiting and paying attorneys' fees. After years of talking to Howard only through attorneys and legal briefs, sitting in a room with together was transformational for her; they were finally able to hear each other's perspectives and respond immediately. In court, by contrast, she would never have had the opportunity to speak. Patricia also felt that this particular judge was integral to the resolution of the case. In addition to the luxury of two full days of a judge's time and attention, the down-to-earth judge put her at ease immediately. When discussing the grandparents' visitation, the judge shared his own experiences as a grandparent, and that personal touch made the process easier for Patricia. She also reported that the judge never critiqued them or their decisions within their relationship. If the person conducting the process had not been a judge, she thought it still would have been successful, but that Howard responded well to the process because the judge brought such credibility. Lastly, like the attorneys, Patricia appreciated hearing the judge's opinion but also being able to make her own decision. She then had more information when she decided how she wanted to proceed but did not feel pressure to come to an agreement. Because she and Howard ultimately controlled the direction and the outcome of the case, she found JDR more empowering than the process of court.

Most significantly, she noted that since the JDR she and Howard have had civil interactions and accommodated each other's requests. They could disagree without fighting and threatening to run to lawyers and they have not had to return to court for any reason. She does not think they would have such a cooperative relationship if they had remained in litigation with continued fighting and no opportunity to sit down and talk face to face. This was an outcome of JDR that surprised her.

Satisfaction and Compliance

As stated, both attorneys believed the quick resolution satisfied both the parties. Patricia was generally satisfied with the settlement, though some details were less than ideal. She was not thrilled that Howard had the children over the summer for two weeks while he was not working and she had the children while she was working. Further, she was unable to see them on some work-free weekends. She was also disappointed that he would pay the back child support in installments, rather than a lump sum, since she had to pay the bills all at once when they were due. However, she was so relieved to settle the case and finalize the divorce that those details became less significant. If they had continued with litigation, she felt those issues would have remained more central to her position.

Ultimately, the JDR resolved the issues of property, child and spousal support, and parenting time, which likely would have been resolved—one way or another—in a trial. However, Patricia felt that only JDR could have allowed a respectful dialogue that enabled her and Howard to move forward and have a productive co-parenting relationship.

Though the parties complied with the agreement, no one had a copy of the order to reference. Perhaps the JDR process instilled enough trust between the parties that they did not need a written agreement. Regardless of whether the order exists in written form, the parties left the JDR with not only a finalized divorce—significant to them both—but also with the possibility to resolve any conflict between them without the intervention of a third party

Capacity to Mediate

Both lawyers and Patricia agreed that the judge's attitude and conduct were integral to the successful resolution of this case. His combination of skilled evaluative and facilitative mediation in dispute resolution was key.

On the evaluative side, all three admit that the parties were much more realistic and reasonable when they heard this respected judge's opinion of their proposals. His evaluative skills in leading a productive conversation where everyone felt heard shepherded the collaborative settlement of the case. Patricia's attorney also noted that the judge's discretion to award court costs in the event that one party was being unreasonable—an option unavailable to mediators—provided an incentive for the parties to work cooperatively.

Just as judicial mediators' orientations vary, private mediators can also fall in various places on the facilitative-to-evaluative spectrum, and they often have a reputation for their style. Parties can therefore choose, maybe more easily than they can with judges as mediators, whether they want their mediator to focus more on evaluating the legal aspects of the case, facilitating a constructive conversation, or a combination of both. Because private mediators are arguably more common than judges, especially in rural areas, parties have more of a choice in the type of mediation they want to participate in when they choose private ADR. Finally, private ADR can occur at any point in the process, even long before the case is filed, possibly removing the need to expend time and money in litigation. Follow-up research could involve comparing JDR and ADR cases throughout Canada and parties' satisfaction with each.

Access

The judge in this case believes that JDR is all about access to justice. Trials are costly in terms of time and money, and JDRs can often be scheduled much earlier than trials. JDR also allows parties to be unrepresented and still reach a favorable resolution. However, access to this form of justice is not always equal. For example, the mandatory ADR rule in Canada is sometimes suspended in rural areas because of the lack of judges or other ADR practitioners. The rule suspension often occurs in direct response to attorneys' advocacy for clients who cannot travel two or three hours each way to find a JDR or ADR practitioner. JDR reduces barriers in terms of time and cost, but it is not equally available across the country. Though at the time of this case JDR was only four months old, if it had been available to her earlier, Patricia would have welcomed participating in a JDR and avoiding two years of litigation.

Although judges in Canada are all supposed to offer JDR, those who do not like to serve as mediators can let it be known that they prefer not to participate. This, of course, impacts access to JDR, making availability dependent on a judge's particular attitude toward the process—and some locales are served by only one judge. Further, judges conduct JDRs in dramatically different ways. In contrast to the judge in this case, for example, some judges tell the parties to resolve the case and call them only if they need to. Thus, even with access to JDR, there is no guarantee that the judge as mediator will take an active role in conducting the JDR. Experiences vary wildly; the evaluative-facilitative orientation that the judge in this case employed was successful, but availability of that specific approach throughout Canadian JDR is unknown.

This case suggests multiple aspects of JDR that can be explored through further research: how many JDR cases rely on trust—rather than traditional enforcement—as a means of compliance after reaching an agreement? How can access to JDR be improved in Canada's rural areas? What mediator orientation is most helpful to the parties to promote a successful resolution? If judges were taught to conduct JDR as part of their judicial training, what would that entail? Until these questions are further explored, few conclusions can be drawn about what mediation methods are most effective in a divorce JDR or in JDR more generally. For now, this divorce JDR was successful in reaching a settlement and securing a long-term, cooperative co-parenting relationship for Patricia and Howard.

THE MOTOR VEHICLE ACCIDENT WITH PEDESTRIAN CASE

Nicholas Friedel

The Facts

Mr. Barton, a plumber from Alpine, Saskatchewan, parked his car on the side of the TransCanada Highway and ran across the road toward a city mall. Barton had traveled to Alberta to visit friends and do some shopping. While crossing the road, Barton was hit by a 1963 GMC truck, causing severe injuries to his head, legs and back, leaving him with chronic pain and in need of long-term care. Following his discharge from the hospital in the early 2010s, Barton brought suit against the driver of the truck.

The truck was driven by Mr. Driggs, an Alberta local, who had been on the road for eight hours that day transporting hydroponic vegetables across the province. He had made this trip without incident several times before and had successfully traversed most of the nationwide TransCanada Highway throughout his career. Despite a long record of safe driving, there is no question that Driggs struck Barton that night.

Barton, the plaintiff, sued Driggs for failing to observe him or to honk the horn as a warning. He alleged that not only was Driggs fatigued and driving in a dangerous and distracted manner, but that the old truck was not properly maintained and had not been equipped with modern braking equipment. Barton would never fully recover from his injuries that had left him in the hospital for almost two months. He sought just over $1 million in damages: $200,000 for general damages, $500,000 for future loss of employment, and $350,000 for future cost of care.

Driggs, the defendant, claimed that Barton had run across the highway without warning and had caused an unavoidable collision. He also asserted that Barton had crossed the road outside of a crosswalk—which was unlawful—and without due care and attention. Driggs further claimed that although he was tired, he had exercised due caution at the time of the accident and that his slow-moving truck was properly equipped for highway driving. Lastly, Barton's sporadic work history made it difficult to estimate any loss of future income the defendant had suffered.

The parties filed timely pleadings through their lawyers. Barton hired a plaintiff-side law firm located in Alberta and filed the case in the jurisdiction where his injuries had occurred. Driggs' direct involvement was brief because his insurance company took over the case and hired a defendant-side law firm with experience representing institutions in personal injury and business-related claims.

The Outcome

Statements filed with the court may have given the impression that this case could not be settled. On the one side, there was heart-breaking descriptions of pain, suffering and loss, with allegations of personal liability; on the other, an equally compelling presentation of a conscientious truck driver regrettably involved in an accident over which he had no control due to the personal fault and negligent behavior of the plaintiff.

Notwithstanding these initial positions, the parties participated in a JDR session attended by Barton, a representative of Driggs' insurer, Driggs' counsel, and a sitting justice on the Alberta Court of Queen's Bench, in which all parties agreed to settle. Barton received a payment of approximately $150,000 and all claims were dismissed.

The JDR Process: Fixing a Date

The JDR took place at the Calgary courthouse several years after the initial claim was filed. The lawyers for both parties had commissioned and shared reports from medical evaluators and experts defending and rebutting the various types of damages and accusations of liability. Prior to the JDR, however, neither lawyer had made a concerted effort to engage in mediation or any form of Alternative Dispute Resolution (ADR). The trial was still over a year away, and as a result, this case was on the backburner for at least one of the two lawyers who had more urgent files with imminent deadlines.

This timeline changed, however, when both lawyers and their clients agreed to a JDR and received a date for three to four months away. Setting the date made the case a priority and brought it to the front of the counsels' dockets, officially starting the process with a clear timeline to analyze, discuss, and aim for a settlement. They reviewed the reports and legal correspondence that had swirled about for the previous few years and scheduled updates with their clients about changing interests and circumstances, all part of preparation to present before a Queen's Bench justice and opposing counsel.

The JDR Process: Setting the Table

The lawyers had agreed on the justice who would oversee the JDR, a decision that provided enough planning time for all. The justice provided each counsel with an overview of the process, detailing the steps and information needed to increase the likelihood of a settlement at the JDR session. Her assistant sent both parties a letter requesting:

- a pre-JDR conference call between the justice and the lawyers;
- a short brief from each party (10-12 pages);
- supporting materials including medical reports, highlighted case law, independent expert reports, family physician notes, and relevant portions of examinations for discovery.

The informal conference call took place several days prior to the JDR, before the justice had seen the statements of claim or defense. The call gave the justice a sense of what the case was about and introduced the lawyers to the justice's JDR style. The justice asked the following:

- What is the case about?
- What are the stumbling blocks?
- Have there been any offers? What were they? Why have they been rejected?
- Is there a disability involved? Language barriers?
- Why has the case not settled?
- Where are they in the case?
- Why do they want a JDR?
- What are the strengths and weaknesses of the case?

The justice wanted to hear directly from the lawyers in their own words. The questions were intended to provide a sense of what counsel believed was important about the case and what issues would likely need to be addressed at the JDR. The answers informed how the justice prepared for and structured the JDR.

The plaintiff's sporadic work history as a consequence of a prior disability was flagged as a stumbling block. The justice noted that in other cases, issues—such as disabilities related to mental health, incapacity to give instruction, inability to understand and instruct legal counsel, and the inability to speak English and communicate—were ideally addressed prior to the JDR. Unaddressed, the JDR process may not be properly adapted to suit the needs of the parties. In this case, there were expert medical reports involved and the justice wanted to know if experts should be on standby to answer questions during the JDR.

Since an insurance company was involved, the justice was particularly interested in what offers had been made: was the insurance company just "kicking the tires" and denying the injury or lowballing the plaintiff with disingenuous offers? The insurance company had made some offers and the justice was satisfied that, though the range given by the insurer may or may not align with the law, they had made the offers in good faith.

During the second part of the call, the justice provided the lawyers with information regarding the province-wide JDR rules and how she would conduct the JDR session. She stressed that each lawyer's client understand the concept of "without prejudice."[1] The justice referred to this as her "JDR intro spiel," drawn from a standard form: no party can be called to trial to testify to the content of the JDR; all parties are attending in good faith; and the justice would not keep any notes on the case or have any part in the trial should the case not resolve. The justice then described how the day would be structured, beginning with a plenary session where the clients state their accounts. She reminded the lawyers to make sure their clients were prepared.

---

1. The without prejudice (WP) rule means that statements that are made in a genuine attempt to settle a dispute cannot be used in court as evidence of admissions against the party that made them.

Next, three or four private caucuses with each party would take place until their 4:30 pm deadline. The justice was transparent about the limited number of exchanges that would occur, making it clear that everyone would need to cut to the chase; there would be no time for posturing. The justice ended the call by asking for any questions and indicating a willingness to adapt the structure of the JDR session to the needs of the case.

After the call and before the JDR, the justice reviewed all of the case materials provided by the lawyers and developed a strategy based around the key issues at play. The justice noted the plaintiff's sporadic work history and liability. The work history meant that it would be difficult to prove future lost income. Though the plaintiff had contributed to his injuries by not crossing at an intersection, he was almost all the way across the road when he was struck, which meant his liability was low.

The justice then ran this strategy by another justice on the Queen's Bench for their input. This is not always possible given the lack of formal channels for sharing information between independent justices. Since the case may be assigned to any judge after the JDR, details of the case must remain confidential to the parties and the JDR justice, so only limited information is shared.

JDR Process: At the Table

The JDR session began with the justice's introduction in a plenary session with all parties. The justice covered some of the same information that was shared during the pre-JDR conference call: the official rules for JDR; no one can subsequently be called to testify about what happens in the JDR; the process would consist of a plenary session followed by shuttle diplomacy or caucusing; and the opening plenary session would last until just before lunch.

The justice took particular care to speak directly to the clients, telling them how she would be involved and that "this is really [the clients'] day in court." The justice's goal was to assure the clients that she was familiar with the facts of the case, she was a neutral party, and she empathized with the parties' difficult situation. To establish rapport with clients and comfort with the process, the justice stated that she had read all of the papers the lawyers had sent and that she might ask questions, commenting: "I hope you don't mind." The justice further explained that she would be taking notes and asking questions in the same way as if she were hearing the case at trial, and that she wanted to know, "what [the defendant] did before the accident, a bit about their work history, education, what [their] goals were, what [their] health was like, how did [their preexisting disability] affect education opportunities, the ability to work at the job [they] wanted, and had [they] always wanted to be a plumber?" The justice assured the clients that she understood their personal story but was obligated to make decisions around law and precedent. The justice then did some framing of the JDR process and tried to empathize with the plaintiff, saying, "They can give you money, but can't make you better. This is just about compensation." She also confirmed that the parties present had full authority to settle the case. After the introduction, the clients were asked to make a statement.

The plaintiff went first and spoke for about forty-five minutes. The insurance representative had a short reply, stating that they intended to settle in good faith. The justice then turned to the lawyers and had a short discussion on the medical reports, asking them to explain their positions and how the reports affirm or rebut them. The justice's goal was to have a general discussion about the reports so that everyone had an understanding about their legal position before caucusing began. The final part of this plenary session involved a review of the case's damages: general damages, loss of earning capacity, and cost of future care. At that point, there had been no discussion about numbers except for the briefs and what the clients shared in their opening statements.

The first private caucus was held with the plaintiff, his lawyer, and the plaintiff's mother, who attended the JDR to provide moral support. The justice sat down with them and reviewed the particular damages to begin deleting items. Some were easy to omit, like the cost of gym passes and vitamins that the plaintiff would have purchased regardless of the accident. The justice reminded the parties of their 4:30 pm deadline, which left only three or four sessions, and that they should get to realistic numbers quickly rather than incrementally moving by one thousand dollars each session. The justice lamented, "If you do not give people a time deadline, they will always have a reason to have another round." The justice had already worked out a reasonable and justifiable number for settlement prior to the session.

The justice described the first caucus session with the plaintiff as risk analysis: discussing what would happen if they went to trial. This can be a challenge, she noted, because JDR is fairly successful and very few personal injury cases go to trial. Due to the high settlement rate, there is not a lot of precedent and as new justices join the bench, it becomes difficult for even experienced justices to tell what will happen at trial. Still, justices are quite aware of the costs of trial and in this case, the justice laid them out and explained the kind of risk analysis that needed to be done and why. The cost of medical bills, updated reports, and testifying experts all increase throughout trial, and insurance companies have the money to fight when the plaintiff does not. Even if the plaintiff won, he might get nothing when the reward is offset by the costs. The justice asked the lawyer to explain these possibilities to the plaintiff, as well as the risks of rejecting an offer and going to trial. She asked the plaintiff to come up with a new offer, which she then gave to the defendant. Breaking for lunch, the justice told them to return for caucusing—the defendant at 1:30 pm and the plaintiff at 2 pm.

In the second caucus, the justice spoke with the defendant and counsel. They conducted a similar risk assessment, discussing the risks of an extended trial and costs in attorneys' and experts' fees that could be avoided by settling that day. The justice then went through the numbers with them to illustrate what various options would cost. She noted that while she is always willing to work with numbers (and enjoys doing so), counsels on both sides of this case were very well prepared and organized so she did not need to play a large role in explaining or completing calculations. The defendant then provided a new offer for the justice to present to the plaintiff.

After the second offer was made, the justice suggested that the parties stop discussing particular damages and the payments associated with each one and instead and look for a global settlement number. (The justice later remarked that it is easier to work with a single number, but that it is preferable to have parties discuss their specific damages for two or three rounds before dropping them.) After getting a global number from the plaintiff, the justice and counsel did further risk assessment around the plaintiff's contributory negligence and sporadic work history. Both parties then exchanged offers in separate caucuses, focusing on a global number and an appropriate risk discount.

Throughout the day, the justice acted as the go-between for the parties by delivering offers, and also as a risk assessor by providing opinions on each party's situation. She was careful to only express opinions in private caucuses and never in a plenary session. One of the lawyers described the justice as candid and more judicial than a typical mediator. Having done several JDR sessions with this justice, the lawyer said that her style might be characterized as "proactive" or "judgmental" since she was willing to share her opinion on what the issues were, how they would matter if the case went to trial, and how a trial would likely play out. Commenting on her own approach, the justice stated that she is willing to tell a party if she thinks they are lying, but she is always careful not to embarrass anyone in front of the opposing party. Respect for each party's dignity and a desire for neutrality made the justice save probing questions that exposed weakness or cast doubt for private caucuses.

The parties came to an agreement in a private caucus in the JDR session, but the final papers were drawn up outside the courthouse which closed at 4:30 pm. The parties walked to one of the lawyer's homes to sign and finalize the decision.

Evaluation

This case settled for a number of reasons. As stated, the JDR gave the case a sense of urgency and priority when it might have otherwise gone unattended until trial. If neither party was willing to set a deadline or put in the same amount of work for a private mediation, this case may not have settled. Empathy played a central role in settling the case; both the justice and the defense counsel honored the plaintiff's need to be heard and respected.

Plaintiff's counsel stated that for many clients it is important to hear what kind of settlement range they would receive at trial from a Queen's Bench justice. Defendant's counsel also stated, "Some people just need to hear it from a judge." Lawyers can tell clients what the law is and has been, but justices can provide a more persuasive assessment of what the law *will be* in their particular case.

The justice stated that the case settled because both parties had agreed to an amount justified by the evidence. Her presence and input played a large role in helping parties understand that justification, especially after having had the opportunity to hear the likely outcome of a trial.

A final reason that this case settled was that it had been lingering for over four years, and the defendant was broke and desperate to settle. Heading into the JDR, he had given his lawyer the instruction, "I'll take anything."

Themes

Fairness and Justice

One lawyer stated that JDR for personal injury cases can be effective by ensuring that neither side presumes an advantage over the other. The defendant's lawyer mentioned that a JDR justice is always distinct from typical mediators; many of the lawyer's insurance clients—who may be in-house counsel for an insurance company—are quite sophisticated in their legal knowledge and push back against counsel's risk assessments and analysis of the law. A sitting justice can assess the accuracy of these challenges and correct them if necessary.

The lawyer speculated that since the parties do not pay JDR justices, the lack of financial compensation may make justices better suited to the process than paid mediators. Believing that mediators with a high rate of settlements are more sought after, he reasoned they may be incentivized to settle a JDR in order to preserve their reputation. He added that some mediators are known among colleagues to lack the mediation—or people—skills suitable for JDR. In contrast, counsel expressed his confidence in the Calgary bench, which was small enough to allow lawyers to get to know the justices' work and trust in their individual expertise and unbiased opinions.

Justice itself played a major role in the effectiveness of this JDR. Defined as "what the courts do," it seemed to be what everyone was interested in finding in the JDR. The insurance adjuster wanted to know what they owed according to the court and the defendant wanted to know what they would get at trial. The justice provided unique insights into how a court would have defined justice. Her opening remarks put that concept in perspective and bears repeating: "They can give you money but can't make you better. This is just about compensation." Thus, in this case, justice meant finding the amount of money owed to Mr. Barton according to Canadian law.

But the case was actually about a lot more than compensation. It was about giving Barton a chance to be heard and for the justice system to respond on a personal level; he witnessed empathy from the justice and from defendant's counsel. It was also about finally ending a four-year entanglement in the courts and taking the next step to recover from the effects of a horrific accident. It was about receiving a fair monetary settlement, resolving "what-ifs," and regaining a measure of dignity and respect. Barton may have been asking for too much in his claim, but going to trial, with the risk of being embarrassed on the stand, would have been its own injustice.

Confidentiality

Confidentiality was a significant factor in this case. It meant that the justice could not be as transparent as she might have liked when strategizing with other justices about the best way to approach this JDR. Nonetheless, she preserved the conditions necessary for the parties to move forward with a fair trial and impartial justice.

Both the justice and defendant's counsel expressed their concerns regarding self-represented parties in JDR. The justice explained that legal representation is a pre-requisite for confidentiality: In cases with self-represented parties, a recorded and sealed record is required. She added that she would not have even conducted a pre-conference call with a self-represented party.

Confidentiality also contributes to a lack of precedent. Given that so many personal injury claims settle, it becomes more difficult for justices and lawyers to review standards and advocate for fair results. However, confidentiality may have been key in ensuring the dignity of the parties and in pushing them to settle; trial can be embarrassing and the process can undermine relationships and injure reputations. This JDR allowed the justice to privately question and expose the weaknesses in Mr. Barton's case and assess the sincerity of the insurance company.

Technical and Scientific Information

In spite of the many medical reports and expert opinions involved in this case, the technical details were rarely mentioned in interviews and did not seem to be a critical component of the case. This may have been because both lawyers were well organized and had laid the groundwork ahead of the session to ensure that technical questions could be answered. Plaintiff counsel's discussion of a possible JDR prioritized the case and may have meant that the counsels spent more time reviewing expert reports, conducting technical research, and familiarizing themselves with the case details to ensure they had strong competency on the technical issues.

The justice's pre-JDR work to identify possible stumbling blocks and adequate resources helped ensure that all parties had sufficient information at the JDR session to reach a settlement. The process allowed for experts to be on standby, for the justice to speak to other justices with different technical and legal competencies, and for parties to find and review necessary case law and technical information in advance of the JDR.

Precedent

As discussed, the lack of recorded precedents complicated the justice's ability to provide accurate assessments of the value of the case. She commented on the challenge of accurately predicting what any given justice might do because of the constant changeover in the bench. It is possible that a lack of precedent makes lawyers and parties less confident in their own assessments and more interested in the JDR judge's assessment. The lack of recorded precedent may also allow JDR judges to be more persuasive. Perhaps this is why such a large percentage of JDR cases settle.

One of the lawyers commented on another way that precedent in JDR can be particularly effective. Many personal injury plaintiffs know of similar claims and their settlements without being aware of the distinguishing facts. A plaintiff might say, "My cousin had a truck accident, and he got $3 million. So, there's no way I'll take less than that." Unfortunately, the cousin's case ended in a settlement without a written precedent, and it is difficult to show a client that the facts in the earlier case were very different, and that their expectations are unreasonable. JDR provides a solution by letting misguided clients hear from a justice what their lawyers (should) have been telling them.

Compliance

Compliance and enforcement were nonissues in this case. Both parties got a copy of the agreement and followed through. The nature of personal injury lawsuits may minimize the need for ongoing involvement of JDR justices, since settlements are usually implemented immediately.

Access

Both lawyers commented on the increasing difficulty of accessing JDR. JDR has become less common than when this case occurred. In May 2014, the Alberta Court of Queen's Bench issued two notices to the profession that changed the priority and frequency of JDR, making it more difficult for personal injury cases to proceed to JDR. Beyond the lack of access to JDR scheduling, the volume of cases is also limited by the number of justices skilled at conducting them. Mediation and ADR training are not widely available, and the independent nature of Canadian justices means that information sharing across the bench is minimal.

Cost

Everyone involved acknowledged that the limited cost of JDR was noteworthy in the case. In Alberta, mediation costs at least $3,000 and comparable mediation by a former judge might cost $15,000. In this case, the JDR was free, aside from the lawyer fees. This may have been crucial to the settlement, since the plaintiff had limited funds and may not have been able to pay for mediation. In personal injury cases, it is standard for the paying party to cover mediator fees if there is a settlement, and for each party to pay their own fees when mediation does not result in a settlement.

A disadvantage of the low cost of the JDR is that it shifts fees to the courts. This makes JDR a target when administrators look to reduce court costs. Some would view JDR services as a redundancy to the private sector alternative of mediation.

Process

Rather than seeing the JDR as a process for settling cases, it may be more fitting to frame it as a procedure for *allowing* cases to settle. Observers might be tempted to overlook JDR's capacity to bring about a resolution, given the plaintiff's willingness to settle. He was only open to settling, however, on the day of the JDR. Without the process of JDR, he may have lacked the chance to settle, and the case may have ultimately gone to trial and resulted in a last-minute take-it-or-leave-it offer from the defendant.

As a result of the JDR, Barton's lawyer prioritized his client, lawyers on both sides re-familiarized themselves with the case to prepare updates for the justice, and Barton got to share his story directly with an empathetic opposing counsel and justice. The JDR was an opportunity for movement by both parties, allowing them to take stock of what had previously been covered in claims and negotiations, and to evaluate their current goals and sticking points. The defendant's counsel noted how valuable it was to have a justice require a recitation of the facts of the case beforehand and receive updates about the status of negotiations. A clear understanding of where the case had been and where it stood was essential to moving it forward. The JDR process brought about an agreement that might not have otherwise occurred, even though it was possible. JDR offers a process for unlocking settlements in ongoing cases that have potential for resolution but lack the procedural movement necessary to pin down an agreement between parties.

4

TEMPERAMENT IN AN ESTATE DISPUTE CASE

Nicolás Parra-Herrera

Facts

On November 8, 2019, before the Court of Queen's Bench of Alberta, two siblings, Tom and Elsa, discussed how to distribute their deceased parents' estate. Their father had died in June 2008, and their mother passed away almost three years later. When the father died, the estate and values consisted of a residence ($345,000), personal property ($4,330), a portfolio of investments ($71,000), and a boathouse cabin ($92,000). Additionally, assets such as personal belongings remained in both houses waiting to be inventoried and disposed of.

The estate also had many costs to cover, such as unpaid municipal taxes for the properties and other management fees. Tom and Elsa were named as the personal representatives of the estate and tasked with liquidating and distributing its assets and liabilities. Agreeing on finances—that is, deciding who gets what, how much, and why—is not easy. Yet, the hardest issues often have nothing to do with money, but with the complexity of feelings involved and the gap of recognition between the parties. This case revolved around "feelings and finances," as Elsa's counsel, Marie, put it.

Elsa had financial difficulties of her own, even before her parents died. To help her out, her parents had let her and her husband live in the residence property until their situation improved—for more than eleven years. She devoted a significant amount of time to helping their parents cope with their physical conditions for many years, and she felt that her time and efforts should have been compensated or at least acknowledged by her brother.

Tom was frustrated that his sister had lived rent-free—without even paying the taxes on the property—and that she continued to delay any agreement by refusing his offer to distribute the estate. She even asked to keep the most valuable asset, the house, for herself. He generated multiple offers to deal with their differences, but none were satisfactory to her; he thought Elsa was uncooperative and messy with numbers.

Though an application for a Grant of Probate was made, they were not able to resolve their differences, partition the estate, and honor their parents. In fact, they were so polarized they could not even agree on language for their parents' gravestone.

Tom filed a petition asking the court to settle these issues once and for all. He requested that his sister be removed from the property and initiated a contentious proceeding to divide the estate. Tom's counsel, John, explained to the justice that his client wanted him to bring the matter to adjudication to resolve it as soon as possible because it had been in limbo since 2011.[1]

Marie, Elsa's lawyer, took the case just a few days before the hearing. She recalled a bulky case file that required a lot of time to draft a proper response. Marie realized that this trial would entail substantial costs for her client, who was not in a sound financial position to begin with. Furthermore, after reading the case, Marie saw that it was about their relationship. This epiphany led her to say something to the justice—in her first intervention in the hearing—that changed the course of the entire case: "In everything I read of this case, it struck me that there were issues, feelings, and finances, and that it would lend itself to either a collaborative approach to resolution or some other alternative dispute-resolution mechanism. I think there should be an effort to resolve this in a way that would not require the court's intervention."[2] Tom's counsel jumped in immediately and insisted that the dispute had existed for several years and his client's mandate was to get a final resolution. "You can still do a JDR," said the justice. Everyone stopped.

The JDR Option

The justice took the floor and shared a story of a case that had been argued for years without any progress. His narrative was aimed at encouraging the lawyers to entertain the possibility of doing either a non-binding or a binding JDR (BJDR). He explained that moving to a BJDR would make it possible to have both a collaborative approach as suggested by defendant's counsel and a final resolution as demanded by claimant's counsel.[3]

His use of narrative and storytelling were persuasive. Reflecting back on that moment, the justice agreed that "storytelling can be the best way to shift people from an adversarial to a collaborative mindset."[4] He added, "It is likely that I use story to engage people into JDR. I suspect I do it a lot more than I am aware of. In family matters, there are always feelings involved. There is always a human element involved, even though in family matters it's more salient."

After offering his story, the justice ordered a break so that counsels could speak to their clients and make a decision. Before letting them go, however, he mapped the array of options from which they could choose: arbitration, JDR, BJDR, mediation, summary trial, or ordinary trial, and still others. Finally, he noted that while JDR is a great

---

1. Court of Queen's Bench of Alberta Judicial Centre of Calgary, Proceedings, p. 2.
2. Id. p. 3.
3. According to the Court of Queen's Bench, BJDR is a dispute resolution mechanism in the form of a confidential pre-trial settlement conference led by a justice aimed at resolving a dispute or limiting the issues on which the parties do not agree. If a settlement between the parties is not reached, then the justice's opinion will be binding (See Court of Queen's Bench of Alberta, JDR, Available at https://www.albertacourts.ca/qb/areas-of-law/jdr [16.03.2020]).
4. All quotes by the justice are from interview on March 6, 2020.

option, the judge involved needs to have "a natural inclination in that direction," and both counsels and clients must voluntarily agree to move in this direction.

Deciding on BJDR

After some deliberation and conferencing with their clients, both counsels agreed to proceed with BJDR. They set a time for a BJDR process with the justice, and meanwhile agreed to move forward with the liquidation of assets, starting with the less contested and more urgent matters, such as payment of municipal taxes. To prepare for their meeting with him, the justice suggested adding to the consent order that the parties would meet at least every sixty days with counsel or an outside mediator to settle whatever they could before the scheduled BJDR session. He wanted to generate momentum for their collaborative approach and persuade them to work together as much as possible before the BJDR. Everyone agreed.

Before the end of the hearing, Marie asked the justice to provide a short explanation for her client, Elsa, who was absent from the court that day. She wanted to read directly from the transcript. He agreed and said:

(1) The parties want to resolve the dispute as soon as possible. (2) They want probably to be heard by a judge at some point. (3) The dispute has been going on for some time and given the nature of the dispute, there are interpersonal difficulties that need to be hopefully dealt with. And I might say that it has been my experience in a few of these [that] it's not uncommon to have someone at that process just say, "I am sorry." It's not uncommon or out of place for one party to say, "well, okay, here's the financial part of it, but here is the personal part of it, one of which is a statement of feelings between each other and they care about each other, they are a family." I have had people actually say, "I am sorry," and do stuff; I've had people hug and cry. It doesn't happen all the time, but it has happened . . . we are here to solve problems as quickly and efficiently as possible.[5]

After this initial hearing, the court issued an interim order requesting that the parties identify an itemized list of the issues to be determined through the BJDR. Particularly, the parties agreed to schedule a meeting to settle: an agreed statement of facts; an agreed exhibit book; a joint statement of the issues in dispute; and a determination of the steps and actions to be taken prior to the BJDR.[6]

Why BJDR for This Dispute?

It is not easy to determine when a case should go to court and when it should be referred to JDR or BJDR. There has been more experimentation leading to creating new Alternative Dispute Resolution (ADR) methods than research about matching cases to specific types of ADR. This case can help us determine three criteria for determining when JDR is a good path to resolve a dispute.

---

5. Transcript. 27-31.
6. See Consent Order. November 8, 2018.

First, Marie was clear from the outset that she did not think this was a matter to be litigated in court. "JDR could provide more latitude to their respective grievances," she said. A more collaborative approach was needed because "feelings and finances" were involved. This suggests that there is a need for counsels to be open to the best forum to meet their clients' needs and interests.

Second, the justice stepped in to persuade the parties that JDR might be a better alternative based on his prima facie reading of the case. Drawing on his own experience, he was able to use storytelling to help the parties imagine a less costly and, perhaps, more satisfactory approach to resolving their differences and coping with the emotions involved. In other words, the justice not only described the possibility of JDR, but also made a case for its applicability in this particular situation. Counsels may have not had much experience with JDR or perhaps they were not fully aware of how it might have been used in this instance. The justice's intervention made all the difference.

Third, in the end, the lawyers had to agree to offer their clients this route as a possible and even an ideal way to deal with the conflict. As Marie argued, "lawyers need to understand the impact of these alternative projects. You need lawyers who understand all the [ADR) options and are willing to recommend them."[7] It is not enough to accept the JDR route; lawyers need to feel comfortable choosing among and operating within various ADR options. There are important differences among mediation, arbitration, JDR, and BJDR. As Harvard Law School Professor Frank Sander put it, echoing Maurice Rosenberg, you need to "fit the forum to the fuss."

In summary, these elements are critical for steering clients and their cases from litigation to JDR: counsels' initiative and motivation; responsiveness and pedagogical input of judges to present the JDR option to the disputants; and counsels' understanding of the varieties of ADR methods and promotion of JDR to their clients.

JDR Process

The BJDR session was held on July 9, 2019. According to John, the justice's decision to focus on the emotional content of the dispute was paramount in moving the dispute-resolution effort forward. The justice ordered the parties to provide financial records and to itemize each of their claims on the estate. This helped each side understand the other's interests. It also gave some shape to the Zone of Possible Agreement.[8]

Although clarity about what was important to each party was crucial, so was emotional guidance and a push for candid conversation. This is why at the start of the BJDR, one of the first things the justice did was to ask the siblings to talk about their feelings regarding the loss of their parents. It turned out that Tom and Elsa both felt tremendous loss and were each grieving in their own way. The justice expressed surprise that they had not been able to agree on what should be written on their parents' headstone. In John's words, by directing the parties' attention to their shared loss the justice found "a clever

---

7. All quotes by respondent's counsel (Marie) are from interview on March 11, 2020.
8. All quotes by claimant's counsel (John) are from interview on March 12, 2020.

way to plant a seed of collaboration." Shortly thereafter, that matter was settled: Tom agreed to Elsa's proposed language and they moved on to other issues. They both knew that if they could agree on one thing, it would be easier to agree on others.

Marie recalled the gravestone issue a bit differently. For Elsa, the problem was not about the content but about communication: She finally had a chance to articulate her feelings about the gravestone. "She needed some catharsis," Maria insisted. "What was important to my client was to express her feelings in a safe environment where she could honor her parents. The justice provided great respect for my client . . . She felt listened to."

The justice then suggested that perhaps it would now be easier to work together to resolve other aspects of their dispute. "I didn't have to do my traditional opening," he confessed. "I usually draw a diagram and say to the parties: 'This is how you might think about the dispute and your positions; no common ground, no shared interests, no commonality whatsoever.'" (See diagram below.) Then he draws diagram 2 and says, "At the very least, you have four things in common. First, you want to resolve this dispute as soon as possible. Second, you want to resolve it with the minimum cost. Third, you want to reduce any litigation risk. And finally, you both want to live a happier life. I often ask people involved in litigation if there is one day that they haven't thought about their dispute. The answer is almost rhetorical: 'Every day I think about it, and it doesn't make me happy.'"

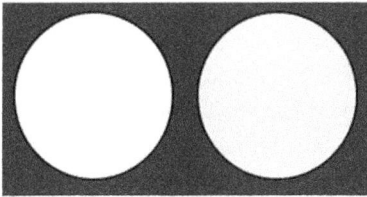 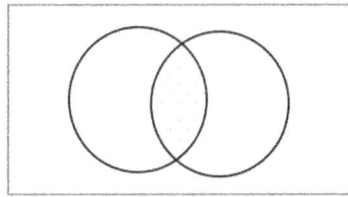

Diagram 1   Diagram 2

Settlement

In the first session of BJDR, the parties did not resolve the main issues they faced, such as the sale of the property where Elsa was living. They drafted a roadmap of the actions needed with respect to each of the assets involved, but they did not reach closure. The roadmap was part of the consent order issued August 13, 2019. The property taxes were paid. The resealing of the Grant of Probate and the instructions to register the property where Elsa lived under both their names were steps toward its eventual sale. The parties agreed to sell the boathouse cabin.

Elsa was permitted to reside in the house until the title of the property was transmitted to the siblings as personal representatives of the estate, and the parties decided on an equalization payment that would allow her to keep the property. Marie said that it was difficult for Elsa and her husband to think of possibly having to leave their home. Lastly, they agreed on consolidating an inventory of the possessions of the deceased to then decide how to distribute, donate, and discard.

In the consent order, the parties agreed to provide an updated summary of the estate administration as well as certain financial information by November 15, 2019. If an item was not resolved or liquidated before that deadline, the justice would arrange a session at which final determinations would be made, particularly regarding the sale of the property where Elsa lived. In short, all matters that were partially agreed upon, and decisions made regarding further actions were included in interim and consent orders. These orders provided a shared point of reference for the parties, who were barely speaking before the BJDR process started.

The justice noted that one of the features of JDR and BJDR is that "there is a possibility to have contingent settlements, that is, settlements which address and solve parts of the dispute." This can be helpful if there are issues that are best addressed through litigation. The parties need to know the justice will ensure compliance. "This addresses the sustainability of the settlement and, perhaps, enhances the engagement of the parties to comply with what was agreed." In some cases, he concluded, "JDR is a path forward; it is a roadmap. This resonates with what was written in the consent order for this case." JDR, therefore, is not only a forum to resolve disputes, it is also a venue to formulate a plan and a timetable.

Lawyers' Perspective on JDR

According to Marie, the JDR worked for two reasons. First, the justice had the capacity, temperament, compassion, and intellect appropriate for the case. Second, the parties' counsels were committed to resolving the matter collaboratively.

This was especially true when, for unknown reasons, Tom changed counsel soon after Marie prepared a draft order in August 2019, delaying the signing of the order until December. Marie tried to secure a date for a final BJDR session before the year ended, but they could not find common availability, despite the fact that she and the justice made themselves available on weekends and evenings. These many exchanges postponed the final date of the BJDR until the summer of 2020.

John was impressed by the justice's capacity to extract commitments from the parties. He spoke vividly of how the justice handled the opening of the BJDR and made it easier for the parties to share their feelings. Without the intervention of the justice, John felt it would have been much harder to promote a productive conversation.

Both parties highlighted that for JDR to work, the forum itself is not enough. Advocates of JDR and other ADR methods often emphasize the virtues of the forum and forget that it requires an effective mediator. Counsels agreed that BJDR worked so well because the justice had the sensibility, temperament, and receptivity to listen to the parties and help them address their differences. They suggested that without the appropriate character or attitude of the moderator, the institutional setting may be ineffective. It is worth considering whether ADR studies should focus more on the character of the intermediary and less on the design of the sessions.

Marie thought they got as far as they did with the liquidation and distribution of the estate because of the mindset of both counsels and the attitude of the justice. "In a

JDR," she said, "so much rests on the ability of counsel, in particular, to be conciliatory and cooperative." Tom's counsel was not available to comment.

When to Caucus?

The lawyers were quite willing to collaborate, so caucusing was not a major component in the process. But at some point, according to John, the justice did caucus with just the parties and their counsels. This was useful, John recalled, because they were able to have candid discussions and test each party's bottom-line assessments. "If your position is out of bounds, he will tell you so," said John. Thus, the justice was able to communicate both in joint session and in caucus in a way that allowed the parties to be more realistic in their positions.

Surprisingly, Marie did not remember any separate caucus occurring; she recalled no need for it due to both counsels' level of commitment and ability to cooperate, at least until Tom replaced his counsel. Whether there was a caucus or not, the fact she did not remember it may suggest it was not terribly important to her. Conversely, John remembering the caucus *and* praising it as an opportunity for each party to express their views illustrates a stark contradiction. This may illustrate that unraveling a JDR's process may be complicated due to confidentiality and imperfect recall, leaving researchers with some gaps in data; parties' memories may be tainted by the dust of time, the intensity of the conversation in the sessions, and their projections about what they would like to have happened.

When Tom decided to hire new counsel just a month before the deadline, they may have lost a lot of the momentum that had been gained from the BJDR session. Marie recalled that it was difficult and slowed things down.

JDR vs Mediation or Trial

One of the main strengths of JDR is its flexibility. "I leave my robes, and put my suit on," said the justice. "My flexibility is coupled with the need of the parties to have an authoritative figure as an interlocutor, who listens to them and knows what they're talking about." Unlike in mediation, the JDR justice knows the law and can readily assess the probabilities of litigation outcomes.

"In JDR there is finality," argued Marie. Also, in BJDR, unlike in mediation, the justice can make a binding decision and help insure compliance with the terms of the settlement. "The parties need to know that I will come back," stated the justice. In this case, if counsels could not settle on the distribution of all the assets, the idea of having a justice present and ready to make a binding decision created a sense of purposefulness.

Maria noted, however, that JDR does not work unless the judge and parties are willing to shift their mindset when necessary. She stressed that the success of JDR is highly dependent on the people leading it. In her view, it requires lawyers who are committed to the process, adaptable, and able to articulate a client's needs and interests in both adversarial and cooperative settings. Further, she said, "The way a lawyer speaks to her client about the alternatives available to deal with his or her dispute will necessarily shape the decision of the client." Pursuing collaborative solutions is a belief rooted in her background as a police officer, work that strengthened her commitment to community conflict-resolution without a fight. While there is a need for more JDR opportunities, there is also a need to cultivate supporting attitudes among those leading it.

Mediation has a disadvantage vis à vis JDR. "In JDR you have a justice listening and guiding you to agree with knowledge and understanding," John explained. Moreover, in some BJDR cases the benefit might double compared to mediation. "In BJDR," he continued, "you have a justice who has the power to write down a binding order with the same effect as a judicial ruling." John felt that a judge's presence, even without his or her traditional garb, "helps the parties to keep their stubbornness restrained and to be more open and realistic about their demands."

In arbitration and mediation, a judge is not facilitating the dispute-resolution session. The first leans toward an adjudicatory and trial procedure; the latter is about a dialogical encounter between the parties to share interests and explore options with the assistance of a third party. In BJDR, parties' awareness of a judge's gaze produces a grounding and self-constraining tone, coloring what parties offer to one another and what they ask for.

"I am not in favor of a non-binding JDR," Marie said. "At the end of the day, you share plenty of information and if no settlement is reached, then the other party can strategize with your case."

JDR and Temperament

Counsels agreed that the success of this JDR was dependent on the temperament of the justice. Temperament is more than the sensibility or character of the moderator; it is a pragmatic notion describing "our individual way of just seeing and feeling the total push and pressure of the cosmos."[9] Or put differently: our patterns and responses to the struggles of the world. One counsel reflected on JDR sessions where the judge conducted it as if it were a trial because that was the default setting for dealing with disputes. The justice in this case, by contrast, had a flexible and open, amenable, and responsive temperament that led him to adapt his legalistic style to an empathetic and receptive one every time he entered a JDR session.

This is why, according to Marie, "judges should be carefully picked for this role, as there is a considerable amount of mediating involved." Parties agreed that it was helpful when the judge gave an initial pep talk about the benefits of JDR, the need for cooperation, active listening, and being clear about both parties' objectives. JDR may be improved if parties and justices understand that the issue is not about being right or wrong, but, as Marie put it, about something else entirely: understanding the other party's perspective. She went on to say that you do not necessarily have to accept that perspective, but you are creating a space that allows divergent views with the shared goal of resolving the dispute and moving on. In this sense, one might argue that JDR is at its best when moderators favor dialogue over debate.

---

9. See James, William, Pragmatism, Lecture I. Dover Editions.

Did Lawyers' Views of JDR Change?

Everyone in this case favored JDR, at least in its binding form. Marie had always recommended BJDR over arbitration, not only because arbitrators do not always understand the law, but also because they do not necessarily provide parties with a forum that encourages talking to each other. "Sometimes clients need some catharsis," she insisted. "It is important for them to be able to express their feelings in a safe environment."

John came to favor the JDR process only after his involvement in this case. He was initially hesitant to support a binding decision, but in hindsight, he realized it was an effective tool for pushing the case forward: "I think in this case the parties and the administration of justice were best served, even if they may not like the result in the end."

Finally, a common takeaway was that JDR generates momentum toward resolving a dispute; if counsels cooperate with each other, the chances of reaching agreement increase dramatically.

Both counsels emphasized that they were close to resolving the dispute on their own before Tom terminated his counsel's retainer. Once you change counsels during a JDR, you lose traction and restarting the process is difficult.

Some practitioners and scholars believe ADR methods like JDR are desirable because they are less costly, provide wider access to justice, and bring more satisfaction to the parties. This might be so but it overlooks the importance of the people running the show; the attitudes of the judge, the counsel, and the parties are key. Both counsels and the justice in this case embodied characteristics essential to JDR's efficacy: an "appropriate temperament," or "a cultivated sensibility."

Decision

The main reason the case was still pending as of 2020 is that Tom changed counsels. His impatience backfired and changed the rules of the game, undermining the collaborative mindset that had been established by the BJDR. The parties have not been able to agree on the sale of the property where Elsa lives and what she will owe if she keeps the house. They are waiting for a final BJDR session or for the justice to impose a binding decision.

5

THE NEGLIGENT LAND TRANSFER CASE

Lucy Prather

Facts

This case focuses on a dispute between Betty and Tom Walker and their three children, Lila, Will, and Ellis. Betty and Tom owned several tracts of land in Alberta, including three parcels of farmland where they lived. Their son Will had also been made the registered owner of these three parcels. Lila was made an owner of only one parcel, the "family home parcel," where their home was located.

In 2006, Ellis spoke with his family about being added to the title of the three parcels of land. His parents, sister, and brother would all need to execute documents adding him to the title of each parcel. Despite a verbal agreement that he would become a co-owner of the land, his brother Will refused to execute the documents. Seeing conflict brewing, Tom Walker hired a lawyer, Laura Simon, to represent him in adding his son to the title for each of the three parcels. Betty, Will, and Lila retained their own lawyer, Terry Harris.

Simon and Harris negotiated a settlement with the family in early 2007 that allowed Will, Betty, and Lila to each retain their quarter interest in the family home parcel. Tom would share his quarter interest in the family home parcel as joint tenants with his son Ellis; when Tom died Ellis would inherit the entire quarter interest. Lila was added as a quarter owner to parcel two, and Tom agreed again to share his quarter interest in parcel two with Ellis also as joint tenants. Ellis was not added to the title for parcel three.

Simon sent the agreement to Harris for his clients to sign, and then Harris sent the document back to Simon for her clients' signatures. Tom Walker signed the documents but Ellis Walker did not. About two weeks later, Simon sent revised documents to Harris for their signatures. The new agreement modified Ellis's quarter share: instead of holding the interest with his father as joint tenants, they held the interest as tenants in common, each holding one-eighth interest in the entire property. At Tom's death, Ellis would no longer have had any claim to his father's one-eighth interest in the property. Ellis was not informed of this change and it is unclear why it occurred.

Simon was responsible for submitting the executed documents to the title registry. Nearly a year after the modified settlement had been executed, she contacted Harris to obtain additional affidavits to support the transfer. While Simon was waiting on those documents, in May of 2008, Tom Walker died.

Betty Walker became the chief executor of her deceased husband's estate. Meanwhile, Harris informed Simon that he was under the impression that the family had resolved the issue privately and there was no longer any need for the affidavits. Simon did not communicate with Ellis, but executed the required affidavits herself, as agent for the plaintiff, and submitted the title transfers for registration. The land titles office rejected them due to a missing form and incorrect land descriptions. Simon requested the corrected land description from Harris, but did nothing else to pursue registration of the title transfers. In 2011, she informed Ellis that the transfers had not been completed and that she thought the matter had been resolved between him and his family. Ellis's family refused to honor the agreement they had negotiated in 2007. Six years had passed, and Ellis was still not listed as a co-owner of any of the three land parcels.

In 2013, Ellis filed suit against his family to compel them to either honor the agreement or compensate him for the value of the land. He also sued Simon for negligence in her representation of him. The family argued that any agreement between Ellis and Tom could no longer be enforced because the statute of limitations barred enforcement actions. They also disputed that Ellis had suffered any losses because he had never owned the properties. Simon denied liability, as well, arguing that she had been retained solely to represent Tom, and had never been Ellis's lawyer. Simon was represented by malpractice attorneys from the Law Society of Alberta as well as one provided by her malpractice insurer.

Lead-up

Ellis's lawyer reported that Simon's attorneys were very responsive and helpful, but that the Walker family's attorney was not prompt in responding and seemed to be trying to prolong the case.[1] It came to light that the family's attorney had received an administrative suspension of his law license for failing to keep up with his law society annual fees; other lawyers reported that he neither paid those fees nor regained his license to practice.

The Walker defendants did not hire a new lawyer when this suspension came to light, which further delayed any action on the case. Ellis's lawyer contacted the family members several times, encouraging them to find a new lawyer and agree to do a JDR in the hopes that the case would settle quickly.

Meanwhile, Simon's attorney had attempted to engage in private mediation, but the former Walker defense attorney had been resistant, and the defendants appeared to be avoiding the conflict. Simon's attorney feared that she and her client would be drawn through a decade of litigation purely because the Walker family was stalling. She, too, was anxious to pursue JDR as a way to get the whole family in the room and encourage a negotiated settlement.

---

1. All quotes from Ellis's lawyer in this action are from interview on March 18, 2020.

Outcome

The defendants were very reluctant to put Ellis's name on the title of any of the three pieces of land that they had fought over. The judge noted that Betty Walker, who was about ninety-two years old and "very sharp," was clearly aligned with Lila and Will. The conflict appeared intractable until the family members agreed to transfer some land to Ellis.

The family owned a fourth tract of land that was recently approved for subdivision. The family ultimately agreed to give Ellis sole title to one of the land's subdivided parcels, but not to add his name to the title of any of the original three parcels that had been in contention.

Ellis's attorney said that the negotiation between the family members was paramount. Once the plaintiff and the defendants were "broadly speaking, in agreement" over the land transfer, Ellis and his attorney turned to Simon to negotiate a settlement amount for her malpractice claims. Simon's lawyer said that once the plaintiff had "extracted something from the co-defendants, which I never thought they would do," it became easier to reach an agreement on the amount that Simon's insurance company should pay out.[2] Simon was more than satisfied with the amount, far below what her attorney had authority to offer.

Process

Prior to the JDR, each party in the dispute filed a mediation brief with the judge laying out their legal positions. Simon's counsel noted that the mediation briefs were not required, but "if you don't do it, you're at a severe disadvantage." The plaintiff's counsel stated that the judge walked into the room fully briefed and prepared for the complexities of the conflict.

The JDR took place in a boardroom with adjacent breakout rooms. The judge introduced himself to everyone, shared some information about how the process would work, and then gave each side a chance to share their opening positions. The attorneys' opening statements were very similar to the legal arguments in their pre-mediation briefs. The judge invited all of the parties to speak as well because, as he said, the case is "not about the lawyers," and having more participation from the parties increases the chances that they reach a resolution.[3] It was also important to him to give the parties a chance to speak because of the nature of the case: "There was a lot of baggage in this family that made [the case] difficult to resolve." The judge needed the whole family to buy into the process if they were going to work through the issues. He told the parties that he was willing to offer each side his honest legal opinion of the case if they asked and promised that he was providing an identical evaluation of the case to the other parties.

After the opening statements, the rest of the JDR was conducted through shuttle diplomacy with each side in their own breakout room and the judge moving between them.

---

2. All quotes from Simon's malpractice defense attorney are from an interview on April 6, 2020.
3. All quotes from the judge are from an interview on April 3, 2020.

Simon's counsel said that this was the "right way to do it because the family members hated each other. Keeping people in the same room was not a viable [option]." The attorneys were also happy to separate out the co-defendants because, as the attorney's counsel said, this was "a family dispute in which a lawyer … got dragged in." Simon's lawyer added that the JDR felt like two settlement negotiations on two cases were occurring simultaneously, though she recognized that the negotiations would influence each other.

The case settled in the afternoon on the first day of the JDR. In total, the process took about four hours.

Comparison with Trial

Ellis's attorney was confident that the claims against Simon would never get to trial because her attorneys were being provided by her insurer, and typically, insurance companies would prefer to settle than go to trial. The case was initially set for a ten-day trial—the sort of lengthy process that Simon's counsel wished to avoid. Simon's counsel nonetheless said, "The only person who would be liked by a trial judge would be my client." Despite being an inexperienced attorney, she felt that Simon's candor, willingness to accept responsibility, and history of personal and professional generosity would win her favor with a trial judge.

The plaintiff's attorney also admitted that his client's case against his family was weak. The judge agreed that it was "very, very unlikely" that a court would give the plaintiff the relief he wanted, namely specific performance of a contract that had never been signed by all the parties. The root of the conflict—a land transfer that left one child out—suggested that Ellis valued receiving land from his family more than any court-ordered monetary compensation. From this perspective, the plaintiff received a better outcome than he would have at trial. Ellis's attorney also said that, as compared to trial, it produced "less strain on the client to go through a more informal process to try and resolve the matter." He was very attuned to the pressures that Ellis was feeling, and how much he "just wanted it done."

The Walker family conceded land in settlement that they would not have had to give up had the case gone to trial, since Ellis had no legal claim to that land. Yet, the Walker family may ultimately have been more satisfied with giving up this land than they would have been if they had allowed the trial to go forward. The lawsuit had persisted for the better part of a decade by the time they settled the case, and a ten-day trial would have added to the family's already significant legal expenses, in addition to the emotional cost of going through a trial against one's family. Settling the case in the confidential forum of JDR likely gave the Walker family more satisfaction than any vindication a trial could have provided.

Satisfaction

Simon was "ecstatic" about the outcome. Prior to the JDR, she and her attorney believed that the intractable conflict within the Walker family meant that they were unlikely to make concessions. If the family could not sort out their differences and reach a settlement,

Simon would remain embedded in litigation. Thus, her insurer had authorized a settlement amount large enough, they hoped, to "get rid of the whole thing." Simon was surprised and pleased she did not need to hand over such a large sum.

In contrast, this conflict took quite a toll on the Walker family. The mood at the conclusion of the JDR was not celebratory. Ellis's lawyer said that the litigation tore the family apart; the settlement allowed them to end the dispute but did not repair the relationship. "My client is sad that the grandchildren will not get to see their grandmother anymore," he said, ". . . not because he's being malicious or anything, but the relationships are gone." Simon's attorney saw Ellis as a successful businessman in contrast to his less successful siblings. The land transfers to his siblings were gifts to ensure their financial stability, and though Ellis did not need help financially, he felt hurt by being excluded. The judge also mentioned the difficult family dynamics, referring to "history" between the siblings and the mother and agreed that the relationships had probably frayed beyond repair.

Role of the Judge

This JDR judge was well suited to the complexities of the dispute. A former defense attorney in legal malpractice cases, he ran a successful private mediation practice prior to becoming a judge. His judicial expertise as well as his mediation skills were both remarked upon favorably by the attorneys. The judge stated that he treats JDRs "very much like a mediation in most cases, with my ability to provide opinions from time to time." He said that sharing an authoritative evaluation of the case with the parties was "a service that the public wants. They really like the ability to hear what a judge thinks."

In this case, however, the parties did not appear to rely on judicial evaluation in order to move toward an agreement. Rather, Simon's attorney raved about the judge's ability to listen, show empathy, and handle the emotions in the room: "This judge was a perfect JDR judge. He's firm, he listens, he's empathetic, he's an all-around terrific person. He's just so good at his job." The plaintiff's attorney also appreciated that the judge could "guide and broker" the settlement by offering his opinion on which legal positions were sound, but felt that the real value was in gathering information from him about "how far the other side is from agreeing."

The family members in this case had experienced a total communication breakdown. They were still fighting in the aftermath of losing a loved one, amidst unacknowledged pain and sadness that was likely exacerbating their conflict. In this context, the judge's ability to listen, to respect the emotions and experiences of the parties, and to act as a conduit between parties who were unable to hear one another brought the case to a resolution.

The judge was also instrumental when it came to generating creative options. He described "one of the beauties of JDR" as allowing him to "think outside of the box a little bit." In this case, that meant that he asked the defendants whether they had any other land they could offer to the plaintiff. Had this case been before the judge at trial, he very likely would not have ordered the land turned over pursuant to the alleged agreement between the Walkers, and he would have lacked the authority to instruct them to give away parcels that were not at issue in the litigation. In his role as JDR judge, he could suggest options to settle the case, as he put it, "with more than money." This creative solution acknowledged that for the plaintiff, the wrong he suffered came before any alleged breach of contract, and instead originated with his parents excluding him. The judge rightly assumed that as large landowners they would likely own several parcels, including some that could be subdivided. And, he likely realized that Simon would remain entrenched in the case if it failed to settle, potentially costing both reputation damage and legal fees. All the parties' interests were met by developing a novel solution that transferred land instead of money.

Though the JDR was nonbinding, the agreement did result in a court order. All the parties concurred that the agreement should be memorialized this way and kept in the judge's file, so that the parties could not, as the judge said, "go behind it." Given the low level of trust between the parties—particularly after the Walker defendants allegedly reneged on the 2007 land transfer agreement—all felt that filing the decision as a court order was prudent. This is one situation in which an agreement made with a judge in the room, rather than one negotiated in a private mediation, may have been more beneficial for the parties. After the fallout from betrayals stemming from a private contract, the parties were confident in their settlement because it had the official backing of the judiciary.

Access

One reason that ADR[4] practitioners encourage mediation over litigation is that it offers potential for repair of ruptured relationships between parties. Dwight Golann writes in "Is Legal Mediation a Process of Repair – or Separation? – An Empirical Study, and Its Implications" that the most important factor in assessing likelihood of relationship repair is the stage of conflict at the time of mediation.[5] The further the conflict has progressed toward litigation, the less likely mediators report reconciliation. First, Golann explains, filing a formal complaint might be perceived by the parties as a line that cannot be un-crossed, making repair less likely. Second, as the dispute lingers, parties' positions and their attitudes toward one another are likely to harden.[6] And third, it is likely that after some time has passed, the disputants have replaced their fractured relationships with new supports, reducing the perceived value of this damaged relationship, and perhaps leading them to believe it is not worth salvaging even where salvage is possible.[7]

This conflict originated from discussions about land transfers that began in 2006. The case was first filed in 2013 and was settled in the fall of 2019. If it had not settled it would have been set for trial in 2021, a full fifteen years after Ellis and his parents first

---

4. Alternative Dispute Resolution (ADR) is the procedure for settling disputes without litigation and may involve arbitration, mediation, or negotiation.
5. 7 Harv. Negot. L. Rev. 301, 325.
6. Id.
7. Id.

discussed adding him to the title of some of the land. This prolonged conflict reduced the likelihood that the relationships within the family could have been restored. Not only had a formal complaint made them refuse to budge from their positions, the plaintiff's children no longer saw their grandmother. The parties likely believed that the work necessary to repair their bond was far more costly than the relationships were worth.

This raises the question of when JDR should be accessible to parties in intimate cases such as family disputes. Because it is a judicial function, JDR is not available to parties prior to the filing of a formal complaint, which in itself may decrease the possibility of a repair. However, in this case the JDR was also unavailable to the parties for several years due to delays caused by the Walker family and problems with their lawyer. Simon's attorney said that the Walker defendants were only spurred to consider JDR after they were "dragged into a case management meeting and the case was set for trial." The circumstances that delayed the option of JDR may have also denied the family a process of reconciliation: they suffered a further breakdown in relations and cemented their opposition instead of addressing the conflict as soon as they entered the courthouse.

If the aim of JDR is simply efficiency for the judicial system, this case mostly achieved that goal. In lieu of a ten-day trial in 2021, the parties spent four hours negotiating and found resolution two years earlier than scheduled. If JDR has other aims, however, such as meeting the parties' needs more effectively than trial, the long delay prior to JDR should raise concerns. A six-year gap between when the case was filed and when it went to JDR represents a potential lost opportunity to address the root cause of the conflict and to provide a space for the parties to repair their relationships. JDRs require the consent of all parties, and here the Walker family only consented once the trial date had been set and it was clear they could no longer avoid it. What would have happened if they had been referred to JDR immediately upon receipt of the complaint in 2013? Perhaps they would have been able to reach a more amicable resolution. That timing, so close on the heels of the death of Tom Walker, may have allowed them to grieve together over their shared loss.

We cannot know how the case might have resolved differently, but research such as Golann's suggests that delay may have played a role in the deep rupture within the family, and that access to JDR earlier in the life cycle of the conflict might have allowed for at least partial repair.

6

THE FALLING ROCKS CASE

Yijia Wang

Facts

This was a ten-year litigation case between a Canadian municipality (the city) and the owners of a private building near the city hall (the building owners). Third parties included architects who designed the city hall and engineers responsible for the building's roofing system and for hiring contractors for repairs.[1]

In December 2004, a storm passed through the city and allegedly blew loose rocks from the private building's roof onto city hall, breaking its glass pyramids. A year and a half later, the city advised the building owners to take immediate action to avoid similar incidents in the future. In October 2008, another violent storm resulted in severe damage to over one hundred panels of the glass pyramids. Ten months later, approximately ten additional panels were broken in another storm.

After the third round of damage, the city hired an expert to investigate and then file a lawsuit against the building owners. The city accused the building owners of nuisance: they allowed the rocks to accumulate on their roof; and negligence: they had a duty of care to design, inspect, repair, or replace their roof. The city sought an injunction requiring the building owners to repair or replace their roof to prevent rocks from blowing off and damages of roughly $1 million. They proposed a trial that would last less than twenty-five days. The building owners denied all of the accusations and described the city's allegations as "embarrassing and vexatious." In particular, they denied responsibility for the damage to the city hall's glass pyramids' panels, citing the negligible size of the falling rocks. The building owners also asserted that they had taken all reasonable precautions to maintain their roofing system. Furthermore, they charged that the city was negligent for constructing a building with high-risk glass panels, and that the damage was the result of defective glass and improper installation. Regardless of the role that rocks on the roof might have played, the building owners also claimed that weather conditions were an act of God and therefore, the city had no right to file

---

1. In the architecture, engineering, and construction industry, architects are mainly in charge of buildings' appearance and project planning; engineers ensure the safety and functionality of the design by focusing on structural, mechanical, electrical, and plumbing systems; and contractors manage installation and construction.

a damage claim. Finally, the building owners asked the city to repair or replace their roofing system if an injunction were granted.

The following year, the building owners sent a third-party notice asking for indemnification and proceeding costs.[2] In this notice, they accused the building's consulting engineers and contractors of breach of duty of care. They also accused the city hall architects of failing to design a building that could withstand loss and damage and failing in their duty to advise the city on measures to avoid these types of damages.

The city updated its claim to include the engineer and the contractor. In response, both parties denied all the allegations, asserted that the city had failed to bring its claim within allowed time limits, and asked for dismissal with costs. The contractor also stated that their work had been inspected and approved.

The case continued to escalate over the next several years. More accusations accumulated as the building owners updated their statement of defense and third-party notices. In response, the engineers claimed that they were retained to design an ordinary management plan, not a rectification plan. Contrary to the building owners' claim, the engineers said they had never been advised of the city's allegation about rocks falling from the roofing system, and that the contractor's work was not within their purview. The contractor continued to deny all the accusations and any responsibility for losses. The architects denied that they had any obligation to the building owners and also claimed that, after the first incident in 2004, they had submitted a proposal for further service, which was rejected.

The case progressed through the usual stages of identifying witnesses, discovery, depositions, expert reports, etc. In 2018, after all the entities involved agreed to a trial date, they decided to explore the possibility of JDR. They secured a justice with whom most of the lawyers were familiar. The presenting counsels included the city solicitor, the insurers' counsels representing the city, a representative of the building owners, the engineer, and the architect.

The case settled in a single day in Jan 2019. The court issued a consent dismissal order requiring that the city and its insurance company receive almost half of the amount they requested, along with a small portion of their litigation costs. They received around $500,000 compensation two months later, marking the close of the case.

Timing and Process

In Alberta, the court's procedure was not designed to be that of "first responder" to litigated conflict; scheduling a formal trial date was the prerequisite for applying for a JDR.[3] Besides that stipulation, the vast caseload and shortage of judicial resources could delay the process. In this complex case, finding a date acceptable to all the parties

---

2. Indemnity is a contractual obligation of one party to compensate the loss incurred by the other party due to the acts of the indemnitor or any other party. The duty to indemnify is usually, but not always, coextensive with the contractual duty to "hold harmless."

3. Tania Sourdin and Archie Zariski, *The Multi-Tasking Judge: Comparative Judicial Dispute Resolution,* (Thomson Reuters, Australia Limited, 2013).

involved was a challenge. JDR's window of available time slots, limited to only a specific period each year, narrowed scheduling possibilities even further. "It's like booking for a popular concert," one counsel stated. Counsels often prefer to choose a familiar judge; this is an option that can make JDR more appealing than trial, and a selling point to their clients—though it's an added step to the process. The longer it takes to set a trial or JDR date, the greater the risk that most parties will maintain their leverage. In this case, there had been an exhaustive amount of exchanges between parties, and it took a year and a half to set a trial date, with the JDR day occurring several months after that.

The intricate nature of multi-party insurance litigation prolonged the case. Four insurance companies were involved with counsels representing both the insurers and insured, and coordination of interactions was necessary throughout the process.

And there were more complicating factors: Multiple individuals living outside the province owned the building in question, and the representative they assigned to take charge of the litigation had a change in circumstance and was unable to continue to participate after depositions; the building owners changed law firms during the course of the litigation; and, except for the counsel for the plaintiff's insurer, all the presenting counsels had gotten involved after case discovery was completed. Between 2011 and 2017, more than fifteen experts contributed reports dealing with geology, meteorology, and construction.

All parties attended two phone meetings during the pre-JDR phase. The presiding judge talked about the logistics of the JDR day, such as the background information that would be shared and the time allowed for each side to present and rebut. The JDR judge read the briefs from all parties. There was no settlement discussion among the parties prior to the JDR, but the defendant and third-party counsels talked a bit about strategy.

The JDR day kicked off with a plenary session in a boardroom that overlooked the city hall's glass pyramids allowing the parties a clear view of the scene that brought them together. The justice assured the attendees that the proceedings would be entirely confidential and nothing they said would be used against them outside the room. The justice received a written summary from each counsel and encouraged each of them to make statements. He then outlined what he saw as the strengths and weaknesses of each side's arguments as well as the key obstacles to resolution. He stressed that the fifteen days planned for the trial—including three full days of work for him—seemed a woefully conservative estimate.

Then the justice split the group into two breakout rooms with the plaintiff and their counsel in one and the defendants and the third parties in another. Everyone remained in their rooms until the final session, with the exception of a few private exchanges in a third room reserved for such conversations or phone calls.

In the plaintiff room, the city's solicitor and insurer's counsel had been working closely on the case and felt that they had leverage. The solicitor was in charge of witnesses and evidence regarding damage claims, while the insurer's counsel was in charge of liabilities, obtaining evidence, and examining the other parties.

Concurrently, in the defendant and the third-party room, the discussion before lunch focused on the substantive arguments. After lunch, they switched to the topic of monetary issues and spent roughly 10 percent of the time determining what percentage each party should contribute. Ultimately, they found the building owners responsible for the largest portion and the architects not responsible. For the remaining time, they bargained with the plaintiff over the entire compensation amount. During these exchanges one party maxed out their authority and had to make a private phone call.

The justice caucused with each party to get a sense of their BATNAs;[4] reviewed their strengths, weaknesses, and practical problems; and offered his opinion on what would happen if the case went to trial. As the session progressed, the justice shuttled between the two rooms at least six times, reviewing the points of disagreement and providing legal opinions when asked—opinions he always shared with each side. Counsels noted that there was enough downtime to work on other projects while waiting for answers from the opposing party.

The architects' counsel behaved more like a facilitator, commenting, "It's weird, we didn't share that much of interest with the defendant even though we were positioned as 'co-defendant' or an 'added character.'" She felt that the architects' low liability, due to the fact that a decade has passed since they designed the city hall, put them in a good position to negotiate.

The defendant's counsel appreciated the third-party counsels' clear communication of their client's position and instructions.[5] The counsels collectively agreed to create mutual gains—even in their opposing positions—by determining how much they should pay the plaintiff rather than competing among themselves.

At the end of the JDR, all presenting parties gathered in the boardroom and discussed the settlement details. Topics included the release and exchange of documents; how much each party would contribute; the timeline for all the necessary actions; and how money would be transferred. The case was resolved with a consent dismissal order, and everything was finalized six weeks after the JDR day. The justice also followed up to ensure that payment was received. Though smaller cost-related issues remained unsettled on both sides, the majority of the dispute was resolved with a non-binding agreement, and there was no subsequent litigation.

The JDR Justice

"I am a big fan of JDR, and nothing in my mind changed when I became a judge," explained the justice, who had done a fair amount of work as a mediator during his tenure as a litigator. He considers himself to be a facilitative-style JDR justice. Sourdin and her colleague note that judges who practice first as lawyers are likely to bring pre-existing beliefs with them to the bench and may be more independent-minded regarding judicial roles and practices.[6] This resonated with one of the counsels who confirmed that in his experience JDR judges who were once litigators have particular opinions regarding how

---

4. BATNA, a term coined by negotiation researchers Roger Fisher and William Ury in their 1981 book, *Getting to Yes,* is a party's "Best Alternative To a Negotiated Agreement," or what a party can fall back on if a negotiation proves unsuccessful.
5. Instructions can include a party's BATNA, addendums they may accept, etc.
6. Sourdin and Zariski, *The Multi-Tasking Judge.*

they run a JDR. Other counsels added that the justice's litigation experience brought a depth to the process and gave the parties a full understanding of JDR.

This justice's impartial and diplomatic manner, his reputation for being an especially effective mediator, and positive experiences among the litigation industry in Alberta all won him the trust of counsels and put their minds at ease when they worked with him in JDR. "One of the risks when going to trial is you will never know who your judge is until the last minute, and that makes a huge difference in terms of preparing for the court," said one counsel. The justice's wide range of JDR experience allows him to diffuse difficult situations—or as he put it, "to shuttle the bomb away"—and to encourage stubborn parties who are "beginning to set traps" to instead work cooperatively.

The justice's approachable demeanor set a friendly tone during initial caucusing. "That made me have more respect for him," said one of the counsels. He added that the justice's conversational style helped clients open up, especially when he encouraged the plaintiff and defendants to share their feelings in the plenary session. Counsels confirmed that their clients needed the opportunity to have their say and be taken seriously. Sitting with the judge at the same table as other parties, as opposed to watching him or her rule from the dais, is a metaphor for access to justice.[7]

The nature of JDR is such that when a judge becomes a mediator his or her words often carry more weight for the clients than that of their counsel. The justice in this case told the parties what his expectations would be if it were sent to trial, hoping each party would reevaluate their BATNAs.

Throughout the JDR process, the justice considers it essential that he recognize and react to how much authority each presenting party has, and said, "The process is very dynamic and moves all the time." For example, when a counsel has to phone clients during a session to clarify an issue, it complicates the mediation process. The justice would seldom weigh in, however, unless a particular action presented a serious roadblock.

The justice asked questions that reminded counsels to reconsider their BATNAs and reach agreement: "Are you sure about this number? . . . If you look at how much you will spend or end up paying if you go to a trial, do you really want to hold out on this topic rather than seek a compromise?" When asked how he estimates each party's BATNA, the justice said, "That's the better part of the day as I have a plan to settle, but I will see how the parties go, and it's often a monetary issue." Years of mediation experience in various roles allows him to discern each party's perspective and employ a fitting strategy. According to Welsh, JDR judges' training and experience contribute to identifying and rectifying process abuses and inequalities of power and capacity.[8] It should be noted, however, that the justice in this case was mindful not to overstep his role and instead focused on facilitation, which allowed the parties to, as he put it, "go through the dance."

---

7. Ibid.
8. Nancy A. Welsh, *Making Deals in Court-Connected Mediation: What's Justice Got to Do With It?*, 79 Wash. U.L.Q. 787 (2001), https://openscholarship.wustl.edu/law_lawreview/vol79/iss3/3.

As for cases that have not settled, the justice suggested it is most often due to unpreparedness, absence of documents (such as expert reports), and/or failure to exchange documents. Although the justice is disappointed when a case fails to settle, experience has taught him that some failure is inevitable.

The justice specifically noted that as JDR has gained popularity, it has become more lucrative for counsels and more complicated for the JDR judges who may have prior litigation experience in the same jurisdiction. He remains vigilant, however, about avoiding any conflicts of interest.

JDR Incentives and Settlement Evaluation

"When all the parties agreed to have a JDR, everyone is supposed to come in with good faith. Hence, it's not difficult to mediate," said one counsel, and that was the tone for the entire JDR.

Counsels agreed that cost was the main obstacle of going to trial: There was always a risk of greater expense for each side. The estimated cost of trial alone was close to the reimbursement the plaintiff asked for. More, dragging out the case and placing financial and mental burdens on everyone were further disincentives. Parties often put more trust in an honorable judge with mediation experience—and who costs each party nothing in JDR—than they do in a skillful yet expensive and unfamiliar mediator. With this type of case—one mainly litigated by insurance companies—there is a similar distaste for a trial; the cost-benefit analysis involves too many considerations including time, risk, and industry reputation.

One counsel felt that this case had a high probability of settling, and finding the trial date was not only a way to schedule the JDR but to get the parties to focus. After all, the closer to the commencement of litigation that settlement occurs, the better.[9]

The participants had unique perspectives when evaluating each other's strengths and weaknesses. The plaintiff's counsel assumed that the multiple scientific reports they had gathered over the years would play a vital role in proving they had a strong case. He also thought that with the imminent trial date, the defendants might have had limited time to reach a "eureka" moment and were instead digging unsuccessfully for favorable evidence and arguments. However, the opposing counsels suspected that there was still uncertainty on the plaintiff's side and that it would be wise for the plaintiff to settle. The justice believed that the plaintiff might have gained more at trial than what they negotiated within the JDR.

Of the five counsels in this case, most had dealt with multiple JDRs, ADRs, trials, and mediations both in and outside of court, and their liability litigation experience ranged from ten to thirty years. Confidentiality, always a priority for the attorneys, was of primary importance for the insurance company's counsel: If the case went to trial, the claim would be publicly disclosed and it would likely provide a potential benchmark for future insurance claims. That scenario would not be in their best interest, so their counsels had a strong incentive to settle.

---

9. Sourdin and Zariski, *The Multi-Tasking Judge*.

Role of Scientific Experts

Scientific reports in liability litigation like this case (or cases involving building collapse, fire, etc.) are essential and taken seriously. The first expert report was created in 2008 before the city filed the lawsuit against the building owners, and more than a decade before the JDR. The intention of this report was to find proof that the rocks used in the building owners' roofing system were blown from a west-north-west direction during the storms. After presenting this report, the plaintiff's counsel followed up with analyses by additional experts: Meteorologists commented on the weather conditions on the incident days; geologists explained the falling rock composition; and engineers spoke about roof and building envelope analysis as well as structural and load calculation on the glass pyramids. The building owners and engineers responded with reports from their experts whom the city rebutted with additional experts.

It is commonly accepted that installing such rocks on roofing systems is an industry practice to safeguard the roof from degrading and cracking over time. Most of the expert reports were trying to prove one side of a particularly heated argument: the cause of the broken glass and whether the force that caused it had originated outside or inside the building. The plaintiff's counsel thought that his own expert provided an excellent rebuttal, strengthened their case beyond the report that he had submitted during the pre-JDR phase, and laid a solid foundation for deciding liability.

The justice left counsels with the decision of whether to summon expert witnesses at the JDR. If experts had appeared, he would have cross-examined them, relying on his experience to call out biased testimony.

Counsels all noted that it is not general practice to have an expert in a JDR. Beyond the issue of cost, the process has the expectation that expert reports provide enough solid evidence to prove opinion. One counsel suspected that since most of the expert testimony would not be available to the public, these experts' scientific reports were more like a game of competing knowledge. Thus, summoning experts was not necessary, and the scientific reports did not take much time on the JDR day.

Insurance Litigation Industry Feedback on JDR

The parties all agreed that the result of a successful JDR will not necessarily satisfy everyone; an agreement everyone can "live with" is considered a reasonable outcome. As such, JDR is not a zero-sum game and does not declare a winner and loser.

The counsels like the freedom to choose whether to settle and one stated, "People want to have wiggle room and a chance to walk away." Counsels also noted that parties do not like to be bound to an outcome; if they did, a binding JDR[10] would lose its advantage.

---

10. A binding JDR (BJDR) is a dispute resolution mechanism in the form of a confidential pre-trial settlement conference led by a justice, and aimed at resolving a dispute or limiting the issues on which the parties disagree. If a settlement between the parties is not reached, then the justice's opinion will be binding. (See Court of Queen's Bench of Alberta, JDR, available at https://www.albertacourts.ca/qb/areas-of-law/jdr [16.03.2020]).

One counsel mentioned that facing a "difficult" lawyer at trial—whose clients hired them for that reason—is a "litigation lawyer's worst nightmare." He said that facing such an opponent can completely change one's strategy in preparing for a trial and may also present a clear threat to the prospect of settling. By comparison, JDR typically places everyone on relatively equal footing and avoids the adversarial tendencies of courtroom litigation.

Two of the counsels suggested removing the plenary session from future JDRs. One counsel reported that everyone's statements at the outset activated the adversarial mentality of a trial. Another added that clients expect their counsels to be staunch advocates during plenary sessions and they might see the typically effective "mutual gains approach" in mediation as weakness in their counsel.

Judges' approaches to JDR can vary widely. Since there are no procedural rules, they decide on all aspects of the process, such as when and how to conduct caucusing, whether or not to present opening briefs, and whether to use shuttle diplomacy. What functions well in one case might not work in another. As Galanter writes, "There is evidence that judges who consider themselves good negotiators tend to get involved in a settlement, and judges have expressed disappointment with counsel lacking settlement skills and the will to settle their cases."[11]

Years of JDR-related work can increase experienced counsels' unwillingness to settle at an early stage, and they may treat JDR as a "mini-trial." This, in turn, can extend the lifespan of many cases, despite the fact that 95 percent of liability litigation will ultimately end in settlement.

The tight availability of judicial resources is not necessarily a downside of JDR. As Fisher and his colleagues suggest in *Getting to Yes*, some parties might use the JDR to determine whether a settlement is a better option than a trial.[12] The JDR process may allow them to discover and refine their BATNA if they are determined to have an eventual trial, but this contradicts the purpose of JDR. If there was no prior settlement attempt or intention, why should a JDR judge be appointed to mediate the case at the court's cost? In this particular case, all the counsels showed up with an intent to settle and perceived the cost-benefit of doing so, but not all cases play out that way.

Perhaps it *should* remain difficult to access JDR. Sourdin and her colleague suggest that JDRs ought to be reserved for cases that have tried and failed at settlement and/or are unlikely to settle without it.[13]

---

11. Marc Galanter, "'A Settlement Judge, Not a Trial Judge': Judicial Mediation in the United States," *Journal of Law and Society,* Vol. 12, No. 1 (Spring, 1985) https://www.jstore.org/stable/1410244?seq=1.
12. Roger Fisher, William Ury, and Bruce Patton, *Getting to Yes, Negotiating Agreement Without Giving In,* (Boston: Houghton Mifflin, 1981).
13. Sourdin and Zariski, *The Multi-Tasking Judge.*

Conclusion

The Falling Rocks Case may not be a textbook illustration showcasing all the virtues of JDR, but it acts as an ideal example for insurance liability cases.

This case clearly illustrates that counsels appreciate selecting judges, and they prefer certain judges for specific reasons. If the court system would allow it, it may be worth encouraging panel discussions among JDR judges for the purpose of sharing individual mediation styles and methods.

An attorney's skill set needed to succeed in a JDR is not necessarily the same as that required in the courtroom. Besides negotiation and mediation skills—which vary widely—presenting counsels must possess a cooperative attitude and a desire to settle. Clients, as well, may benefit from understanding distinctions among counsels' abilities so that they hire based on a good fit for JDR, not just trial.

If all parties foresee that a case will drag on, it might be cost-effective to consider a JDR sooner rather than later. As one counsel concluded, "At some point, people just want to move on with their lives."

THE MEDICAL MALPRACTICE CASE

Tara Boghosian

The medical procedure giving rise to this action and successful JDR was a vitrectomy that took place in Alberta, Canada. The plaintiff, Smith, had been suffering from impaired vision in his right eye, which was minorly affecting his work as a laboratory technician. In March 1999, a licensed ophthalmologist recommended that Smith undergo a vitrectomy surgery to his right eye to improve his vision. Upon this recommendation, Smith opted to have the ophthalmologist perform the surgery in June 1999.

When Smith arrived for surgery, the anesthesiologist determined that topical, rather than general anesthesia, was appropriate for the surgery. The anesthesiologist administered the anesthesia and then inserted a needle to the right eye, causing Smith extreme pain. The anesthesiologist subsequently administered stronger anesthetic to his right eye. Smith still alleged that the treatment was not strong enough to numb his right eye, but the ophthalmologist went ahead and began the vitrectomy surgery. Smith again experienced extreme pain and moved suddenly, causing the ophthalmologist's needle to perforate the globe of Smith's right eye, resulting in vitreous and preretinal hemorrhage. Further sedation was added to the eye, and the ophthalmologist completed the vitrectomy successfully. However, Smith had to undergo several more surgeries to attempt to correct the damage resulting from the eye's perforated globe over the subsequent two years.

Major Issues in Dispute

In plaintiff Smith's Statement of Claim against the ophthalmologist and the anesthesiologist for negligent medical care, he alleged that his right eye's vision had become even more impaired than when he initially sought care from the ophthalmologist. He claimed that this increased and permanent vision impairment further hindered his ability to do his job as a laboratory technician, which required analyzing details under a microscope, and led to loss of past and prospective income. He also claimed that he was unable to complete regular day-to-day tasks and required home care and other services. Finally, he asserted that he suffered depression as a result of his injuries and had begun taking medication. In total, he sought damages approaching $5 million.

Neither of the defendants disputed the majority of factual events giving rise to the claim, but they challenged that any damages suffered by the plaintiff resulted from the doctors' negligence or other misconduct.

The Litigation Process and Leadup to the JDR

The leadup to the JDR in this case was longer and more eventful than most, which is essential to understanding why the JDR was far more attractive to both parties than trial, and why it was ultimately successful. The case began in 2000 and did not settle in JDR until 2013. Smith had changed counsel more than once throughout the duration of the litigation but was ultimately represented by one attorney leading up to trial and the JDR. Another attorney represented both the ophthalmologist and the mutual defense fund.

Initially, when counsel took on the plaintiff as a client, she felt that the case was strong and that the ophthalmologist had been "clearly wrong" in performing the surgery and perforating the right eye globe with insufficient anesthesia. She also employed an investigator who gathered compelling evidence, including testimony from the ophthalmologist's office intern who asserted that the doctor did not always exercise the requisite level of care in treating patients.

At the outset, the defense counsel considered settlement the best option because the case would not be easy to defend and would involve less time and money. Plaintiff's counsel felt that the parties ultimately agreed on most facts, including some mistakes made in the doctors' care. However, the parties and their economic experts disagreed about the amount of damages owed to the plaintiff—and more specifically about whether the injury that he suffered and the resulting loss of sight in one eye prevented him from continuing his work in a lab. Further, there were different estimates of the plaintiff's pre-injury and post-injury income, which made the two parties' total damages estimates further inconsistent.

Ultimately, as the case developed, two factors emerged that added significant pressure for both lawyers to settle rather than go to trial. First, the ophthalmologist had moved abroad and would only be available to testify via videoconference if the case did go to trial. According to the defense attorney, the logistical challenges of a remote connection at the time, combined with the fact that the ophthalmologist was no longer living and practicing in Canada, would have weakened his testimony.

More important for prompting the JDR settlement, however, were the plaintiff's credibility issues—which each lawyer discovered independently. The plaintiff's counsel was first alerted to these issues when witnesses who were going to testify to Smith's loss of capacity at work and in his daily life began backing out. Plaintiff's counsel then realized that her client would likely not come across as credible at trial, and the calculus of whether to go to trial changed. She felt that she could not withdraw from the case completely, but neither did she want to possibly harm her own credibility and professional ethical obligations by taking her client to trial and allowing him to testify if there was little evidence to support his claims (and more evidence to the contrary) about his ability to work as a result of the injury. Thus, she decided that her best option was to settle and end the matter as soon as possible. She formulated what would be a fair settlement number at JDR, but there was still some disconnect between her and the plaintiff's view of the matter: he remained set on a much higher number of damages and did not agree about the high risks and costs of going to trial given the credibility issues.

Through their own investigation, defense counsel also became aware of Smith's credibility issues and that he was likely not as incapacitated by his injuries as he claimed. Defense counsel intended to leverage these findings during the JDR—and at trial, if necessary—to undermine his credibility. However, defense counsel did not want to expressly notify the plaintiff about the exact nature of the evidence in case they did ultimately go to trial.

The leadup to this JDR involved both counsels—but particularly plaintiff's counsel—beginning the process with an almost certain intention of settling. The biggest barrier to their settlement in JDR, however, was reconciling the high amount of damages that the plaintiff asked for with the more moderate number that plaintiff's counsel thought was fair—and the even lower number that the defense wanted to pay. Fortunately, the justice's JDR process gave the plaintiff the opportunity to see the weaknesses in his case and understand why he should settle, while facilitating efficient and principled negotiation between counsels about settlement numbers.

The JDR Process

Overview of the justice's typical JDR process

The justice uses a fairly consistent process for non-binding JDRs. She is facilitative and nondirective on substantive issues, but more structured regarding the JDR procedure. Typically, prior to the first JDR session, the parties submit short briefs of around five pages summarizing the case. The justice reviews these briefs prior to an initial meeting with the parties. Both lawyers in the case emphasized that the justice does significant preparation for her JDRs and always comes to the session fully briefed on the major issues.

Before the JDR session, the justice meets briefly with the plaintiff and defense counsels to review the basic facts. She may also ask if the parties have had any settlement discussions yet, and if they have not, she tells them to come back to JDR once they have. If the parties have engaged in settlement discussions, she asks each party to disclose their last offers. Sometimes in this conversation a lawyer will disclose that his client is not being realistic about the case, which helps the justice determine where she needs to put her energy in working toward settlement during the JDR.

The JDR officially begins with the justice addressing the parties together for a brief introduction to the process. For the remaining time together the justice almost exclusively caucuses with each party and their lawyers. These conversations are confidential, but sometimes she will encourage parties to share information with each other. In particular, if there is an information asymmetry, she believes that resolving it can bring the parties closer to settlement. Further, she finds that it can be more effective for a party to hear the "bad news" about the case directly from the other side rather than mediated through their own lawyer, which may make a party feel that their lawyer is not fully on their side. Thus, the justice is not only highly conscious of the need to reality-check the parties, but also of the different relationships in play and what source of information a party might find most credible.

At her initial meetings with each side, the justice asks the party to tell her about their experience. For example, in a personal injury case, she might say to the plaintiff, "Give me a snapshot of yourself before the accident, versus now." She will drill down on specifics: how did the plaintiff know x? How did y feel? Her goal is to get to know the party, build rapport, get a sense of how they would fare as a witness at trial, and how sharp their recall is. If a party seems to be a poor historian the justice may suggest, "I have a sense from the ten minutes that we talked that you find it difficult to go through dates and times and places." She will then caution him that remembering dates while testifying is a necessary part of trial, and that trial might be especially stressful if he has trouble calling up details. She will also ask the lawyer to tell their client how they think he will fare at trial.

The justice also works with each party to make a list of issues that would be important if the case went to trial, such as negligence, standard of care, different types of damages, etc. She will then ask the lawyer to "give me summary of what you would say at trial about standard of care." She will also ask what the lawyer thinks the best and worst parts of the case would be at trial. Lawyers may be reluctant to discuss the weaker parts of the case in front of their client, which makes this exercise even more useful for reality-testing.

If the justice notices that an issue is particularly weak for one side after holding caucuses, she will share her concerns with that party. The purpose of caucusing is to provide parties with a structured process to critically analyze the strength and weaknesses of their case; to correct information asymmetries that are barriers to settlement; and to weigh the costs and benefits of going to trial over settling. The justice generally tries to avoid offering her own opinion on the merits of the entire case, which tends to halt settlement conversations between the parties rather than induce them. However, if there has been discussion and unsuccessful attempts at coming up with a settlement number, she might be more evaluative of the overall merits of the case.

In addition to caucusing with both sides, the justice engages in shuttle diplomacy. Each round, she asks each party to come up with a new offer. The justice has found it effective to do this simultaneously because parties are often quite reluctant to be the first one to make an offer. She then emphasizes that "it is not a sign of weakness" to provide a new offer, and that the point of the JDR is to "get to a crossover."

She said, however, that she still has not figured out a surefire way to help the parties avoid positional bargaining, particularly at the beginning of the process. If the parties get deep into positional bargaining and the progress is slow but gradual, the justice might say, "You don't need me to do this ... call me when you're settled or stuck." If the parties get to numbers that are no more than $10-15,000 apart, the justice will say, "This is going to settle, you don't need me anymore," and that will generally spur the lawyers to make the final offers that settle the case.

However, if the JDR has progressed to some degree but the parties' numbers remain very far apart, the justice asks the plaintiff for the absolute lowest number that they would accept and asks the defendant for the absolute highest amount that they would pay. The parties are expected to stick to these numbers and cannot renege. The justice keeps the exact numbers confidential, but based on those amounts, will recommend whether the parties should keep discussing settlement numbers or go home. If the parties' sums are the same, she will ask the parties' permission to be directive and if permission is granted, she will reveal that they gave the same number.

Overall, using this process, the justice estimates that around 75 percent of cases settle in JDR. Sometimes, if a party makes what she considers to be a very fair offer but the other party does not accept it during the course of the JDR, she will ask the offering party to hold open their offer for two weeks and she will tell the other party to think seriously about whether to accept. Thus, some of the cases that do not settle in the JDR settle afterwards.

The justice keeps paper records of the JDR process and the parties' documents but shreds them immediately after the JDR process is complete, unless the case does not settle and the justice and counsels have indicated that there may be a follow-up session. If the parties do settle in JDR, the justice has the participants and counsels sign a sheet detailing the terms of the settlement, which she keeps for two years.

The JDR process in this case

The plaintiff and defense lawyer had participated in JDRs before and remarked that choosing the right judge was essential to the ultimate success of the JDR. Together, they chose a justice who they felt was highly skilled in a variety of areas.

Per the justice's usual process, she held a pre-JDR meeting with counsels to generally discuss the issues in the case and the character traits of parties who would be in attendance at the session. The lawyers also exchanged briefs prior to the JDR, although plaintiff's counsel noted that she felt the five-page limit was too short to summarize a nearly decade-long case and submitted a much longer brief.

By the time the parties had determined that they would participate in JDR to try and settle the case, they were "trial ready" and had exchanged several expert reports. Each party had engaged a medical and an economic expert, and all of the resulting expert reports had been shared between the parties, though no expert attended the JDR itself.

On the day of the JDR session, the justice made her opening remarks to the parties together. Plaintiff's counsel described this as a "relatively informal plenary session" where the two sides met and the justice reviewed the basics of the JDR process. Then the justice separated the parties into different rooms and the rest of the JDR—which lasted the better part of a day—proceeded through shuttle diplomacy.

The lawyers felt that the justice's strengths as a JDR practitioner made the process far less painful than it otherwise might have been and led to a principled settlement. They especially admired and respected the justice's "firm but fair" and efficient process, her thorough preparation and knowledge of the case, and a "no nonsense" approach to negotiation.

The justice expected the parties to work hard to come up with settlement offers, but she did not expect them to do so unaided. As the plaintiff's lawyer described, during each round of shuttle diplomacy, the justice worked diligently with each side to come up with a new offer that would bring the parties closer to settlement. Indeed, defense counsel indicated that the justice ensured that each offer was evidence based and supported by "principled reasons." They went on to say that she pushed back against huge positional numbers and insignificant concessions that might aggravate the other side and stall the process. The justice was able to evaluate the fairness of each offer thanks to rigorous groundwork and assimilation of the facts, evidence, and relevant law in the case.

For example, the plaintiff's attorney noted that because the justice had experience litigating and adjudicating cases involving medical malpractice and insurance pay-outs, the justice had a general sense of the typical ballpark of damages for the specific injury that Smith suffered. The justice therefore did not pressure the plaintiff to settle for an exceptionally low number, which had happened to the plaintiff's attorney in other Alternative Dispute Resolution (ADR) and JDR sessions.

Both lawyers noted that this justice understood the importance of "getting into the weeds" of the case, made clear in her detailed and probing questioning about the facts, strength of the evidence, and legal arguments. Knowing in advance that the justice operated in an efficient and evidence-based manner encouraged the parties to come into the JDR well aware of their bottom-line numbers and the principled reasons supporting them. The parties' lawyers appreciated and complied with the justice's established norm of principled rather than positional negotiation.

In contrast, both lawyers noted other JDR or private ADR sessions in which a judge or mediator did not seem well equipped to assess whether criteria-based reasons or evidence supported both parties' positions. A JDR/ADR practitioner might lack the substantive knowledge—of either the facts and history of the case itself or the background law—to evaluate whether each party's subsequent offer is fair, principled, and supported by the evidence. An ineffective JDR/ADR practitioner might just superficially admonish the parties to "work something out" or urge them to "halve the baby." Sometimes, they might even display bias toward one party or type of claim. Defense counsel noted that these approaches are particularly inadequate with certain clients who are evidence-based and will go to trial if a JDR judge pushes a settlement number unsupported by a well-reasoned argument.

Both counsels reiterated that the justice in this case was a uniquely capable JDR practitioner because she did not rely solely on her inherent authority to help the parties come to a settlement; rather, she studied the case so that she was in a position to help the parties evaluate offers against objective criteria. Her willingness to delve deeply and work with the parties this way was key to persuading the plaintiff to reassess the amount of damages that he would accept in a settlement.

The defense counsel not only felt the evidence suggested that the plaintiff was not as debilitated by the eye injury as he claimed, they further recognized that it was the plaintiff, rather than the plaintiff's lawyer, who was being hardline about claiming the high number of damages. Yet, defense counsel did not want to explicitly disclose the nature of the evidence in case they went to trial. In contrast, the justice's approach is to encourage parties to share information—particularly important information—insofar as possible. So, defense counsel and the justice agreed that the justice would take an "inkling" of information back to the plaintiff to imply that credibility-damaging evidence existed without expressly saying what kind of evidence. It was enough information for the plaintiff to understand that evidence may have shown that he could likely continue his work as a laboratory technician even with the eye injury. It appeared that the plaintiff was able to hear and accept this information from the justice, a trusted authority figure who had genuinely listened to him. Further, concrete evidence meant that contradictory reports regarding the extent of the plaintiff's incapacity could not be chalked up to a difference in opinion.

Ultimately, the plaintiff was convinced that he should accept a much lower settlement because his initial claim had been undermined and rendered unjustified by the defense's evidence. After all, the bulk of requested damages included post and prospective loss of income, as well as damages to cover care services to assist the plaintiff with daily tasks.

The confidential settlement consisted solely of monetary damages and costs. The plaintiff's lawyer said the settlement amount was fair but not huge. The funds were delivered without any issues from the defendant's insurance company to the plaintiff's attorney within fifteen days, and without the need for the justice to assist with compliance. There was no admission of liability by the defendants and the settlement did not become a court order. The justice required the parties to sign a settlement sheet, which she kept for two years following the JDR but she did not keep any other record of the settlement.

Benefits of JDR for This Case

Both lawyers mentioned the general benefits of JDR over trial: JDRs are far less time consuming, require less preparation by the attorney, and are less costly for the client.

Another asset of JDR, and one more specific to the way JDR worked in this case, was the justice's facilitative yet efficient manner: she helped the plaintiff recognize his case's weaknesses and come to his own decision to accept a lower settlement. Because this took place during JDR, the plaintiff got a preview of what would likely happen at trial, without the risks of actually going to trial and potentially being unable to recover any damages.

Further, by settling within the confidential JDR process, the plaintiff and his lawyer avoided a public trial process that could have been very costly, not just financially and emotionally, but reputationally as well. Moreover, the lawyer did not intend to go to trial with her client at all, given that she suspected he might not testify in complete honesty, and she did not want her own ethical obligations and credibility to be jeopardized as a result. Indeed, had this plaintiff opted to go to trial he would have likely needed to find new counsel, which would have further increased the costs and length of the case.

Lastly, the private JDR process was also beneficial for the defendants in this case. The settlement number was confidential and they did not admit liability. Had this case gone to trial and the judge rendered a decision against the doctors, that information would have been made public and had reputational and precedential impacts.

Thus, looking at this case overall, the justice's experience, tone, and commitment to the process was crucial for ensuring that the JDR served the parties' interests, and that the case did not become even more complicated, costly, and time-consuming. The question, then, is whether other JDR practitioners can replicate the success of this justice's process.

8

THE POWER POLE CASE

Zac Smith

Facts

On a spring day in the late 1990s, three individuals drove a grain feed truck on or near the Happy Valley Farm Ltd. in central Alberta. The truck was mounted with an unloading auger which, when extended, carried feed out of the truck bed through its spiral shaft. While driving underneath power lines, the still-extended auger—usually retracted during transport—collided with the lines, damaging them. Happy Valley hired a journeyman electrician to repair the damage. To access the lines, he climbed a nearby power pole, which suddenly broke and fell on top of him.

As a result of the fall, he fractured his left pelvis and right elbow. He also suffered major contusions and additional minor injuries. The injuries required several surgeries and extensive physical therapy. On top of the expenses and lost income related to medical care and rehabilitation, as well as the damages associated with his pain and suffering resulting from the fall, he alleged that his injuries inhibited his ability to perform basic household tasks, leaving him dependent on the assistance of others. Further, he claimed that the lasting effects of his injuries would render him unable to fully compete with his healthy co-workers, disadvantaging him professionally and limiting his opportunities for future advancement. Because his injuries were sustained on the job, he received some disability benefits from the Workplace Compensation Board (WCB), a provincial agency responsible for administering disability insurance. These benefits were limited, however, and terminated several months after the accident.

Seeking to recover damages, the electrician sued Happy Valley, claiming that the farm, as owner of the property on which the power pole stood, had been negligent in ensuring the premises were reasonably safe for visitors. In particular, their failure to inspect the pole, take necessary steps to ensure its safety, and to warn or advise the electrician of the risk, led to his injuries. In total, he claimed nearly $7 million in damages.

Because he was injured on the job and received WCB benefits, the electrician's claim was limited by the WCB legislation. Therefore, he had to withdraw the claims he had originally filed against the three individuals for damaging the pole in the first place, because the legislation prohibited suits against other individuals covered by WCB legislation (i.e., other employees). Moreover, the conduct of the suit itself was governed by the third-party claim provision of the legislation, and the WCB adjuster had the final decision on the amount they would settle for and what percentage would be given to the complainant (instead of collected by the government).

The defendants denied liability. Happy Valley asserted that, as an expert electrician trained to repair powerlines, the electrician had inspected the pole prior to climbing, and had therefore assumed the repair job's inherent risk.

Process

Prior to the non-binding JDR session, the parties (which included the electrician, his lawyer, Happy Valley's lawyers, as well as a WCB adjuster), filed JDR briefs with the judge mediating the case. According to the judge, these briefs articulated fairly rigid positions similar to those an attorney would argue in court. Based on these briefs, the judge prepared a Scott Schedule,[1] which listed all the issues to be decided and the position of each of the parties on each issue.

On the day of the case, the judge invited the parties to present fifteen- to twenty-minute opening statements. He explained that beyond arguing the legal points presented in their briefs, this was an opportunity for the parties to explain why the case was important to them in more personal terms, as well as emphasize the relative strength of their case. Following the opening statements, the judge explained that he would allow clarifying questions, but not arguments. One of the lawyers reported that a broader scope of response was actually permitted, beyond simple technical answers, that allowed the injured plaintiff to "get things off his chest" and feel heard by the other side.

Then, the parties broke into private caucus rooms. After an initial opportunity for the parties to talk amongst themselves, the judge began a private discussion with the plaintiff. At this stage, he avoided providing his own assessment of the case, but instead went back and forth between the parties, a stage characterized as "shuttle diplomacy." One of the lawyers explained: "A good mediation justice will let them go through the process," and organically adjust their expectations. Over the course of these discussions, the judge said the Scott Schedule allowed him to identify where disagreements persisted.

Though the judge initially refrained from providing his own assessment, he stated that—as is usual in his mediation experience—the initial discussion did not move them far beyond their initial positions. He then began to "reality test" their assumptions and offer an opinion on whether the requests were realistic or fair. None of the individuals involved mentioned invocation of specific precedents during this phase. In fact, there seemed to be a general reluctance to invoke them for fear of entrenching parties and falling back into positional bargaining. At this juncture, the judge summarized the discussions and asked each party for their "best number," or what they would be willing to

---

1. A Scott Schedule, named after George Scott, Official Referee of the United Kingdom High Court of Justice, 1920-1933, is a table used in ADRs that outlines the differing types of damage as well as the monetary amounts claimed for each one. According to the judge in this case, it provides a useful outline and tracking device throughout the process.

settle for. Once these numbers were in the same ballpark (around $90,000), the judge stated something to the effect of: "I think you can get a deal for that number," which provided some confidence for the parties to approach each other and settle.

Interestingly, one of the lawyers mentioned that after both parties had reached a number, the other party sought to gain additional small concessions to test their resolve and see whether they would cave in the interest of closure. The lawyer therefore said he had to be "ready to walk" if they would not hold to the number that they initially agreed to.

The case settled at the JDR for a monetary payment to the electrician of under $100,000 (delivered shortly after the session), in exchange for which the electrician signed a standard release and discontinued the suit. Though the WCB had at first planned on retaining the entire amount, the electrician received some share of the settlement and the WCB adjuster also agreed to reinstate his WCB benefits. The electrician felt satisfied with the process but was frustrated with the restrictions imposed by the WCB.

Role and Capability of the Judge as Mediator

Both counsels felt that this particular judge was an essential part of the JDR's success. When testing the assumptions of the parties during the session, the judge was an impartial authority. For example, when he began to question the size of some of the plaintiff's damage claims, his experience with similar disputes and the general aura of respect that surrounds the judiciary provided credibility that would not necessarily have been present with other non-judge mediators. Furthermore, the fact that he was a *sitting* judge carried even more weight. This was likely due to the respect garnered by the office and also a recognition that this judge, or one similar, would hear the case should it go to trial. The parties therefore felt that, when the judge did give his opinion on a matter, it was due significant deference.

All the parties reported that—beyond trusting this judge's opinions—simply having a judge as mediator increased their faith in the process. When discussing important issues of liability or compensation with an outside party, there is inevitable suspicion of what may inadvertently make it back to the other side. Given the citizenry's trust in judges, this seemed to be less of an issue and allowed the judge to have frank conversations with each party. The trust the lawyers placed in this particular judge—established through past interactions and his reputation as an effective mediator—was mentioned as a factor over and above the trust they generally felt with judges.

The judge noted that, generally, when one party is particularly far off from what he believes is reasonable, he will bring the lawyers and insurance adjusters into a caucus discussion. He prefers this to a broader discussion because it allows a more candid evaluation of the merits of each side's arguments. In such cases, the authority of the judge would presumably weigh significantly for the parties.

Role of Precedent

As mentioned, the parties' initial briefs and opening arguments appeared to be the part of the JDR most laden with precedent. Past cases can reinforce initial positions and inform what is considered fair, but prior results can also block resolution in the case. Thus, it seemed that much of the judge's work was aimed at disentangling the parties from their initial positions (based on the precedents cited by their lawyers) and focusing on the facts and needs of the case.

The judge did indicate that occasionally, when one side's demands are particularly high, he will speak to the lawyers separately and invoke relevant precedent to the counsels to bring their demands into more realistic territory. Because of the high sum initially demanded in this case and the relatively low settlement amount, and based on interviews with the parties, it appears that the judge enacted such a strategy in this case to lessen the demands of the plaintiff. Precedents are important external indicators of fairness and a yardstick of what can reasonably be demanded as damages; however, precedential jousting can hinder the process.

Relative Cost and Stakeholder Incentives

All parties indicated that cost reduction was a significant appeal of JDR, which limited the likelihood of drawn-out proceedings and a trial. While the judge discussed the prominent role insurance representatives play in similar litigations, they are often making decisions on the side of the defense. In this case the WCB adjuster had the final say for the claimant and, according to plaintiff's counsel, was seeking a swift and risk-free resolution. While the case was likely to settle at some point, prolonging the case would only have increased the legal fees and uncertainty for all involved. Consequently, the WCB had a strong incentive to settle, and the plaintiff had reasonably little discretion over continuing the case. The plaintiff did, however, receive some relief outside of the case itself when a separate conversation with the WCB adjuster led to an agreement to restart his WCB benefits.

On top of these incentives, though, are the reputational costs of an action, both between lawyers and as perceived by a judge. Such norms—particularly in a legal market where litigators will almost certainly appear before a judge again in another matter—shape the demands on all sides and increase the likelihood that lawyers will opt for a more cooperative, agreeable stance in a JDR.

Comparison with Other JDRs

Although the judge did not have specific notes on this case, according to the lawyers involved, his typical JDR process mirrored this case. Counsels said the judge's commitment to the process and knowledge of the case were crucial to a satisfactory settlement.

The lawyers identified three primary shortfalls they had experienced in other JDRs. First, if the judge does not let the parties gradually reevaluate their own positions and instead appears to side with one party early on, parties may become distrustful and unwilling to settle, regardless of how reasonable the offer. The reality is that these processes take time and the judge cannot necessarily take short cuts because the emotional expectations of the parties may not yet allow them. Even if the ultimate outcome is the same, dispute resolution involves much more than numbers on a piece of paper.

Second, one counsel mentioned familiarity with the facts of the case as a simple yet pivotal characteristic of a successful mediator. Such cases often require significant review time because of myriad facts, proliferation of potential precedents, and a mass of evidence. In other mediation cases, particularly private ones, counsel identified insufficient review of materials as an occasional problem, due to case overload and client expectations of fewer billable hours. In such situations, a mediator's attempt to provide an authoritative view actually hurts the process; if a mediator gives an opinion without a sufficient grasp of the material, he could baselessly strengthen the resolve of one party and exacerbate the gap between the parties. This kind of anchoring, if not based on the strength of the case itself, only draws out the process at great cost to all. Though the judge in this case had a particular reputation for reviewing materials closely, it is also possible that judicial norms around case preparation may well increase the likelihood that JDR judges (as compared to private mediators) have thoroughly reviewed the material.

Finally, judicial buy-in is another important element of JDR. One counsel mentioned that, in some cases judges may not be particularly enthusiastic about performing their roles in mandatory dispute resolution and may see it as outside of their job description. In such cases, JDR may amount to little more than an insistence that parties talk it out with little input from the judge. While this type of process this may lead to settlement in a few cases, the lawyer indicated that if it was merely a matter of talking between the parties, the issue would have been resolved before coming to court. When judges are not interested in the process, JDR seems little better than a pro forma waste of time, decreasing the likelihood of success—as well as support—for JDR in general. If applied properly, however, the intervention of a judicial mediator, through procedural and substantive contributions, is critical to dispute resolution.

Satisfaction

The JDR was one of the few meetings between the parties following the accident (including between the WCB representatives and the injured party). In the interim—amidst the flurry of legal letters—tensions and demands rose as the lawyers corresponded via email. The proceedings lasting only a day was beneficial to all parties and provided closure that otherwise could have been delayed. Happy Valley was satisfied with the settlement.

Although the plaintiff was disheartened by the WCB's imposed limitations to the case—which he felt weakened his claim and limited the potential damages—he had resolution. Articulating his experience of the injuries in his opening statements not only proved cathartic, it increased the WCB adjuster's sympathy for him and led to a resumption of his benefits. His lawyer suggested this outcome may have been more valuable than his final share of the settlement. Overall, the judge's cooperative tone at the outset and his emphasis on conciliation created an atmosphere where the plaintiff's physical and emotional injuries could be acknowledged.

9

THE WELL FIRE CASE

Lucy Prather

Facts

Hydraulic fracturing, or "fracking," involves injecting an acidic solution at high pressure into a well in subterranean rocks in order to create deep, under-ground fissures and release oil, natural gas, geothermal energy, or water. As fluid and vapor are released in this process, the gaseous returns are vented and collected in a tank.

At a fracking site in Alberta in the late 1990s, a fire broke out when the collected gases escaped from their tank and alit on a diesel engine sitting two feet away. Allegedly, the tank was the wrong kind of vessel for flammable gas storage, as it was not equipped with any kind of venting mechanism to release pressure in the tank, and this led to the leakage. The placement of the engine near the tank and the crowded layout of the fracking site made it difficult for firefighters to maneuver around the blaze. The firefighters lost precious moments when the fire truck stalled, and making matters worse, they may not have had enough training, fire retardant, or water at their disposal in order to quickly extinguish the fire. All told, the fire caused more than $3.3 million in damage to equipment, as well as a loss of profit due to the shut-down and clean-up operations required after the fire.

At the time of this case, the regulations governing fracking in Alberta included a schematic drawing of how a fracking site should be laid out to prevent fires and to allow emergency personnel to respond to fires. The design requirements at these sites were of particular importance in this case: Flammable vapors captured from wells were required to be properly stored seven meters from equipment such as diesel engines that might cause those vapors to ignite.

These requirements would have been common knowledge among all parties on the job site. However, there was also an unspoken norm that workers on fracking sites would be blacklisted from future jobs if they raised safety concerns that might slow or halt production. The site in this case was operated by one company, owned by several others, staffed by engineers and operations consultants from three other companies, and two companies were also brought in to provide safety services. Any of these companies and their employees may have recognized the myriad safety violations that led to this fire, but none of them raised alarm. This culture of silence meant those individuals could be found jointly and severally liable for the cost of the damage caused by the fire.

The owner of the well filed suit against all of the companies mentioned above, as well as the individual site supervisor, who had allowed his professional license to lapse and was thus operating illegally. The defendant companies denied responsibility and pointed fingers at one another; several of them responded by claiming that the owners of the well were contributorily negligent, which would reduce defendant companies' liability.

All of these entities had insurance, including the site supervisor. The well owner's insurance company had paid out to cover the damage at the site but was looking to recover some of those costs. Though this lawsuit named companies and individuals, it was litigated almost entirely by lawyers appointed by their insurers.

JDR Process

Prior to the JDR, the parties filed briefs with the judge, which included expert reports on any material evidence that may have been relevant to the outcome of the case were it to go to trial. The JDR was scheduled over two days and took place at the Court of the Queen's Bench building.

At the start of the JDR session, the judge asked lawyers for opening statements that laid out their positions. One attorney noted that these statements may bring up feelings, but that he tries to keep his emotions in check. "Sometimes it just pisses you off . . . but you never want to look angry because the whole point of the meeting is to settle, and you don't settle by being obnoxious."[1] Each party also had a chance to speak, and though some of them said they had nothing to add, others shared how this case had affected them emotionally, professionally, or financially. The attorneys noted that this moment can be cathartic for parties and can add a human element to negotiations. It may also signal to the judge that a party might be "asking for the moon" when they are "only going to get the stars."

The judge then moved the parties to separate rooms where they remained for most of the process. One attorney said that he interpreted the judge's choice of who to caucus with first as an indication of that party needing a "reality check." In this case, the plaintiff's attorney was a former oil engineer and argued aggressively for his case. The judge caucused with him first, and the other attorneys guessed that the judge encouraged him to approach the issue with a more flexible position on liability if he really wanted to settle the case. The judge described the plaintiff's attorney as a "one-man band" who "had to play tough" because "everyone was against him."[2] He recognized that the plaintiff was in a difficult position and would not want to make concessions too early.

The rest of the process was primarily shuttle mediation between the parties in separate rooms, though the judge at times called them together. When the judge was in a private caucus with a party, the rest of the attorneys sat with their clients and waited.

---

1. All quotes from attorney for individual defendant and attorney for corporate defendant are from interviews that took place on March 18, and 26, 2020, respectively.
2. All quotes from judge are from interview on April 6, 2020.

One attorney described passing the time by doing a crossword and chatting with the client. Attorneys also said that the downtime allowed them to step out into the hall and chat with one another about the process without their clients present. These informal check-ins allowed the co-defendants to share information with one another about what the judge had told them, whether they believed their clients would budge, and how much time the judge was spending, comparatively, with each party.

At the end of the first day, almost no progress had been made toward settlement. One of the co-defendants—a company with such limited exposure to liability that the cost of the JDR was higher than the amount of damages they were likely to pay—sought permission to leave. The judge allowed it but did not share his decision with the other parties. Early on the second day, when all parties were in the conference room, the co-defendants' absence was apparent. Once they broke into private caucuses, one attorney who knew the absent counsel called him to ask why he had left and to ensure that the sum of money that the co-defendant had offered to contribute toward a settlement was still on the table. Reassured that it was, the JDR process continued.

A settlement seemed imminent once the judge informed the plaintiff that the defendants were feeling angry and frustrated by his counsel's refusal to budge from his hardline stance on liability. Eventually, the plaintiff's counsel was ready to reduce the liability that defendants would be accepting if they settled, and the defendants then found it easier to negotiate among themselves as to who would contribute toward a settlement.

However, the JDR closed on the second day without a finalized agreement; the plaintiff's lawyer continued to insist that the defendants had not offered a sum he could settle for and that the case would have to go to trial. The case did ultimately settle, and though the defense counsel could not recall the exact time frame, they credited the JDR process with persuading the plaintiff's lawyer to accept a lower number.

Outcome and Comparison with Trial

The site supervisor and the site operator assumed the majority of the liability, and the rest of the defendants were assigned "descending levels of contribution." The liability assignment was based in large part on guidance from a supreme court case that had come down the previous year, a precedent which made the deal feel fair overall.

Some aspects of the settlement, however, may not have felt just to all parties. The attorney who left after the first day did contribute some money toward the settlement pot, despite evidence indicating that his client was not liable for the damage. This contribution may have been key in reaching a number high enough for the plaintiff's attorney to accept, but had the case gone to trial, the attorneys and judge all agreed that no liability would have been assigned to that party. Interestingly, that party was able to cap the level of contribution to the settlement amount based on insurance policy limits, an option not available at trial. Liability is based on fault, not on capacity to pay. In the unlikely event that this party was found liable for any of the damage, the amount recoverable from that party might have exceeded the party's policy limits.

The attorneys felt that the plaintiff probably came out a bit better through JDR than they would have at trial. The plaintiff's company had a professional engineer on staff who may have known, just as the other companies working on the site may have known, that the well site setup was dangerous. This fact would likely have opened the plaintiff up for a determination of contributory negligence that could have significantly reduced the amount recoverable at trial. There were, however, too many variables for the defense to know that for sure. A different judge may have brought about a different outcome. For the site supervisor, a settlement opportunity that was under his insurance policy limit—thereby protecting him from any personal liability—was too good to pass up.

Ultimately, though, the relevant comparison might not be with hypothetical results of a trial. After all, the case was being litigated primarily by insurance companies, who typically do not favor a protracted trial when they could instead settle a case. One defense attorney said that most cases settle, "it's just a question of when." The trial date for this case was set for nearly two years out due to the overwhelming caseload in Alberta. Had the case dragged on for another year or two, each party would have owed thousands more in legal fees. They might have reached a different—even better— settlement at trial but would have suffered more by having to sink money into the case in the intervening time. Using this framework, the attorneys came away quite pleased with the outcome; it reduced their clients' cost burden and provided them peace of mind when their lives had been disrupted by the stress and uncertainty of a complicated lawsuit.

Technical Information

The JDR process did not rely heavily on expert testimony and other technical expertise that might have played a key role at trial. At trial, the plaintiff and the defense would have presented their own expert testimony about oil well safety, proper equipment and vapor storage, firefighting preparedness, and other issues relevant to determining each party's responsibility for the damage. These experts would then be subject to cross-examination. The judge would weigh the expert testimony, assess credibility, and issue a decision and appropriate damages.

In contrast, the JDR process allows each party to submit a written expert report highlighting key sections that support their positions. Typically, there is no in-person expert testimony through which the judge might assess credibility, nor any mechanism established for asking clarifying questions. Primarily, it is the written document and each party's brief that shapes the judge's assessment of each argument's relative merits. The judge then uses these documents to develop a "Scott Schedule" in preparation for the JDR that lists each party's position and supported reasoning on each issue in the case. This document was designed to "try and hit the high points" of a case to ensure the judge understands the central issues without getting ensnared in the technical minutiae.

In this case, the "ex oil-engineer" lawyer for the plaintiff had leaned heavily on his technical background when arguing that the defendants should be held liable for the full amount of damage caused by the fire. That expertise might have been helpful at trial and could have intimidated the defense counsel during informal settlement negotiations. Here, however, the judge repeatedly told him that this case would not settle until he was willing to budge. He reoriented the conversation around what the parties were willing to accept in the future and away from the plaintiff's expertise about what had occurred in the past.

To some degree, this de-emphasis on technical expertise comports with the reorientation of the JDR proceedings away from the judge as the arbiter and toward empowering the parties, who may not all agree on what happened but might agree on how to move forward. The judge's ability to evaluate the relative strength of each party's case, however, is potentially weakened by limiting technical input to the written briefs. Judges may find it difficult to decipher these reports, and their level of preparation with regards to the expert reports could shape how accurately they evaluate the relative merits of the case. One value of JDR is giving parties a reality check: A well-prepared judge with an understanding of expert testimony and a measure of their credibility may be in a position of telling the parties that their cases are not as strong as they think. Though the lack of expert testimony in this case did not impede the judge's ability to advise the parties, some examination of its role in JDRs may be worthwhile.

Relative Cost

A major reason that the parties opted for JDR was the anticipated cost of trial. The case, initially scheduled as a ten-day trial, promised to be complicated and expensive. Further, after the trial each of the parties would have run the risk of having to bring additional enforcement actions, particularly between co-defendants who might hope to recover from one another a portion of the judgment they paid the plaintiff.

The uncertainty of the result of a trial meant another vote in favor of JDR. The insurance policy limits of each defendant are not admissible during the liability phase of a trial. A judge or jury could, therefore, find that a defendant was 100 percent liable for damage caused even if the amount awarded was far more than that defendant's insurance could pay. For the site supervisor, who was the only individually-named defendant, the possibility of the plaintiff recovering the full judgment from him was particularly worrisome. His insurance policy would only cover a portion of the $3.5 million in alleged damages; a judgment beyond that amount would eat into his personal assets, such as his house or retirement savings. And even if responsibility was apportioned between the defendants in a more even split at the liability phase of a trial, under Canada's Tort-Feasor Act all the defendants would be jointly and severally liable. Functionally, this allows the plaintiff to recover the full amount of damages from each of them in an enforcement action, even if the outcome of this case allocated primary liability to someone else. All of these unknowns can weigh heavily on clients, and the attorneys agreed that one benefit of JDR is to provide certainty for someone who has been losing sleep worrying about how the case might turn out.

Another type of cost associated with JDRs is lawyers' reputations. The lawyers in this case were concerned that rejecting a settlement that was, broadly speaking, acceptable to their client would open them up to accusations of participating in JDR in bad faith. This fear of reputational harm may cause attorneys to accept a settlement agreement even if they believe they could eventually do better at trial. And, the structure of the JDR may introduce another kind of reputational risk to attorneys: When the entire process is structured to produce a settlement, walking away from the table feels like a failure. The pressure to come to a settlement might be even more heightened for attorneys because their clients are seated in the same room, listening to and participating in the negotiations. This dynamic might create conflicting incentives for attorneys by compelling them to save face and accept settlements for their clients that are worse than what they could negotiate in later rounds.

Role of the Judge

When asked to place himself on a spectrum from facilitative to evaluative, the judge said, "I'm kind of in the middle." He is happy to give parties an honest evaluation of a case, when asked, and added that refusing to do so would be an abdication of his role as a JDR judge. "Some judges . . . don't give opinions, and people want the opinion of the judge. They want judges to weigh in and give some guidance." He insisted, however: "It's not about me; it's about you [the parties]; so, you settle it," and stressed that he would not impede settlement negotiations by rushing to give an opinion before a party solicited it.

The attorneys were quite satisfied with the judicial guidance they received from the judge and felt they selected well. Attorneys "shop around" for judges whose style and expertise fit the case type, and then decide on a JDR schedule that makes it more likely they are assigned to their preferred judge. Unlike private mediation, parties to JDR are not guaranteed a particular judge as their mediator, so attorneys have learned to use the scheduling information to game the system. This strategy is important because attorneys reported significant variation in quality of JDR judges, both in terms of their familiarity with the applicable law and their willingness to step out of the role of decider and instead empower the parties to come to an agreement themselves.

The attorneys further noted that the judge's evaluative role was a particularly effective method for resolving this dispute. A recommendation from a judge holds significant weight and can encourage parties toward settlement. One attorney described *The Well Fire Case* as "a lot of finger-pointing," which could really use "some sort of judicial direction . . . a reality check."

The attorneys were particularly satisfied with the judge's handling of "asymmetric" expertise. The technical expertise of the plaintiff's attorney could have intimidated defense counsel into accepting a worse deal if they had assumed his interpretation of the facts was more likely to be the correct one. Being able to frankly ask a judge how he would decide the case ensured that the plaintiff's attorney's confidence did not push the defense to accept a poor deal. Similarly, one attorney described being in other JDRs, such as personal injury cases, where the defense attorney was an insurance lawyer with expertise in the case type, while the plaintiff's attorney was newly barred and had no experience in that area. The judge's ability to counsel the plaintiff attorney and his client to accept a nominal settlement allowed him to save face in front of his client.

Judges can also play an important role for clients by acknowledging their pain. The attorneys confirmed the value their clients place on being heard by "a real live judge," a human element that predisposes some to settle for less than their original claim.

Precedent

The settlement in this case was structured to conform with a recent opinion in the Alberta Court of Appeal that provided guidance for allocating liability for a series of negligent acts. The case, Heller v. Martens,[3] outlined a "comparative blameworthiness" standard for allocating liability. That opinion grounded the parties' discussion in this case about how to go about structuring a settlement and provided a helpful standard of legitimacy against which they could assess whether the agreement was fair compared to what they would have achieved in court.

The judge described himself as taking a "principled approach" to JDR mediation, which may have moved the conversation toward tying a settlement to a broadly acceptable standard of legitimacy. He stated, however, that not every case can be settled by looking to the law: "Sometimes you can do it on the law, and sometimes you can do it on the evidence." Sometimes, the facts put forth by a party may be compelling enough to spur a settlement that does not conform with legal precedent. Parties who tell a compelling story in their opening statements or who otherwise win the sympathy of the judge may be advantaged by this willingness to deviate from precedent when other principles, such as fairness or compassion, motivate the judge employ a more flexible approach.

---

3. https://ca.vlex.com/vid/heller-v-martens-681372145

INDEX